RETHINKING ECONOMICS

RETHINKING ECONOMICS

Reflections Based on a Study of the Indian Economy

C.T. KURIEN

SAGE PUBLICATIONS
New Delhi/Thousand Oaks/London

Copyright © C.T. Kurien, 1996

First published in 1996 by

Sage Publications India Pvt Ltd
M-32 Greater Kailash Market-I
New Delhi 110 048

Sage Publications Inc
2455 Teller Road
Thousand Oaks, California 91320

Sage Publications Ltd
6 Bonhill Street
London EC2A 4PU

Published by Tejeshwar Singh for Sage Publications India Pvt Ltd, lasertypeset by Daya Shankar Sharma, New Delhi and printed at Chaman Enterprises, New Delhi.

Library of Congress Cataloging-in-Publication Data
Kurien, C.T.
    Rethinking economics: reflections based on a study of the Indian economy / C.T. Kurien.
      p. cm.
    Includes bibliographical references and index.
    1. Economics. 2. Economic policy. 3. India—Economic policy—1947- 4. India—Economic conditions—1947- I. Title. HB171. K826 330—dc20 1996 96-6134

ISBN: 0–8039–9309–9 (US–hb)   81–7036–546–5 (India–hb)
          0–8039–9342–0 (US–pb)   81–7036–581–3 (India–pb)

Sage Production Editor: Pramod Kumar Singh

CONTENTS

PREFACE

This work is an exploration into the relationship between economic problems and economic theories. There is likely to be general agreement that the role of economic theories is to analyse economic problems and to be of aid to economic policies. But from time to time there have been instances where the very nature of economic theory has prevented it from performing this role. Why does this happen and what needs to be done to make economics as a branch of knowledge more responsive to real-life problems is the theme of this book.

Throughout my professional life my main concern has been with the economic problems that the people of India confront in their day-to-day lives. In trying to probe into them, I have constantly turned to economic theories to throw light on them. Reacting to what I felt was the inadequacy of mainstream economics to be an instrument of such probing, I wrote *The Economy: An Interpretative Introduction* (1992b). It was not meant to be a contribution to economic theory as such, but a way of perceiving the changing profile of the Indian economy and of focusing on its central problems, especially the manner in which growth has been generating both affluence and poverty among different sections of the population. The book received two kinds of reactions. Administrators, doctors, engineers, lawyers, journalists, politicians, and social workers who, in their professional work have to deal with specific types of economic problems have been immensely grateful to have a book that expounds the working of the economy in a language they can follow. During the past three years I have participated in a number of study groups of such professionals who were interested in using the book to understand the underlying interconnections.

The reactions of professional economists to the book so far have been very guarded. At a meeting of economists, one senior economist, an old friend of mine, referred to the book as an example of the 'interdisciplinary approach' to economics. It was not clear whether he was commending it or cautioning the profession against such misdirected efforts. So in a private chat I asked him for a more detailed comment. He hesitated for a moment, then stated candidly: 'I found it difficult to react to your book because you have changed the nature of the discourse.' 'That was not altogether an accident', I replied.

In this work, addressed mainly to professional economists, I discuss why it is necessary for economics to change the nature of discourse. I recognise that, as a specialised field of study with a community of scholars devoting their lives to its pursuit, economics will have a vocabulary of its own. It is understandable too that enriching this vocabulary will be part of the work of professionals. But, then, there is the possibility that in the process it may get detached from the substantive issues that may not have the rigour and elegance of an increasingly refined language of professional discourse. As is well known, many leading economists in different parts of the world have felt that, as a field of study, economics has been showing the tendency to distance itself from real-life problems in the attempt to develop its universe of discourse.

It is this disjunction that I reflect on based on my attempts to understand and interpret specific aspects of the Indian economy. As I see it, the source of the malaise can be traced to the conceptualisation of the economy that the pioneers of neo-classical economics put forward in their attempt to shape economics as a science similar to Newtonian physics.

This conceptualisation forming the pre-theoretic vision which underlies much of what is even today considered to be economics is, in my view, ill-suited for perceiving and analysing real-life economic problems because it assumes away the essential features of real-life economies. I attempt an alternative conceptualisation of the economy more in tune with the working of real-life economies, particularly those like the Indian economy.

The implications of the new conceptualisation and the manner of enquiry it will necessitate is also spelt out. If I am right, the logical culmination is a restructuring of economics as a tool for studying economic problems. However, I do not undertake the task for which I cannot claim competence. In any case, there is a prior stage to go through: to discuss whether economics, in fact, stands in need of reformulation. The best that can be hoped for is that this work will stimulate a studied discussion of this question.

This book was written during my tenure as the National Fellow of the Indian Council of Social Science Research. I am grateful to the Council for the honour, the freedom given to decide what to work on, and for the generous financial support. Others who have directly helped in the production of the book are L. Celine who did the typing and S. Juliet Vinolia who attended to the proofreading and the compilation of the bibliography. But for their devoted service and the willing cooperation of the administrative and library personnel of the Madras Institute of Development Studies, I would not have been able to concentrate on my part of the work.

Malcolm Adiseshiah, T.D. Felix, Josef James, S. Neelakantan and Yasodha Shanmugasundaram have gone through parts or all of the earlier drafts and given their comments. I am grateful to them. Adiseshiah who had become enthused about my project and had seen the drafts of the first two chapters passed away while I was organising the material for the third chapter. His demise has been a great loss to me.

My greatest indebtedness in the writing of this book is to Koilpillai J. Charles who patiently went through the drafts, made several comments on substance and style, and spent long hours discussing the issues that I have dealt with. His generosity has been a great source of encouragement to me.

As this work is, in one sense, the product of many years of reflection, I am not in a position to name many others—teachers, students, colleagues and a large circle of people from all walks of life whose direct involvement in economic activities has been an important source for my studies—who have inspired me, challenged me and helped me in my professional work. I must also record the emotional support I have received over the years from friends and members of the family, especially my parents, daughters and wife. During the nearly four decades of our married life my wife has patiently shared my travails and has been a willing helper and friendly critic.

A scholar who chooses a life where his work is not of immediate use to others is dependent on charity, in one form or other, for his life and livelihood. Looking back on the four decades and more of my professional life I realise that I have been sustained by the contributions of many people, known and unknown. I take this opportunity to express my sincere thanks to all of them.

Madras
30 August 1995   C.T. KURIEN

1

ECONOMICS AND THE ECONOMY

In *Economics and the Public Purpose* Galbraith draws a distinction between an. *economic system* and *economics* which does not usually receive the attention it deserves. According to Galbraith the purpose of an economic system (which we may shorten to an *economy*) is to provide the goods and render the services that people want. It is a system 'that grows food, processes, packages and distributes it, manufactures cloth and makes clothing, constructs houses, furnishes them, supplies educational and medical services, provides law and order, arranges the common defence ...' (1973: 19). This descriptive account of the economy could be extended and edited to say that any economic system or economy addresses itself to a set of common fundamental issues as indicated in Samuelson's *Economics*:

What commodities shall be produced and in what quantities? That is, how much and which of alternative goods and services shall be produced? ...
How shall goods be produced? That is, by whom and with what resources and in what technological manner are they produced? ...
For whom shall goods be produced? That is, who is to enjoy and get the benefit of the goods ad services provided? (1976: 17–18)

Of course, this is not the only possible edited version of the economy. I have proposed a more inclusive description of the economy as a structure of relationships among a group of people, in terms of the manner in which they exercise control over resources, use resources and labour in the production of goods, and define and settle the claims of the members over what is produced (Kurien 1992b: 20), emphasising that while the economy is concerned with goods and services, it should be recognised essentially as a set of social relationships.

Such distinctions drawing attention to different aspects of the notion of the economy are important to arrive at a more adequate understanding of what this complex entity is, and more shall be said about them in this book. For the moment I wish to emphasise, as Galbraith has done, the more significant distinction between these statements about the economy and the definitions that economics as an area of enquiry has come to have. There are many such definitions as can be seen from the introductory chapters of most Indian textbooks on economics. By far the most widely accepted one (certainly in textbooks) is the 'scarcity definition' of the subject as 'the science which studies human behaviour as a relationship between ends and scarce means which have alternative uses' (Robbins 1935: 16). Again, a critical analysis of this definition is not my immediate intention. Rather, I wish to draw attention to the difference in the languages used to depict the economy and economics. The economy is usually described in terms of concrete characteristics; the definition of economics is in more formal and abstract categories. Consequently, the characterisation of the economy is immediate and matter of fact; economics, on the other hand, gets defined in terms of categories that are removed from day-to-day experience. The economy is an experiential reality; economics is a propositional entity.

The differences in language noted earlier are related to two different worlds, for language is the expression of a *universe* of discourse. It is obvious that the language of the economy is the language of everyday life. It has arisen from day-to-day human activities. Human beings engage in the production of goods, they render services, get paid, use the earnings thus made for the purchase of goods paying a price, if they have a surplus they lend it directly or deposit it in a bank, they pay taxes, and so on. Since all human beings are in one way or the other involved in many of these activities, day-to-day language has terminologies referring to them. The purpose of economics may be considered as an attempt to edit the everyday language about economic activities or the economy. However, it is more than that. The language of economics belongs to a different universe of discourse—to a different world. Jacob Viner is credited with the statement that economics is what economists do. There is much truth in it. The language of economics is the language of the economists, generated by them, and mostly also used by them. This is true not only of economics but also of other academic disciplines. It is a community of professionals who generate and utilise the universe of discourse of a discipline.[1] Phyllis Deane draws attention to the fact that while Adam Smith's *Wealth of Nations* published in 1776 is considered to be the first major work in economics or political economy, it is only after the establishment of the Political Economy Club in 1821 where members started meeting regularly to discuss the book, came to share a common set of concepts and agreed on the problems that should engage their attention, that something like a well-established subject of political economy received recognition (Deane 1978: Ch. 6). Even today, economics as a discipline is mainly the concern of the varieties of 'clubs' it has—university departments, research institutes, professional associations—and their publications. It is not surprising that academic activity consists primarily of reading, writing and talking.

What happens when a discipline gets increasingly professionalised through the discourse of its votaries? No doubt there will be more to talk and write about because of the arguments and disagreements, and thus the subject will grow and, hopefully, become more refined. But what of the links between the world of the professionals and the world which is the basis of their being? There is no doubt that in the beginning, and for a long time thereafter, the language of professional discourse in economics was *about* day-to-day economic problems and issues. Its purpose was to throw light on such problems and make them more intelligible because their complexity had to be comprehended through simpler approximations. In a subject like economics, so closely linked to everyday experiences of human beings in general, it is legitimate to expect that as it becomes more refined and advanced it will be able to fulfil its original purpose with greater clarity and precision. However, the opposite is also possible. As it comes to concentrate attention on its own language, the world that the professionals set up may snap ties with the other, and the two may drift apart. Then professional language may not only fail to illumine the problems of the world of experience, but may also obfuscate and distort them. A reflection on the evolution of economics and of the contemporary situation will show that this ominous possibility is not merely hypothetical.

II

These considerations show that professional economists have two worlds to reckon with—the world of experience that they share with fellow human beings and the universe of discourse which they share with their professional colleagues, which they also help to build or at least to sustain. It is as though the professional economist has a dual citizenship. Exercising this responsibility of relating the world of theory to the world of problems is not easy.

It is possible to identify three different patterns of reaction under such a situation. The first is best illustrated with reference to a personal anecdote. In the early part of 1986 I was invited by the North Western University in the United States of America to give a talk on the Indian economy. Readers will recall that this was just a year after Rajiv Gandhi had become Prime Minister and had started *his* New Economic Policy of liberalisation. What was expected of me was to comment on the changes in India's economic policy and to indicate whether it was influenced by what in those days was known as 'Reaganomics', the economic policies associated with President Reagan. The lecture was sponsored by the Department of Political Science. Even so some faculty members of the Economics Department were present. After the lecture, one of them came up to me and said: 'You may wonder why your lecture was not organised by the Department of Economics. I don't want you to think that it is because of a lack of interest in the *Indian* economy. As a matter of fact, we are not interested in any *real* economy.'

Perhaps, this comment was not meant to be taken too seriously. Yet it is true that in many centres that claim to be doing advanced work in economics, the subject has shown a tendency to become 'a scholastic game of logic-chopping and puzzle-solving', as Ashok Guha (1981: 31) puts it. Certainly, modern economics has this tendency to cut itself off completely from real world economic problems and to become exercises in abstract logic supported by high level mathematics. Introducing a collection of essays on 'growth economics' in the early 1970s, Amartya Sen recalled the practical context of the immediate post-Second World War years in which interests in growth revived after it was sidelined for a while by the emphasis on the allocation of given resources. He referred to the desire of the war-damaged Western economies to reconstruct fast, the eagerness of the Soviet Union and its socialist associates to overtake the capitalist economies in terms of growth, and the effort of the newly emerging underdeveloped economies to initiate and sustain economic development.

With this immensely practical motivation [observed Sen] it would have been natural for growth theory to take a fairly practice-oriented shape. This, however, has not happened and much of modern growth theory is concerned with rather esoteric issues. Its link with public policy is often very remote. It is as if a poor man collected money for his food and blew it all on alcohol (Sen 1970: 9).

Hicks also had expressed a similar verdict.

Modern growth theory [he said] has been fertile in the generation of class-room exercises; but so far as we can yet see, they are exercises, not real problems. They are not even hypothetical real problems, of the type, 'What would happen if?' where the 'if' is something that could conceivably happen. They are shadows of real problems, dressed up in such a way that by pure logic we can find solutions for them (Hicks 1965: 183).

In the 1970s many other leading economists, Wassily Leontief (1971) and Joan Robinson (1972) the most prominent among them, expressed their frustration and indignation at the preoccupation of economists with all sorts of questions except those that were of vital interest to ordinary human beings. This concern has also been expressed more recently.[2]

Why economics, which many of its early proponents claimed to be a study of an important aspect of daily life, comes to be almost totally detached from concrete economic problems is a subject worth examining. One reason for it is the innate fecundity of logic and mathematics to set up universes of discourse of their own. Although economic problems, whether so recognised or not, have been coterminous with human civilization as such, the emergence of economics as a separate field of study is closely related to the attempt of the early writers, Adam Smith himself and more so David Ricardo, to discern logical interconnections among such problems and thus to distil a coherent corpus of propositions as constituting the central core of the subject. But it is easy for the delicate link between economic problems and *their* logical interconnections to snap and for the logic to emerge as an independent realm of discourse. Counterfactual economic logic can come to have a self-contained language of its own. When this kind of logic is combined with mathematics, which generates its own language, new kinds of academic issues and further enquiries based on them emerge. Economics then becomes a very interesting, challenging and exciting intellectual exercise. This gives rise to prestigious clubs and the discipline continues to grow often without any links with the world of economic reality.

The problem is not with the use of mathematics and logic in economics per se. The question that Walras raised while presenting his mathematical model of the economy is pertinent even today.

> Why should we persist [he asked] in using everyday language to explain things in the most cumbrous and incorrect way, as Ricardo has often done and as John Stuart Mill does repeatedly in his *Principles of Political Economy*, when these same things can be stated far more succinctly, precisely and clearly in the language of mathematics? (Walras 1954: 72).

Indeed! Though I have not done much work in economics involving mathematics, I remain indebted to many who have used this language in expounding and clarifying many deep and intricate issues in economic reasoning. However, I share Sen's view that in a great deal of modern economic analysis 'mathematical exactness of formulation has proceeded hand in hand with remarkable inexactness of contents' (Sen 1987: 2). As for logic, I cannot see how any systematic process of thinking can be done without it. So, the mere fact that a great deal of economics is now couched in mathematical and logical terms is not a matter of concern.

And yet one must take note of the built-in tendency that economics has abundantly demonstrated to take flights into fancy and set up pseudo worlds of its own. In his day, Marx detected this tendency in psychology and asked: 'What are we to think of a science which airily abstracts from this large part of human labour and which fails to feel its own incompleteness, while such a wealth of human endeavour unfolded before it . . .?' (Marx 1959: 102). We may say the same about economists who claim to be 'pure theorists' and who in their devotion to logic and mathematics find no place for human beings and social relationships in their approach to economics.

III

As long as the attempt to get away from the real world is seen as a mere intellectual exercise done for its own sake, we may just overlook it as simply the personal preference of some who find it interesting in itself or a respectable way of making a living. However, as already hinted, there is lurking danger in this. The artificially created world may come to be viewed as the real world or as what the real world should 'ideally' become. That is the second pattern of link between economic theories and economic problems, to thrust economic theories built up on the basis of their convenient assumptions and presuppositions on the real world. Again, the criticism is not against model-building per se. In a discipline like economics where it is impossible to conduct laboratory experiments to isolate and control variables, mental experiments of drawing inferences from stated premises can play a major role in clarifying the nature of interconnections among what are considered to be key variables. It is part of the process of abstraction which constitutes a major procedure in all branches of knowledge and virtually unavoidable in those that deal with societal relationships.

However, while abstracting enables one to get away from the immediate proximity of real life problems to gain a perspective from above, or from outer space, so to say, it then raises the problem of 're-entry' to tackle those problems with better insight. For whatever reason, while abstraction and model-building seem to come naturally to economists, few seem to worry about 're-entry'. This is the biggest professional vice among economists—that they tend to confuse the artificial world of their creation with the real world itself and are often unaware that they are doing so! The best example of this vice is the manner in which the (abstract) theory of competitive markets is used to canvass support for 'market-friendly' policy regimes and the related claim that markets bring about 'efficiency' in view of the correspondence between perfectly competitive markets and Pareto optimality. It is forgotten, or overlooked, that the theory of competitive markets is based on a large number of highly simplifying assumptions about information, mobility, nature of the distribution of economic power among the participants, and so on, and that Pareto optimality provides veto power to every single individual so that it becomes virtually impossible to think of any economic conditions, other than the existing one itself, which can 'pass' on the basis of the

Pareto criterion. And so, inferences drawn from arbitrary or simplified premises are presented as 'scientific laws' to guide economic policies.

The reason this pattern is so common in economics is not far to seek. Once a logically sound and mathematically rigorous corpus of economic theory is built up, it serves as a convenient pedagogic device and is easily passed on to successive generations of students irrespective of whether it is relevant or adequate to deal with concrete problems of the real life economy.[3] However, the world of affairs expects the professional economists—except those who contract out claiming to be 'pure theorists'—to respond to real-life problems and assumes also that professional knowledge has the capacity to solve them. When caught in such situations, it is not surprising that professional economists turn to the easy way of imposing their acquired knowledge on the real world partly because such knowledge was based, to some extent at least, on the real world conditions, though of an earlier period. Galbraith points out that the image of an earlier economic society serves admirably the instrumental purpose of a later one.

IV

The third approach that professional economists have taken and continue to take in view of their 'dual citizenship' is to enter into a critical dialogue with the two universes of discourse, especially pitting the facts of experience against the inferences and even premises of received economic theory. This is the procedure that Keynes had adopted in the *General Theory*.

> Classical theorists resemble Euclidean geometers in a non-Euclidean world who, discovering that in experience straight lines apparently parallel often meet, rebuke the lines for not keeping straight—as the only remedy for the unfortunate collisions which are occurring. Yet, in truth, there is no remedy except to throw over the axioms of parallels and to work out a non-Euclidean geometry. Something similar is required in economics (Keynes 1936: 16).

Whether Keynes in fact worked out a 'non-Euclidean economics' is beside the point.[4] He did show a way of exercising the dual citizenship using a pressing economic problem of the real world for a critical scrutiny of the world of theory, going down to its explicit as well as implicit presuppositions.

Whether such critical scrutiny will always and immediately lead to reformulations of theory's universe of discourse is doubtful. But, granted that professional economists have their being in two worlds, it is a necessary task. Its purpose is to enable theory to play its legitimate role of making sense of practical problems and to let the world of reality constantly bombard it to prevent its universe of discourse from becoming petrified.

The Indian tradition in economics has been essentially of this third pattern of guarded application of theories, generated elsewhere, to the analysis of Indian problems and the critical evaluation of the theories arising from such exercises. Recalling and reviewing the contributions of the early pioneers, B.N. Ganguli has reminded us (Ganguli 1977) that Rammohun Roy was a contemporary of Ricardo, Malthus, Mill and Marx and had participated in a lively debate on the population problems triggered by Malthus' work. Ranade had, similarly, pointed out in the second half of the nineteenth century that the Ricardian theory of Rent was true only of farmers' rents and was wholly inapplicable to the Indian *ryots'* rent. He had responded to the writings of Mill as well. He also supported the German Historical School, especially Muller and List in their rebellion against 'the orthodox creed'. The writings of the people of this period also showed a search for an 'Indian economics' which could provide a conceptual frame for the spirit of economic nationalism which had grown in the wake of the nationalist movement towards the end of the century. And, of course, as shown by Naoroji's work, poverty was a central problem of analysis. Ganguli's overall evaluation is that 'the Indians who speculated on economic doctrine developed a healthy respect for the historical and comparative method of reflection, a deep concern about concrete economic reality and an enthusiasm for studying Indian economic problems in an Indian setting' (ibid: 81).

That much the same trend continued in the first half of the twentieth century is confirmed by Bhabatosh Datta (1978) in the companion volume to Ganguli's. The deep concern about concrete economic reality continued but became more diversified. National income and population studies assumed a prominent role. There were special treatments of the problems of agriculture and industry. Monetary economics, public finance and international trade received considerable attention. However, Datta expressed the view that 'compared to the extent and high quality of the Indian economists' work on theoretical economics in the 1950s and later, the first 5 decades of the century were relatively sterile' (1978: 159), which he considered surprising 'because the Indian scholarly mind has always delighted in abstraction' (ibid.). Malcolm Adiseshiah, in the Foreword to Datta's work, observes: '. . . from Mahadev Govind Ranade onward Indian economists were uneasily aware that the economic theories and laws that had been developed despite their claim to universality, were in fact generalisations arising from the capitalist industrial economic structures of Europe and North America, and as such could not be applied to the economic and social dualism or pluralism that characterised the Indian economy. What was missing in their work, which later economists in the country have attempted and are attempting successfully, is the necessary modifications both in the premises and parameters of the theories in relation to the Indian reality' (Datta 1978: Foreword).

In the second half of the present century professionally trained Indian economists like Amartya Sen have made significant contributions to economic theory and such contributions have become integral parts of what may be considered the global literature on economics. But there is hardly any Indian economist who would claim to be a 'pure theorist' concentrating exclusively on the logic of economic theory. Perhaps the reality of the Indian situation has been so overwhelming to let that happen and that, certainly, is a healthy sign. Consequently, what has been referred to as the Indian tradition of critical evaluation of received theories in the light of the Indian reality has continued.

An early and leading contribution of this kind was V.K.R.V. Rao's attempt to show that identifiable features of the Indian economy prevented the straight application of Keynesian economics (Rao 1952; 1953). Specifically, he expressed doubts whether the Keynesian multiplier would function the way it was expected to because of the supply inelasticities in the Indian economy. That sort of reservation was expressed by others also who followed Rao's lead. Subsequently, K.N. Raj (1979) and Sukhamoy Chakravarty (1979) showed ways of interpreting Keynesian economics to deal with problems of developing agrarian economies. A more comprehensive writing of this kind is Mihir Rakshit's attempt to bring into a neo-Keynesian frame many aspects of the Indian economy, both its real and monetary components (Rakshit 1982). From other theoretical perspectives Bagchi (1982), Bhaduri (1984), Bharadwaj (1974; 1978), Brahmananda (1974), Das Gupta (1974) and others have also wrestled with the problem of adapting received theories in the light of Indian realities. Within the Marxist tradition, the 1970s particularly witnessed the Mode of Production debate, now conveniently brought together as a volume by Utsa Patnaik (1990), which was again an attempt to re-examine a theoretical system on the basis of problems arising from the Indian situation.

V

The present volume can also be situated broadly within the Indian tradition of critically evaluating received economic theories against the concrete and experiential realities of the Indian situation. However, there is also a difference. Unlike most others mentioned earlier, I am not a theoretical economist in the sense that I have not been directly concerned with generating economic theories or even extending or adapting them to accommodate Indian conditions. I would describe myself as one who has constantly sought the help of economic theories to illumine economic problems. My role has been that of an analyst, one who negotiates between economic theories and economic policies without being either a theorist or a policy maker. To put it differently, I have been a self-appointed representative of the many who actually experience economic problems and try to make sense of them. In this task I have posed questions to both theorists and policy makers from the perspective of my 'clients'. The reflections contained in this book have arisen from such dialogues—the dialogues between the world of theory and the world of experience. They are not answers. They are further posers, or pointers at best, mainly to professional economists who take their 'dual citizenship' seriously.

My position is that if economics as a field of study is to become relevant to experiential economic problems and related to the ever changing character of real life economies, a conceptualisation of the economy, distinctly different from what standard economic theory is based upon, is called for. My point of reference is neo-classical economic theory partly because that was the basis of my learning and teaching economics and also because it is economics par excellence in most academic institutions in India and in many parts of at least the Anglo-American world. In Chapter 3 a selective expedition into the evolution of economic theory is made, setting neo-classical economics against the classical tradition on the one hand and the new institutional economics on the other. The contrast is between the abstract logic of a timeless economy which neo-classical economics deals with and the substantive logic of economic evolution that Adam Smith had tried to build up. The new institutionalists have been brought in to demonstrate the futility of the attempt to graft selectively substantive aspects on to the formal logic of neo-classical economics and to suggest that, if the emphasis is on substantive issues, what is called for is not a reformulation of some theories but a conceptualisation of the economy in tune with the realities of the situation.

In Chapter 4 I try to establish that as the economy is a manifestation of some aspects of social relationships it must be approached with an evolutionary perspective. Economic evolution, of course, is a difficult problematic and many issues related to it are contested and controversial. However, it seems that in the usual epochal treatment of the subject a very important aspect of economic evolution tends to get neglected, namely, the changes that come about in the organisational patterns of the economy over time. It is this theme that is concentrated on, almost to the exclusion of all other aspects of the vast and intricate problems relating to economic transformation. In order to get into the changing organisational patterns of the economy a scanning of it in terms of its basic units and their interactions must be done. A units-and-links analysis of this kind provides a micro-global view of the economy. For this purpose I enter into an identification of the basic units of the economy, trace the differentiation they experience and the changes that come about in the manner of their interactions. Special significance is attached to the processes of intermediation that emerge over time. It is also suggested that empirically identifiable aspects of economic evolution are the changes in the unit mix of the economy, in the internal structure of the units and in the patterns of their interaction.

Such a conceptualisation of the economy as an evolving complex system makes it possible to probe into the working of the economy and its differential impact on different sections that constitute it. In Chapter 5 the implications of viewing the economy in this manner are drawn out and four interrelated substantive issues that call for clearer understanding in order to come to grips with economic problems in the future are discussed.

These views on the economy are not the result mainly of theoretical or logical considerations. My studies in the past have all been related to specific aspects of the Indian economy. The reflections on the nature of the economy have resulted from grappling with these problems—especially the poverty of the masses—over the past four decades or so. Chapter 2 contains a critical assessment of my studies on the Indian economy. At the end of this Chapter I indicate that the treatments in the three subsequent chapters are further developments of themes that emerged from these studies. The problem that I have been wrestling with, and continue to wrestle with, is how to have a theoretically informed procedure to identify and interpret the empirical manifestations of transformation in economies such as India's.

Notes

1. This theme is further discussed in Chapter 5.
2. On the occasion of the centenary of the *Economic Journal*, some leading economists were invited to contribute short pieces on 'The Next 100 Years?' The January 1991 issue of the journal consists of these pieces. Many of those who responded made use of the opportunity to comment on the present state of economics. E. Malinvaud said:

   > On this occasion I believe it is more proper at the beginning to question whether economics meets with the expectations one entertains about its ability to contribute to solving some of the problems raised by the organisation of our society. From this point of view the past fifty years were obviously marked first by a wave of optimism, then by the painful realisation that most of the initial beliefs were the product of delusion (1991: 64)

   Joseph E. Stiglitz's observation was:

   > In spite of . . . methodological triumph, the subject does not bear all the hallmarks of some of the other sciences. Most strikingly, while economists of many persuasions may agree about the tools to be employed, there is no agreement about the basic economic model for describing the economy (1991a: 134)

3. When Gilbert Slater arrived in Madras in 1915 to head the newly started Department of Economics of the Madras University, he recognised the danger of the students learning Marshall's *Principles* in 'parrot fashion' and decided that they should learn economics by observing the living conditions in their own villages.
4. According to Phyllis Deane '. . . Keynesian theory has come to be interpreted in textbooks in exactly the opposite sense to which Keynes saw it himself, i.e., it is treated as a special case of neo-classical theory, the case of unemployment equilibrium' (1978: 180). Dasgupta expresses himself even more strongly when he says: '. . . Keynesian economics, in spite of the author's invectives against his predecessors is a return to the classics, while the analysis that it involves is based on the marginalist technique' (1983: 12). Chapter 3 (section XV) will show that my evaluation of Keynesian economics is different.

2

ECONOMIC PROBLEMS AND ECONOMIC THEORIES: A RETROSPECTIVE ACCOUNT

Issues of Allocation

I

My decision to take up the study of economics as an academic discipline was made in 1947–48. I was then in the final year of high school in a small town in what was then the native state of Travancore. During the early months of that year, academic work was disrupted by the political situation in the State. The independence of the country was imminent and there was considerable excitement in looking forward to the emergence of Free India. However, the Dewan of Travancore, Sir C.P. Ramaswamy Iyer, had announced a plan to declare Travancore an independent country *outside* Free India. This was opposed by the people at large, and the State Congress which had been demanding Responsible Government in the State now shifted its demand to the merger of the State with India. In June and July 1947 the popular agitation in the State intensified with students from schools and colleges also joining in. Strikes in educational institutions became a regular feature followed by meetings and speeches. As a senior student of the school and a member of the school's debating team, I became heavily involved in all these activities which finally led to the resignation of the Dewan and the decision of the State to remain within India just a few weeks before 15 August thus enabling the people of the State to greet Independence as citizens of the Indian Union.

For the flag-hoisting ceremony in the school on that bright Friday morning attended by many prominent members of the public, I was selected to make a speech representing the students. Political freedom is only a prelude to the economic freedom of the masses was the theme of my speech. Though this statement was frequently heard in those days, I had not given much thought to it till then. However, as I was preparing my speech it occurred to me that the study of economics, to see how the economic freedom of the masses could be made a reality in independent India, would be a fascinating and challenging task. Minoo Masani's *Our India* was one of the books prescribed as a non-detailed text for our English course. Through it I was able to get some glimpses into Indian economic reality and I decided to take up economics as my course of study at college. I discussed the matter with my teachers. None of them knew what academic economics was and many of them expressed disappointment that I was not going into the physical sciences in which I was doing very well.

Economics was not a subject taught in the Intermediate Course in those days (at least in the many south Indian colleges where I had made enquiries). The advice I was given was that as economics was one of the 'arts' subjects it would be better for me to do logic and history at the intermediate level as a preparation for the study of economics. This I did in St. Joseph's College, Bangalore, in 1948–50. I joined the Madras Christian College in June 1950 for the BA (Hons) course.

The Honours Course in Economics at Madras University at that time had six papers (and a general essay) and the pattern in Christian College was to do two every year. During the first year the two papers were Principles of Economics and Economic History with four lectures in each per week which left considerable free time for reading in the library. I turned to Principles with great eagerness and expectations, but the theory of consumer behaviour with which the course started (after a very brief and vague discussion of Lionel Robbins' *An Essay on the Nature and Significance of Economic Science*) appeared to be far removed from the concerns I had in my mind—poverty of the people of India and related aspects—and I began to feel restless. Before the end of our course, specifically in the final year, 1952–53, our attention was frequently drawn to the discussions on planning that were becoming prominent in the country at that time. But it was clear that the vocabulary of that discourse was distinctly different from all that we were learning, with the possible exception of the paper on public finance which had some reference to policy issues. Public Finance and Rural Economics were the two papers in the final year. I found it initially impossible to link up all the 'theory' I had learned till then and the treatment of some major aspects of Indian reality dished out as descriptive accounts in Public Finance and Rural Economics.

When I completed the BA (Hons) course (recognised as equivalent to MA by the Madras University) I felt strongly that there was much more to be known in economics than what I had learned. My only hope in the circumstances was to take up teaching and continue the learning of the subject on my own. I was invited to join the Department of Economics in my own College immediately after the results were published. Since teaching, as such, was not very demanding, I was able to devote considerable time to reading (without much guidance, however) and writing occasional articles relating to economic problems. I studied V.K.R.V. Rao's critique of Keynesian economics which was one of the first attempts, that I had seen, evaluating received theory in the context of Indian reality. With the preparations for the Second Five Year Plan in 1955, planned economic development had become the general theme of economic discourse in the country. There was a lively discussion in the *Economic Weekly* on the problem of choice of technology in which Joan Robinson, K.N. Raj, Amartya Sen and others participated. As I was, at that time, trying to go abroad for advanced studies in economics, I paid special attention to the debate.

II

In September 1958 I joined Stanford University for a PhD programme. The studies at Stanford were very demanding which I initially found hard to cope with because my training till then had been confined to economic theory (mainly Marshallian economics with brief introductions to Hicks' *Value and Capital* and Keynes' *General Theory*), but had not taken me to its underlying logic. The core of the training programme at Stanford was the logic of neo-classical economics expounded by Kenneth Arrow, Melvin Reder and others, and its analytical tools handled by Hendrik Houthakker, Marc Nerlove, Irma Adelman and Hollis Chenery. Bernard Haley taught the history of economic thought. Lorie Tarshis dealt with Keynesian economics and Ellis Shaw gave an introduction to Patinkin's attempts to rehabilitate classical economics and also to the Gurley–Shaw theory of finance which was at its formative stage at that time. The three people dealing with economic growth and development were Moses Abramovitz who was analysing aspects of US economic growth, Hollis Chenery specialising in inter-industry economics and Paul Baran providing a Marxist analysis of the political economy of backwardness. Baran was one of the very few Marxist economists in any US university at that time. Baran introduced me to an alternative analytical framework within which the problems of poverty and exploitation which exercised my mind could be examined.

When the time came for the choice of a topic for the PhD dissertation, I had no doubt that it would have to be some applied problem relating to the development of what was then called underdeveloped economies, but narrowing it down was not easy. I did extensive reading on the problems of 'surplus labour' and in the area of the choice of technology. I sought the help of Bagich Minhas who was a couple of years senior to me at Stanford and who was in the final stages of his PhD thesis which subsequently received considerable attention as the Constant Elasticity of Substitution (CES) production function. A possibility he suggested to me was to take an Indian industry to test the production function and I did some work along that line. The cotton textile industry suggested itself as the natural choice. I discussed the matter with Hollis Chenery (who was one of the scholars associated with the CES production function) and he thought it was a good idea. He also agreed to be my PhD supervisor.

The main source of data for Indian industry studies was the Census of Manufactures and as I started processing the data pertaining to the cotton textile industry, it looked as though the industry was subject to increasing returns to scale with the smaller units using more inputs per unit of output in comparison to the larger ones. This posed a problem for me as the CES production function had constant returns to scale as one of its basic premises. A more serious problem also occurred to me. If the smaller units were using more inputs per unit of output, they were technologically inefficient, and if they continued to coexist and compete with the larger ones, the factor markets could not be taken to be perfect. This line of thought turned the focus of my attention to a more serious study of factor market structure and imperfections.

That markets, particularly factor markets, showed many forms of imperfections in underdeveloped countries was a widely accepted proposition at that time. The explanation offered was that factor markets were characterised by immobility and ignorance which could be recognised as facts of life, but which could not be analysed as they were considered to be non-economic in nature. I was not willing to dismiss these as non-economic issues and decided to probe further into them.

I turned to a study of 'small scale units' and found that, in many instances, they were indeed technologically inefficient. It became clear also that many of them were proprietorships or partnerships in which the labour and other resources (capital) available to the owners were jointly utilised in production. This was seen as a common feature of many of the small scale units whether they belonged to the 'modern' or the 'traditional' sector. Since such units formed the vast majority of the industrial enterprises in a country like India employing the bulk of the labour force in the manufacturing sector, I arrived at the conclusion that the joint utilisation of labour and non-labour resources by the owners should be considered as a characteristic feature of the factor markets in an underdeveloped country.

From then on my attention shifted from the purely technological aspects of production to the organisational aspects. Around this time Hollis Chenery left Stanford to join the Kennedy administration and Moses Abramovitz became my supervisor. He showed great interest in the manner in which work on my dissertation was proceeding. When I brought in the handloom sector of the cotton textile industry as well into my analysis, two aspects became clear to me; first, that the industrial scene (in India) was characterised by the coexistence of a large spectrum of diverse technologies, many of them being technologically inefficient; and second, that this was a reflection of 'surplus labour' as those who could not find work tended to employ themselves with whatever non-labour resources they had at their disposal without considering whether such utilisation was efficient or not.

I gave a seminar on these issues providing what I considered to be an economic explanation for the widely prevalent pattern of self-employment in labour abundant economies. Some who were theoretically oriented, however, considered that self-employment was a 'cultural' manifestation, the unwillingness of people to work for others. I took the line that wage employment, which economic theory accepted as the norm, could also be interpreted as a 'cultural' feature, the unwillingness of those who had both labour and capital to utilise them directly and their eagerness to rent out their capital *and* their labour to others. I proceeded further and argued that if it was the case that the joint utilisation of own labour and capital would bring a larger total income than the sum of the earnings separately from the renting out of capital and labour, it was an eminently rational economic activity even if in the process obsolete and inefficient technologies came to be in use. Such indeed was likely to be the situation where, in a macro sense, labour tended to be redundant with its marginal productivity approaching zero. There was general recognition that I was able to provide an economic rationale for factor market imperfections in underdeveloped countries, particularly those said to be characterised by surplus labour. This finally became the central argument of my PhD thesis, *Factor Market Structure and Technological Characteristics of an Underdeveloped Country: An Indian Case Study.*

I did not succeed in providing a rigorous theoretical formulation of the issue. I only showed that in an economy where the equilibrium price of labour was zero, the labour markets would be imperfect as labour had a positive 'existence price' and that the resulting disequilibrium in the labour market would have its bearing on the market for other factors as well, thus providing the basis of overall factor market imperfections. This formulation, however, gave rise to a new problem. Where labour and non-labour resources tended to be used jointly by those who owned them, market categories themselves have analytical limitations. In particular, in as much as the owners themselves are striving to ensure the highest possible joint returns, it is not possible to decompose their earnings neatly into wages and profits. And because of the established basic disequilibrium, even shadow pricing of the factors has limitations.

These issues came up for discussion from time to time, especially with the members of my doctoral committee, but I did not have enough expertise to negotiate them adequately. One member of the committee cautioned me against getting lost in difficult and uncharted theoretical issues and wanted me to concentrate on the empirical aspects of my work and the rationale I was providing for the continued coexistence of technologies of different vintages. This aspect had been generally neglected in the debate on choice of technique which had become very much of a 'planning problem' in the sense that the major issue was considered to be the determination of criteria for the choice on the assumption that once that decision was made the right kind of technique could easily be adopted. Here was a clear case of a 'logical' approach without reference to the realities of the situation, or a concern with 'rational' choice without addressing the question of the

extent to which choice was feasible, and without distinguishing between rationality as viewed by the actors themselves on the one hand
and by the analyst on the other.

What I considered to be the theoretical aspects arising from my
work could not easily be pushed away from my mind. But those who
were dealing with development issues did not address some of these
fundamental problems while theorists were not familiar with the kind
of empirical situations I was dealing with. Towards the final stages of
my work at Stanford, in fact after my final draft was with the members of the doctoral committee, I had a discussion with Kenneth
Arrow. I had taken courses with Arrow and he was on the panel that
examined me for the 'comprehensives' after I had completed the required course work. However, while I was working on the dissertation
I had practically no contact with him. The problem I posed to him was
whether the fact that labour must have a positive share in output even
when it was seen to be a redundant factor (with an equilibrium price
of zero) posed any threat to general equilibrium analysis. I brought to
his attention a rather obscure footnote in Schumpeter's *History of
Economic Analysis* where he had stated that one of the instances
where the general equilibrium analysis would break down was under
such conditions.[1] Schumpeter, however, had not explained why. Arrow had not seen this reference and stated that general equilibrium
analysts had not considered the problem in this manner because it was
generally assumed that such problems would not arise. He pointed out
too that in the paper on the existence of competitive equilibrium, that
he had done along with Debreu (Arrow and Debreu, 1954), they had
made this assumption quite explicit. I had not seen this paper because
Econometrica was not one of the journals I was consulting. Soon after
our conversation I looked up the paper and found it not easy to follow.
I reported this to Arrow who told me that there was a paraphrase of
the paper in Koopmans' *Three Essays* (Koopmans 1957). Going
through this book I noted that Arrow had drawn my attention to what
Koopmans had referred to as the 'survivor problem'. I went back to
the Arrow–Debreu paper and the significance of the two basic assumptions of competitive equilibrium suddenly dawned on me. I was
very happy indeed to note that what I had hesitantly considered as a
theoretical problem was indeed a crucial one, although even then it
was not clear to me how it was to be communicated. I resolved to do
some more work on the problem.

III

My dissertation was accepted in April 1962 for the award of the Ph.D. degree and I returned to Madras Christian College. However, for nearly two years it was impossible to get back to the research that I was so keen to continue as I was entrusted with administrative responsibilities as Head of the Economics Department. The opportunity came in 1964 when the Economics Department of the Annamalai University hosted a University Grants Commission (UGC) sponsored seminar on 'The Theory of Economic Development'. I wrote a paper on 'Some Problems of Factor Allocations in an Underdeveloped Economy' (Kurien 1967) about which I said in the abstract: 'The purpose of this paper is to show that the factor allocation problem in an overpopulated underdeveloped economy is significantly different from the treatment of the problem in received economic theory. The paper does not develop an alternative model for factor allocations, although it discusses at length some special features of factor allocations in an underdeveloped economy. It is but an interim report of research already undertaken in this field and of work now going on.' What I did was first to provide a restatement of the pure theory of competitive equilibrium essentially of the Walras–Cassel model, deriving from it the familiar theoretical propositions regarding the allocation of resources. In particular, I pointed out that if a factor was in excess supply in equilibrium it would become redundant with its equilibrium price equal to zero.

I then turned to attempts in the literature to make the mathematical model economically relevant. I entered directly into the Arrow–Debreu issue of survival, the attempt to establish that the participants in the system, particularly the consumers, can both survive and participate in the market. Arrow and Debreu establish this by making two basic conditions: first, that the total quantity of goods produced is more than necessary for the survival consumption requirements of all participants and, second, that each consumer can survive on the basis of the resources he holds and the direct use of his own resources. The significance of the former is quite evident and a model of general equilibrium that did not satisfy this condition certainly would not have economic relevance even if it could be claimed to be mathematically correct. The second condition, however, is of a different nature because it deals with the 'initial endowments' of *each of the participants*. The assumption that each participant has enough resources to survive and enter into market relations is required for a market economy but not for an economy where the production and distribution decisions could be separated. For, under such conditions the total output (which is greater than required for the survival of all by virtue of the first assumption) could be distributed according to some non-market principle. I, therefore, argued that the general equilibrium conditions of optimal factor allocations that could not be satisfied in a market economy (in the absence of the second Arrow–Debreu condition) could be satisfied, for instance, in a socialist economy.

Arrow and Debreu had taken their second condition to be satisfied on the assumption that even if a consumer had no non-labour resources, as long as he could utilise his labour directly or via exchange, it would be adequate. It is on this basis that they proceeded with the rest of the exposition. However, where 'surplus labour' was considered to be a basic feature of underdeveloped economies such as India, to assume that participants would be able to make a living solely on the basis of their labour would be to assume away the problem itself. The problem that surplus labour posed to equilibrium analysis had received some attention in earlier works. Rosenstein–Rodan, the first to use it in the analysis of economic backwardness, had stated that the existence of surplus labour constituted an 'important instance of the Pigovian divergence between private and social marginal product' giving rise to 'external economies'. In any case, since I had argued that the second Arrow–Debreu condition for survival was not necessary for equilibrium analysis as such and since it seemed to go against the very nature of overpopulated underdeveloped economies, I decided to see what would happen if it was dispensed with.

As noted earlier, a Lange–Lerner kind of socialist economy could dispense with the second condition by resorting to a macro redistributive arrangement. While this is a theoretically sound argument, it did appear somewhat artificial to think of the total product (arrived on the basis of an optimal allocation of factors) being first pooled and then redistributed among the participants. Hence, I decided to search for a micro 'solution'.

In the paper presented at Annamalai, my argument was that a micro solution to the survival problem could be found if it was maintained that those who owned the non-labour and labour resources would use them together so as to engage in production *and* the necessary redistribution to ensure survival. Since this appeared to be difficult, if not impossible at the individual level, I went on to claim that the household (which was the basic unit of ownership of resources even in the Arrow–Debreu model) should be taken as the basic production unit at the micro level both as the economic and social arrangement to ensure survival in an overpopulated underdeveloped economy. If so, the household would become an owning, producing and consuming unit blurring the neat separation that the Arrow–Debreu model was trying to maintain between consumption and production decisions, entrusting the former to the households and the latter to the firms. The non-fulfilment of the 'boundary condition' (between producers and consumers) already posed problems to the Arrow–Debreu model. I pressed further and claimed that if labour and non-labour resources had to be jointly utilised to ensure survival, it was no longer possible to maintain the free mobility of factors in search of the highest remuneration. In other words, a different (and certainly more realistic) arrangement for survival made it impossible for some of the other conditions of competitive equilibrium analysis to prevail. I, therefore, concluded that while the new survival postulate would make survival of all participants possible, it would fail to achieve competitive equilibrium and the optimal allocation of factors that was considered to be its logical corollary. It was also necessary to point out that the failure of the competitive system in this case did not arise from ignorance, inertia, irrationality or any of the many 'imperfections' that allegedly made it impossible for the competitive system and its sole institution, the market, to function properly in an underdeveloped economy. My claim was that I had established a theoretical case to show why competitive equilibrium analysis was not applicable in the case of an overpopulated underdeveloped economy though I had not provided a counter model to detail the working of such an economy.

There was not much of a discussion of the paper at the seminar. Many of the participants were not familiar with the type of analysis that the paper had attempted. I sent a copy of the paper to Kenneth Arrow. His response was very encouraging. He said: 'I think you have put up a most interesting discussion in elucidating, with the aid of modern resource allocation theory, the nature of the dual economy. In the course of the discussion, you contribute a number of insights on the empirically observable economic effects of this situation.' But he went on to point out:

However, I feel that in terms of logical structure, and indeed in terms of economic significance, there is a gap in the present version of your argument. You claim that all of the consequences you discuss flow from the redundancy of labour and from that postulate alone. However, I really think that you need in addition the assumption which you refer to in footnote 41 as that of an 'existence price'. Indeed, whenever there is involuntary unemployment, one must admit the existence of some force preventing the wage level from falling in the presence of an excess supply of labour. It is indeed today conventional to interpret Keynesian unemployment also as the product of price and wage rigidity.

In the rest of the long letter he went on to elaborate this point. We exchanged several letters discussing the issue. I pointed out that my main argument was that under the conditions described there could not be an equilibrium wage rate as such and that where resources were jointly utilised it was not particularly meaningful to talk about 'wages' if it meant payment made to hired-in labour. Arrow saw the point and said:

Suppose now we ... assume that some of the would-be workers are propertyless while others have property. Again at zero wage, there will still be zero supply of labour. However, ... at any positive wage whatever, there will be a positive supply of labour from the propertyless workers, possibly even sufficient to meet the demand. If this is literally true, there could be no equilibrium wage strictly speaking. At zero wage there is an excess demand for labour, and at any positive wage an excess supply. I would expect this situation to lead to the one envisaged in your dissertation, that is, a minimum conventional wage gets established and maintained but employment is rationed in some arbitrary way (first come, first served, family connections or something like that) ... I have puzzled for a long time on the question of the dual economy and I do not know that any theoretical coherent explanation exists. That does not mean of course that we cannot simply assume some imperfection in competition and try to examine its consequences as you did in your dissertation and has been done by Lewis and earlier by Rosenstein–Rodan.

IV

I was happy to see Arrow take this position though I puzzled over his resort to the 'dual economy' because I thought that a 'dual economy' concept was not compatible with a general equilibrium approach. But, of course, it could be argued that under the conditions of the redundancy of labour which must have a positive claim on output for survival, the economy would *decompose* into a dual economy kind of set-up. I decided to work further on this problem.

This I did in the Father P. Carty Endowment Lectures of the Madras University that I delivered in February 1966 entitled *A Theoretical Approach to the Indian Economy* (Kurien 1970). In the first of the three lectures I spelt out the implications of the postulational method in economics ending with some reservations about the claim that it is *the* scientific method in economics. After dealing with the connection between economic theories and economic systems in the second lecture, I attempted in the third to set up an 'Indian economic system' as one where the quantum of non-labour resources (identified in the 1964 paper as 'property - P') was so low in relation to labour that while the average productivity of labour was above the level required for survival, the marginal productivity was below it so that a competitive allocation of resources was not possible because the wage rate would have to be equal to the marginal productivity of labour which, however, was less than necessary for survival. The basic argument of the lecture was that under such conditions the functioning of the economy, especially the organisation of production, would depend on the pattern of ownership of P. Three types of ownership units ('households') were recognised:

A-type which does not have any P.

B-type which has some P so that the average product of labour is greater than the survival level of income, but the marginal product below it.

C-type which has enough P so that both the average and marginal products are above the survival level of income.

On this basis the following observations were made about the organisation of production and the structure of the economy.

1. There will be a market for labour in the economy as the A-type households can earn a living only by working for others, and at least the C-type households will be eager to hire labour.

2. Some observations are possible about the level of wage rate that will get established. If the wage rate (per eight-hour day) turns out to be below the survival requirement, A-type households will have to

increase the supply of labour in order to achieve the required level of earnings for survival and the lower the wage rate the larger will have to be the supply of labour. Thus, at any positive wage rate below the survival requirement, there will be excess supply of labour reducing the wage rate further and pushing it down to zero. But at zero wage rate, of course, there will be no supply of labour. However, there will be positive demand for labour, thus resulting in excess demand for it. Hence, an equilibrium wage rate is not determinate.

3. If under these conditions, the actual wage rate gets established at the survival level, by some (institutional) method, the B-type households will also be supplying labour. But not all labour willing to be hired can be hired as the C-type households hire labour only to the extent that the marginal productivity in *that* sector becomes equal to the imposed wage rate. But if the marginal productivity of labour in that sector becomes equal to the survival wage rate, and the marginal productivity of labour in the B-type households still continues to be below that level, in the economy as a whole marginal productivity of labour is not getting equalised and there is, therefore, no optimal allocation.

These findings were used to question the relevance of some standard models to depict an underdeveloped economy. The competitive market economy model can be applied only where all ownership units are of the C-type. The application of the Lewis-type dual economy model also raises problems. For example, how does the 'subsistence sector' manage to have a subsistence income? Is there any factor in this sector which cooperates with labour in the production of this income? What is the principle of factor allocation in this sector and in the economy as a whole? If the subsistence income is produced by labour alone in the subsistence sector, does that not in itself constitute a solution for the practical problem that all the 'overpopulated underdeveloped economies' face—that of providing a bare minimum level of living for their people?

Certainly, I was not getting any closer to a more satisfactory theoretical depiction of an underdeveloped economy. However, I was able to provide a theoretical critique of the standard models that were widely in use for not only describing and analysing the problems of underdevelopment, but even for making policy recommendations allegedly based on such analyses. I found prescriptions based on faulty diagnosis difficult to accept.

These critical exercises also had a major positive impact on my thinking. They brought home the crucial role of the distribution of the ownership of non-labour resources ('property', including land and capital) in understanding the problem of underdevelopment. At Stanford I had seen two different treatments of the problem of under-development. Those who based themselves on the neo-classical general equilibrium theory (practically all members of the faculty except Baran) had viewed it essentially as an allocation problem, specifically as a problem of imperfections in allocation resulting from 'institutional' factors. Baran's approach, on the other hand, was basically in terms of ownership of land and capital and of vested interests with little light thrown on problems of allocation. For long, I was not able to reconcile the two approaches. I had worked with the allocation problem and through it arrived at the nature of ownership as the central problem in understanding underdevelopment. For quite some time I had a schizophrenic frame of mind. The 'theory' I was teaching in the classrooms was primarily the logic of competitive resource allocation. The Indian reality I was getting acquainted with through a factual appreciation of a variety of 'development' problems seemed to point increasingly to the ownership issue as the underlying factor. I would finally settle for an ownership based appreciation of the problem of development and underdevelopment, but not without going through a great deal of introspection and experimentation as will be seen later in the chapter.

Preoccupation with the 'survival problem' in a technical sense had another spin-off effect. It became clear to me that shorn of all the academic analysis and sophistication, the development problem is essentially the struggle of vast sections of the people for sheer survival and that no analysis which did not take serious note of this fact can be considered valid however brilliant and scholarly it may be. And if development in this sense is the reality of the majority in our country, and possibly throughout the world, economics itself cannot be properly enunciated apart from this reality. It is not surprising that many of the neat arguments and theorising in economics are derived by first *assuming* that every participant has enough resources at his command to ensure survival and some surplus to be able to enter into market operations. Yet, from a realistic perspective what a far-fetched assumption this is!

Growth and Change

V

In the Annamalai paper I had indicated (as I had done earlier in my dissertation) that the empirical manifestation of surplus labour was not visible unemployment, as it might be suspected, but the presence of large numbers of work-sharing and income-sharing economic units which I had designated as 'producer households' (the B-type households in *A Theoretical Approach to the Indian Economy*). The distinguishing feature of such households, it may be recalled, is that though the marginal productivity of labour is below the survival income level, the average productivity is above it. They are, therefore, not mere 'subsistence' units, but potentially capable of devoting part of their income for purposes of future growth. I had used this finding to critique the Arthur Lewis model of the 'dual economy' consisting of one sector where labour somehow survived, supplying labour at (constant) subsistence wage rate to the other sector where capitalists using labour at subsistence wage were making profits and reinvesting them to generate growth. The presence of the B-type households spoils this neat dichotomy of the model. On the 'classical' assumption that 'workers do not save and capitalists do not consume' such models could also 'predict' growth, which is simply a function of the share of profits in total income. But if B-type households (which are not only producing and consuming units, but could also be saving and investing units) dominate the system there is no way of determining growth a priori. It, therefore, occurred to me that the B-type households play an important role not only in the allocation of resources in an economy such as India's but also in its growth and development over time. This aspect was going to be the next phase of my enquiry.

Empirically identifying the B-type households in the Indian economy and arriving at an assessment of their quantitative significance, in terms of employment, output savings and investment, was not going to be easy. However, since many households engaged in agriculture and the 'cottage industries' were known to be of this kind, the initial presumption had to be that they would be a major component of the Indian economy. I recalled also Professor P.C. Mahalanobis's statement: 'Indian economy is basically one of small household units of production; and most of the enterprises are run by self-employed persons' (Mahalanobis 1955: 16).

The most readily available information pertaining to this segment of the economy was, rather surprisingly, about savings. This was simply because the national accounting of domestic savings of India had divided the economy (as was the practice in the developed economies of the West) into three: government, corporations and households, the third being the residual sector. One of the early estimates of savings and investments in the Indian economy for the 1950s showed that over the decade the saving–income ratio had moved up from 5.7 to 9.7 and, more importantly, that in most years the household sector accounted for over 75 per cent of the savings—in some years, in fact, over 80 per cent (Khatkhate and Deshpande 1965). This empirical finding seemed to go against the then widely held 'theoretical' opinion that the basic problem of the underdeveloped countries was their *inability* to save. It also seemed to point to a rather unexpected *source* of savings, viz., the households. True, the household sector was a residual one including unincorporated enterprises (which in a more refined division of the economy might have been brought under the 'corporate' sector) but because I had already recognised the category of 'producer households' as an important component of the Indian economy, I decided that the savings behaviour of this composite sector may be more significant than was immediately obvious. The matter required more careful scrutiny.

The literature on savings and investment in the economy at this time had shown that the early stages of development were characterised by division of labour in production but not in savings and investment and that disaggregated studies of national savings indicated that entrepreneurial groups had a higher propensity to save which could arise from the need or desire to finance their own investment (Friend and Kravis 1957; Gurley and Shaw 1967). There was also recognition of 'the potential danger in constructing aggregate saving or consumption functions without distinction between entrepreneurs and other individuals, and in assuming that savings and investment decisions are independent for individuals as a whole' (Friend and Kravis 1957: 290). The estimate of Indian savings and investment for the 1950s had shown that in the early stages physical assets constituted over 80 per cent of the savings of the households and although there was a sharp fall subsequently, even in the early 1960s it was over 50 per cent.

I tried to bring together these somewhat disparate bits of information drawn from widely different sources and arrived at the following hypotheses:[2]

(*a*) The clue to the understanding of the savings of the Indian economy is to be sought in the savings behaviour of the households;
(*b*) the fact that many Indian households are producer households has a bearing on their savings behaviour;
(*c*) the entrepreneurial character of such households would imply that they would directly invest much of their savings; and
(*d*) investment opportunities would, therefore, become a significant determinant of savings decisions.

The first three of these were based on the intrepretation of the available macro data on savings in the economy; although they, especially (*b*) and (*c*), also involved giving an interpretation of the data different from what was widely held at that time. The fact that a very high proportion of savings was in the form of physical assets was considered as indication of the unwillingness of households to part with their savings or as the result of the absence of intermediaries to mobilise the savings. My interpretation depended crucially on the behavioural characteristics featured in (*d*) for which the literature provided some justification, but which could not be substantiated solely in terms of *ex post* data. It related to the savings decision and not to the extent of savings as such and was a departure from the standard Keynesian view which expressed consumption (and savings) as a function of the level of income. Official statistics also did not distinguish between producer or entrepreneurial households and others and hence there was no easy way of probing into the matter further.

Conducting an investigation specifically into the hypothesised savings behaviour was the only way out. The small town of Tambaram in the vicinity of the city of Madras provided a good location where informal enquiries could be held about the 'entrepreneurial' characteristics and savings–investment behaviour of a variety of producer households. These enquiries appeared to support the claim that was made in (*b*) and so I proceeded to do a systematic study of a random sample of small household production units in the city. Because of financial and time constraints the survey was of a very modest nature confined finally to 100 units which, however, were engaged in the production of some 40 different types of goods. With an average annual income of close to Rs 7,000, the saving–income ratio of the sample as a whole was seen to be as high as 37 per cent with the ratio showing a clear positive correlation with the level of income. The study also lent 'confirming support, though not conclusive proof, that investment opportunities have an overwhelming influence in the determination of the savings' of the units (Kurien 1969: 64).

To me the study was significant for a variety of reasons. In the first instance, it strengthened my conviction that the producer households constitute an important component of the Indian economy. Because of their role in employing a very high proportion of the work force, a large share in the output, a large fraction of the savings and investment, I designated them as the core sector of the Indian economy. Second, because of the presence of these units with characteristics distinctly different from what economic theories of different kinds (neo-classical, Keynesian and 'classical' dual economy) depicted, I felt that it was important to further explore the nature of the Indian economy. In this search, I noted also that a distinguishing feature of the Indian economy was that it consisted of very diverse kinds of primary units and that, therefore, the Indian economy had to be studied at different levels of aggregation for different purposes. Finally, I was also led to think that the underlying growth processes of the Indian economy, again, was likely to be different from what development theories and growth models of the time suggested.

VI

This last point had to be given further attention immediately as it appeared to be quite relevant to the planning procedures the country was following at that time. The First Five Year Plan document had recognised the need to step up savings in the economy not only in the long run, but also immediately. With the Mahalanobis strategy for planning adopted from the Second Five Year Plan onwards, the emphasis shifted to investment and the allocation of investment to the different sectors of the economy. The Mahalanobis model was a real economy model of centralised investment decisions. On the financial implications of the model, Mahalanobis admitted:

> On the question of raising adequate financial resources for investment, our theoretical model cannot give any specific guidance . . . .

At this stage our main task has been to work out a tentative solution in real terms, leaving it to the financial experts to work out the details of the monetary counter-part. *We have taken our stand on the obviously true proposition that if something can be shown to be feasible in physical terms, then the financial and fiscal machinery can always be adjusted to supply a satisfactory monetary counter-part (provided there is no difficulty in making necessary institutional changes)* (Mahalanobis 1955: 50 emphasis added).

The 'obviously true proposition' had found a prominent place in the planning procedure in India at that time. It was essentially a proposition valid in the context of socialist planning where the planning authority had enough control over all the resources and operations of the economy so that a fairly simple 'translation' of a physical model into financial and monetary terms could be achieved. But in economies such as India where the planning authority did not have full control over the economy, the Mahalanobis proposition could not be treated as 'obviously true'. However, foreign advisers to the Planning Commission who were familiar only with socialist planning could not appreciate this difference. Even Michael Kalecki who was quite familiar with the Indian economy stated:

It is sometimes asked how can the government 'get hold' of private savings in order to use them for financing of investment [and went on to say] the question is wrongly put; one should rather ask how can the government restrain private investment to the level allocated to it in the plan. If this condition is fulfilled private savings over and above private investment may be absorbed by the government without causing inflationary pressures . . . . The absorption of private savings by government investment will proceed automatically (Kalecki 1963: 63).

He then went on to show how this was a simple banking operation of transfer of savings from those who save to those who invest. But such a smooth and automatic procedure of getting hold of savings rested on what may be called the Keynes–Kalecki description of an important feature of an advanced capitalist economy that *those who save are not interested in investment and those who invest do not generate the savings*. The financial experts of the Planning Commission would have readily accepted this as it followed from Keynesian macroeconomics which was the sole basis for any macroeconomic thinking on financial and monetary terms at that time.

In *Indian Economic Crisis—A Diagnostic Study* (Kurien 1969), I brought these aspects together and contended that the process of planning in India was proceeding at two different levels—a physical level of allocation of investment in real terms *on the assumption that the planning authority had full control over the use of resources in the economy* and a financial level to show that the savings of the economy could be readily mobilised for centralised investment *on the assumption that those who were responsible for savings had no interest in investing them directly*. On the basis of empirical evidence about the Indian economy, I contested both these underlying assumptions, the first that came from socialist planning and the second from Keynesian theory, and argued that this fundamental confusion was the basis of the emerging Indian economic crisis.

In particular, I pointed out that the attempt to achieve the targeted centralised investment by attempting to force the transfer of savings to the public sector via deficit financing (on which both the Second and the Third Plans had relied heavily) would turn out to be highly inflationary. My critique of the Indian planning process was quite different from the usual, but since it was theoretically informed and based on a crucial feature of the Indian economy which had not received much attention, *Indian Economic Crisis* was widely commented upon. I was, of course, rather naive in suggesting that theoretical misrepresentations were the major factors underlying the crisis of the Indian economy.

This foray into the planning process was incidental to my main plan which in the preface to *Indian Economic Crisis* I described as a journey to discover the Indian Economy. But on this journey I was running into a problem. If categories such as wages and profit had limited application where self-employment was the basic pattern, the categories of savings and investment were not particularly helpful to deal with a situation where the intermediation between the two was limited. I felt that categories more appropriate for an adequate depiction of the Indian economy would have to be found. But how was this search to be organised?

VII

I turned to this question when I had an opportunity to spend a year at Yale University in 1968–69 as a visiting fellow. Much of the time was spent reading the classics—Adam Smith, Ricardo, Mill, Marx, Say— and it struck me that the primary concern of the classical writers was to deal with the concrete economic problems of their times using 'theory' to illumine those problems. Thus, they—not even Ricardo, the most explicit theorist among them—did not separate the abstractness of their logic from the concreteness of their substantive issues. In this sense I would include among the classics not only Keynes's *General Theory*, but also Chayanov's *The Theory of the Peasant Economy*, the English version of which, edited by Daniel Thorner, had then just become available. I was particularly excited about Chayanov because his treatment of the Peasant Economy was the only work I had seen till then which had a direct bearing on what I had described as the Core Economy. I felt, though, that Chayanov was restricting the domain of his analysis to peasants who were using their labour on their own land while the Core Economy included all those who were utilising jointly their labour and any or all other non-labour resources they had. I corresponded with Daniel Thorner on this issue, but he felt that it was much better to deal with Chayanov in terms of what he actually did rather than making attempts to generalise his analysis. I wrote a paper on Chayanov specifically for the *Indian Economic Journal* which was accepted for publication; however, I withdrew it later because I was not quite satisfied with it.

A second aspect that struck me about the classics was the much broader range of issues that they brought into their analysis of economic problems, in particular, the ownership of resources and the associated class structure of society. It occurred to me that neo-classical economics whose rigour I had come to appreciate since the Stanford days achieved that by abandoning, or treating as extraneous, these crucial factors and making an attempt to reconstitute economics around the unifying principle of exchange. To verify this I turned to Walras and was pleased to see that such indeed was the case and that Walras, before reconstructing 'pure economics' solely on the basis of exchange, had quite explicitly stated that he was leaving out all questions of 'property' as being extraneous to his analytical system (Walras 1954: 257). I recognised that while Walras was quite within his right to leave out 'property questions' for the sake of his model or system, later neo-classical economists were not justified in pretending that questions of property, ownership, etc., were beyond the concern of economics as such. I felt that this emptying of the substance of economics for the sake of what was considered to be analytical rigour was the main reason for the sterility of economics about which Adolf Lowe had written around that time (Lowe 1965).

I felt that what was jettisoned out of 'pure economics' had to be brought back if the purpose of economic theory was to throw light on real economic problems instead of producing a surrogate version of the economy with a set of imposed regularities that provided the basis for 'scientific' analysis. By this time I had also become convinced that the nature of the Indian economy could be understood only by dealing directly with the problem of mass poverty. So, I wrote a set of notes with the general title: 'The Economics of Poverty and the Poverty of Economics', mainly finding fault with the widely prevalent neo-classical approach to the problem of 'underdevelopment'. As poverty was not part of the vocabulary of economics at Yale, I did not succeed in persuading many scholars there to interact with me on those notes. However, I had some very stimulating discussions there with Koopmans, Tobin and Lindblom about matters of mutual interest.

Soon after I returned to Madras Christian College, one of my first academic tasks (other than the full load of teaching) was to study and review Myrdal's three volume *Asian Drama* at the special request of my friend Prof. Yamaoka of Waseda University, Japan, with whom I had spent some time on the way back to India from the United States. I was very eager to go through *Asian Drama* for a variety of reasons. I had greatly admired Myrdal's *American Dilemma* and his penetrating insight into the race problem in the US. I had decided that poverty was going to be the focus of my personal research from then on. And I was searching for a 'classic' on the subject, a status which Myrdal had claimed for his work. So, I turned to *Asian Drama* with great expectations and patiently worked through the 2,000-odd pages. My reactions to it were very mixed indeed.[3] I admired Myrdal's comprehensive coverage of the Indian economy and the mass of material he had assembled on not only the specifically economic aspects such as agriculture and industry (especially small scale industry where I found the treatment particularly helpful), but also on topics such as education, corruption and the nature of the state. In this sense the attempt, certainly, was to return to the 'classical' tradition. But I did not find in the work the analytical focus of a classic which is vitally necessary when diverse aspects are brought into discussion. In particular, I did not find Myrdal's 'institutional theory' given in Appendix 2 of Volume III particularly satisfactory (Myrdal 1968). Hence I made a critique of that theory the focus of my review. I shall not go into details here (as a detailed treatment of Myrdal forms part of Chapter 3). Myrdal's 'social system', it may be recalled, consisted of six broad categories: (*i*) output and income; (*ii*) conditions of production; (*iii*) levels of living; (*iv*) attitudes towards life and work; (*v*) institutions; and (*vi*) policies. In other words, he added three broader 'social' elements (*iv–vi*) to what he considered to be the limited Western economic factors (*i–iii*) to produce the 'social system'. The argument was that development problems of countries like India required certain peculiar social characteristics ('low levels of work discipline, punctuality, and orderliness; superstitious beliefs and irrational outlook; lack of alertness, adaptability, ambition, and general readiness for change and experiment; submissiveness to authority and exploitation; low aptitude for cooperation; low standard of personal hygiene; and so on' [p. 1862] in addition to conventional economic factors as explanatory variables. I found the procedure unsatisfactory because seldom did Myrdal himself succeed in properly bringing these elements together. On the other hand, it gave him the opportunity to press into service *either* the economic *or* the non-economic factors to explain specific development problems. The review picked up several examples from the work to substantiate the critique. I, therefore, argued that Myrdal's 'social system' disintegrates into two, 'purely economic' and 'cultural', and went on to show how this dichotomy also influenced his understanding of the problem of development itself and the mood of pessimism that runs through the entire work. I said: 'In sum, while radical policy measures are required in South Asian context to bring about change, the social structure, cultural and religious attitudes of the people and their institutions make it impossible to have radical policies. Revolution is necessary; but revolution *will not* come and *cannot* be brought about! This is Myrdal's Asian Dilemma (Kurien 1974: 140). I found *Asian Drama* a very useful book of reference, but I doubted whether it would have much of an impact on Indian economic thinking and analysis.

This is not to say that I was dismissing the work. It influenced me somewhat indirectly. From the Stanford days I had come to think of 'surplus labour' as not only the chief characteristic but also the main cause of the underdevelopment of countries like India. Working through Myrdal helped me to understand that such aggregative characterisations of an economy were not particularly helpful and that the economy had to be viewed from different vantage points and probed at different levels to come to grips with its problems. Second, and perhaps more important, I began to feel that if the very nature of the economy called for such a multi-pronged approach, then no single integrated theoretical model was necessary or sufficient to come to grips with all its features. I was, certainly, not implying that a complex conceptual entity like the economy could be comprehended without 'theory' in some sense. But I had to figure out what the nature of such enquiry was to be. I have wrestled with this issue since then and all my subsequent writings have been attempts to deal with it.

VIII

For a while I felt that there was nothing to hold on to. In teaching I resorted to a strategy which, I thought, would help me resolve my dilemma. Over the years I had become a specialist in teaching 'theory' both at the graduate and undergraduate levels. At both levels teaching theory meant simply expounding what others had written. Hardly ever was there any deep involvement with what was being discussed. Occasionally one did come across a puzzle or two, but it was not necessary to draw students into them. I felt this sort of teaching was not enough for me. Hence I decided to give up the teaching of theory at the undergraduate level and opted to teach the paper on 'Indian Economic Problems' (IEP). My colleagues were surprised because IEP at the undergraduate level was usually handled by the junior-most member of the faculty. Anyway, for the change I wanted, I did not have to step on anyone's toes! What I was looking for was an opportunity to learn with the undergraduates and to test how much and what kind of theory was needed to understand Indian economic problems.

However, even for this purpose one had to have some working notion of what 'theory' was. For this I turned to Myrdal who had indicated that theory was a logically correlated system of questions addressed to the problem to be tackled. All the work I had done so far and my reading of the classics had led me to see that one of the basic questions to be asked of Indian economic problems was about the manner in which non-labour resources were owned and controlled—the 'Who owns what' question. When I started using this question to understand mass poverty it became clear that the 'who owned what' question had a tremendous bearing on the 'Who got what' aspect also. Soon it became clear too that since what one got depended very much on what one did, a third question too had to be considered, 'Who does what?'. Soon I was telling my undergraduate students that three interrelated questions had to be asked to enter into and understand the Indian economy (any economy for that matter, I claimed, without trying to 'prove' it): 'Who owns what?', 'Who does what?', 'Who gets what?', the 'what' in each case was meant to suggest that the question would have to be examined in some detail—land, machinery, financial resources, etc., in terms of ownership; farming, fishing, manufacturing, etc., in terms of 'doing', and so on. Pretty soon it became clear that in fact more details were necessary: it made a big difference whether land was wet or dry, for instance. I was coming to have some basis both for my teaching and my writing.

For a while I turned away from the discussion of the Indian economy as a whole and started looking at specific problems—the green revolution, prices, trade and self-reliance, environment, higher education, etc. This was necessitated partly because the papers I was writing at this juncture were, practically all of them, at the request of periodicals, organisers of seminars and other groups who suggested the topics. However, I made use of each opportunity to approach the particular topic, to the extent possible, in terms of my three basic questions. About this time, somewhat unexpectedly, poverty emerged as a topic of public discussion following the acceptance of *'garibi hatao'* as the Congress party's slogan in the crucial general elections of 1971. The publication of the Dandekar–Rath (1971) study estimating the extent of poverty using the National Sample Survey's data on consumer expenditure made it a topic for discussion by economists also. Economists were mainly concerned with estimations and suggesting remedies. I concentrated on explaining the prevalence of mass poverty. I started insisting also that the problem that needed to be analysed was not the poverty *of* India, but poverty *in* India, drawing a sharp distinction between the mass of people who were recognised as being below the poverty line and a small minority well above this level. A juxtaposition of these two groups was necessary to understand the phenomenon of poverty, I argued. It followed too that if such was the nature of poverty, development, seen to be the remedy for poverty, should not be perceived as an undifferentiated national objective. In the introductory chapter of *Poverty and Development* which brought together some of the pieces I had written during this period I said: 'For me, linking up development and poverty also meant de-linking of development and nations. Poverty is not of nations, but of people .... When development in its economic sense is recognised as dealing with the problem of the poverty of some people *and* the affluence of others within nations and between nations, it is bound to assume new dimensions and pose new questions' (Kurien 1974: 9–10). All through the 1970s my attempt was to identify these new dimensions and questions relating to poverty and development.

IX

The procedures I adopted were determined to a large extent by circumstances. In 1972 I was marginally associated with the newly set up Tamil Nadu Planning Commission. I was shocked to see that in order to prepare a twelve year perspective plan for the eradication of poverty in Tamil Nadu, the effort in the Commission was to produce a 'Mahalanobis kind of model of growth' for the state. I felt that I had to challenge both the concept of growth underlying such approaches and the facile assumption that if growth could be stimulated, poverty would automatically decline. For the country as a whole the famous Fifth Five Year Plan model of poverty eradication had come out around the same time. Although that model had postulated a transfer of income from the top 30 per cent to the bottom 30 per cent as a poverty eradication strategy, it too had uncritically accepted the standard concept of growth. In response, I wrote two related papers, 'What is Growth?: Some Thoughts on the Economics of *Garibi Hatao*' (Kurien 1972a) and 'Framework of a Plan to Eradicate Poverty in Tamil Nadu' (Kurien 1972b). In the former I argued: How commodities are valued in an economic system is at the basis of the concept of growth. An anti-poverty programme via 'growth' is self-defeating because unspecified 'growth' in a system where the vast majority are poor and a few are rich and where the process of valuation is based on economic strength, can only be to the advantage of the rich. The chief concern of an anti-poverty programme must be to spell out a pattern of production to achieve the objective rather than an undue obsession with 'growth' in the abstract. A precondition for any such plan is a drastic reduction in the concentration of ownership and control of the physical resources of the economy.

This was a clear articulation of my position about the theoretical and practical aspects of growth, poverty and related matters which I have continued to hold on to and explicate in different ways since then.

As for poverty eradication itself, I made an identification of those coming below the poverty line in terms of their occupations (agricultural labourers, small and marginal farmers, those engaged in household industries) and their locations (at the district level) and suggested what kinds of policy measures were necessary if poverty eradication was to be achieved. I argued that aggregate and abstract concepts like 'growth' would have to be translated into disaggregated and concrete entities for a proper understanding of problems from a policy perspective.

This led me to take up, along with my colleague Josef James, a more detailed study of economic change in Tamil Nadu. We argued that value categories such as income and growth had very limited application to make an assessment of economic change in an administrative unit such as the states in India within a national economy and that, to the extent possible, a physical analysis was called for (Kurien and James 1979). We, therefore, resorted to a functionally and regionally disaggregated analysis unscrambling the economy of Tamil Nadu into economic activities, basically agriculture and industry and within them looking for changes in cropping pattern and productivity (agriculture) and diversification, location and technological change (industry). These were supplemented by an examination of changes in occupational patterns and in the process of urbanisation. In each one of these we went down to the taluk level and thus produced an elaborately detailed account of economic change (preferring the neutral term change to the more familiar terms such as growth and transformation). Our 'interpretation' of these changes was in terms of the patterns that the data themselves seemed to indicate resorting to cluster analysis for this purpose. It was an out-and-out empirical work, very different from anything I have done before or since.

In spite of what the authors considered to be some very innovative procedures utilised in the work, it failed to generate any discussion or even attention. I can think of two reasons for this. The first was the fact that it was one of the early studies done on the economy of a state at a time when economists did not pay much attention to analysis at that level. Second, cluster analysis that we relied on as the main tool had not been used much in economics and hence it might have been difficult for most economists to follow the work intelligently. Perhaps the study appeared to be somewhat technique oriented, but it set out a procedure for scanning the economy of a region for greater understanding and as the basis for the formulation of policies.

Changing View of the Economy

X

While the study was in its final stages in 1975, I was offered a National Fellowship by the University Grants Commission for a period of two years. The fellowship relieved me of my teaching responsibilities and I utilised the time to write *Poverty, Planning and Social Transformation* (Kurien 1978). In it I pressed into service the propositions I had put forward in 'What is Growth?' However, I had decided that the work would be different from most other contemporary works on poverty. First, it would try to explain the nature of mass poverty and its stubborn persistence in spite of what appeared to be determined efforts, at least from the beginning of the planning era, to eradicate it. I felt that such an approach was required as most of the studies on poverty at that time were, quite understandably, concerned with estimating the extent of poverty. However, my involvement with growth and poverty had led me to see how easy it was for quantification to cease being a way of assessing symptoms and become a substitute for conceptualisation. This, I found to be quite dangerous in as much as it was the first step towards numerical prescriptions without adequate diagnosis which called for an understanding of the underlying processes. My approach to poverty was going to be processual. Second, the professional preoccupation with measurement had also made much of the literature on poverty beyond the comprehension of non-professionals. A stage had been reached where, even on a topic like poverty, economists could talk only to fellow economists. My writing was going to be accessible to anyone who was genuinely interested in the problem of poverty and its eradication. This meant I had to 'translate' a great deal of professional jargon into day-to-day language. In doing so I had to coin some new expressions also.

My reading of the classics, my understanding of what happened to the Indian economy during the colonial period and the awareness that the bulk of those who are now poor are those who had a place in an old economic order but are getting displaced by a new one (artisans, for instance) led me to situate poverty in the context of the onslaught that a capitalist system was making on pre-capitalist economic arrangements. But terms like 'capitalism' and 'pre-capitalism' are heavily loaded and, even granting that economists can identify the package of characteristics for which these expressions are used as labels, I was not sure that an interested lay reader could, without some guidance, distinguish between them. I, therefore, designated pre-capitalist economies as 'need-based' and capitalist economies as 'want-based', and went on to describe the manner of their working. I described poverty as a situation where some people lose their place and claims within need-based economies as a result of the aggressive penetration of the want-based economy on them. I showed that what is generally described as 'growth' is a further manifestation of the aggressive expansion of the want-based economy propelled by, and to the benefit of, the few who own and control non-labour resources. This led me to characterise poverty as a situation where the many cannot have their needs satisfied while the wants of the few are growing and being met. My contention was that poverty is not merely a form of physical deprivation, but a social malady seen by the fact of the growing affluence of the few while the many remain at near subsistence level. Hence I described 'growth' itself as a process that conferred benefits on the few and misery on the many.

The work received considerable attention in the country and outside. Many agencies, especially voluntary agencies dealing with poverty, found the exposition very helpful.

In *Poverty, Planning and Social Transformation* I had not, except in very broad terms, submitted the approach to empirical verification. But while I was writing it, I was also working on a study of poverty in Tamil Nadu that the International Labour Organisation (ILO) had asked me to write for inclusion in their volume on *Poverty and Landlessness in Asia* (Kurien 1977). My examination of the Tamil Nadu situation had given empirical support to the claim that 'growth' was simultaneously generating affluence and poverty.

I followed these two studies immediately with *Dynamics of Rural Transformation: A Study of Tamil Nadu, 1950–1975* (Kurien 1981). This was an attempt to reconstruct the process of transformation that was going on in rural Tamil Nadu since independence, relying solely on the variety of secondary data that was available. If *Economic Change in Tamil Nadu* (Kurien and James 1979) arose in response to the kind of approach that the state's Planning Commission was taking towards the state's economy, *Dynamics of Rural Transformation* was meant to make a critical assessment of 'Integrated Rural Development' that had become official policy in 1976 and had also become something of a global slogan thanks to the sponsorship that it had received from the World Bank. Integrated Rural Development claimed that a holistic approach to development via the application of science and technology would stimulate growth which would eradicate poverty. I contended that deeper issues were involved in rural transformation and went on to examine the pattern of land holdings and asset structure in the rural areas, the changes that were taking place in agriculture, the rapid growth of agricultural labourers, the rising prices and stagnating real wages, and state policies relating to all these aspects. I set poverty and consumption levels against such a background once again to show that evidence coming from the experience during the first quarter of planned economic development was the growing affluence of the few and the continuing misery of the many.

In *Poverty, Planning and Social Transformation*, I had used a literary style. However, *Dynamics of Rural Transformation* was heavily data based, and I made use of a variety of statistical techniques to analyse the data and draw inferences. The Indian Council of Social Science Research (ICSSR) had financed the study and after its report was considered by the Council a decision was made to commission similar studies in the other major states. I was invited to coordinate the research programme, which I readily accepted. Kerala, Karnataka, Andhra Pradesh, Orissa, West Bengal, Uttar Pradesh, Punjab and Rajasthan were taken up for study mainly in terms of the availability of scholars. The programme made a good start with three meetings of the scholars held, first to agree on a common methodology, then to evaluate the data and the third for interim reports. The idea was to complete the studies at about the same time and to bring them out as a volume with an introductory piece making a comparative evaluation. During the second meeting it became evident that some scholars were not keeping in step and at the third meeting it became clear that there was no possibility at all of the studies being completed at about the same time. Hence its collective approach was abandoned and each study was to be treated as a separate project. I was disappointed about the outcome but was glad that in the second half of the 1980s many of the state-level studies did in fact get published.

While I was mentally organising the Tamil Nadu studies in the mid-1970s, I had received an invitation to take up the Directorship of the Madras Institute of Development Studies (MIDS) started at the beginning of the decade by Malcolm Adiseshiah and which was being reconstituted as a national research centre within the framework of the ICSSR. I had no intention of leaving the Madras Christian College which had an excellent atmosphere for the kind of work I was interested in doing and had declined several invitations. However, by mid 1970s I had become very restless about the incompatibility between the economics that I was still teaching and the economic problems I was dealing with both in the classrooms (the papers on Indian Economic Problems for undergraduates and Planning for the postgraduates) as well as in my writings. The shift to MIDS, I thought, would enable me to give up teaching and reflect on the ways to resolve my intellectual crisis and so I had responded positively to the invitation on the condition that I would join the Institute only in 1978 after putting in one more year of teaching in the college following the UGC National Fellowship. This was agreed to both by the MIDS and the ICSSR and so I viewed the Tamil Nadu studies also as a kind of 'homework' preparing myself for the new job.

XI

It was my expectation that the Directorship of a small institute would provide plenty of spare time for my personal research. However, that is not how it turned out. The administrative work was not particularly demanding, but involvement with building up a new institution— recruiting the faculty, drawing up the ground rules, developing the programmes, etc.—did not give me enough opportunity to concentrate on what I wanted to do. Ten years of Directorship, therefore, interrupted my personal research considerably. The best I could do was to respond to some of the many invitations I was getting to participate in academic seminars in the country and outside. In the 1980s, the economic scene in the country took something of a sudden turn with an emphasis on 'liberalisation' as a means to stimulate growth and to tackle the problem of poverty through an essentially redistributive measure. This 'growth plus' strategy spelt out in some detail in the Sixth Five Year Plan (1980–85) document had become the basis of economic policy. I had done enough homework to see that if eradication of poverty was the real objective, this strategy was not much better than the earlier 'growth' strategy. I chose my seminar participations carefully to be able to develop my critique of the strategy keeping in view the relationship between growth and justice as the main issue.

The first thing I did after relinquishing Directorship in 1988 was to make a selection of my writings of the 1980s which Oxford University

Press brought out in 1992—*Growth and Justice—Aspects of India's Development Experience* (Kurien 1992a). I would touch upon two specific problems on which I had initiated enquiries. The first was in response to the Report of the Committee to Review the Working of the Monetary System, 1985 (also known as the Chakravarty Committee Report) which had come to the conclusion that 'the nature, composition and growth of financial assets or claims indicate the sophistication, development and growth of the financial system and hence the overall financial development of the economy'. From the work I had done earlier on the composition of the savings in the Indian economy, I was not sure that it was proper to interpret the changes as reflecting a change in the character of the economy as a whole. For one, contrary to the expectations of an earlier period, that as economic development takes place the share of the household sector in total savings would *go down*, the finding was that even after the overall savings had gone well over 20 per cent of GDP, the share of the household sector was still dominant and that, in fact, it had marginally gone up from 73.7 per cent in 1950–51 to 74.3 per cent in 1983–84. But physical assets which constituted 63.6 per cent of the savings of that sector during the First Plan period had come down to 45.9 per cent in 1983–84 with financial assets correspondingly going up to 54.1 per cent. The Committee had interpreted this change as reflecting the growing separation of the functions of savings and investment in the economy. However, the Committee had not examined what percentage of households was responsible for that sector's savings. Since this question was not considered to be important, there were no official estimates about it either. I pieced together whatever fragmentary and unofficial estimates that were available and came to the conclusion that about 25 per cent of the households were responsible for the entire savings of that sector, and that the top 10 per cent accounted for close to 70 per cent of it. If so, what the Committee had interpreted as the growing sophistication of the economy had to be seen as reflecting the growing incomes and wealth of 'the island of affluence' within the economy, as I came to refer to this upper crust. I also showed that the shift from physical assets to financial assets was partly a consequence of the growth of 'the service sector'—a very striking phenomenon of the 1980s—which gave to the upper crust some distinguishing features. I was led to conclude that a very small segment of the population was beginning to exercise prominent control over the economy via its control over finance and that this was an aspect that I had not sufficiently taken into account in my own approach to the economy which still remained essentially in 'real' terms.

The second issue I had taken up for study during the 1980s was the process of marketisation and the relationship between state and markets. I have been greatly influenced by three studies on the development of the market (or of exchange as an activity); Karl Polanyi's *The Great Transformation,* Hicks' *A Theory of Economic History* and Marx's analysis of the metamorphosis of exchange. While all these had dealt with the epochal evolution of markets as an (or *the*) economic institution, I had felt it necessary to appreciate marketisation as a contemporary and ongoing process in India with tremendous socioeconomic consequences. Along with one of my colleagues, Sarajit Majumdar, I did a study of 'The Characteristics and Consequences of Market Penetration' as an ICSSR project where we examined, at the theoretical level, some of these aspects. When Rajiv Gandhi launched his 'new economic policy' in 1985, suddenly the 'market' appeared on the Indian academic and political scene as a mysterious power capable of producing miracles as had happened in Japan and Germany immediately after the Second World War and as the four 'Asian tigers', South Korea, Taiwan, Hong Kong and Singapore were said to have demonstrated more recently. Without entering directly into the policy issues, I examined the relationship between the state and the market in capitalist countries using 'initial endowment' as the clue to understand the operation of the market, the political power that the state wields and the class divisions of society. I also pointed out the way in which these interact and modify one another.

Early in the 1990s, I developed some of these issues further in the R.C. Dutt Lectures, *Markets in Economic Theory and Policy* (Kurien 1993a). In the lectures I used Polanyi, Hicks and Marx to critique Walras and to move from market in economic theory to the market 'as is, where is'. I indicated the need to see the market as a social institution situating it along with two other institutions in the social realm, the household and the state. As against the standard view that the economy is the domain of the market, I argued that the economy should be envisaged as the constant interaction between this social trio.

It is this perception of the economy that I have attempted to develop in *The Economy: An Interpretative Introduction* (Kurien 1992b). But before I turn to that I would touch upon one more aspect of my work of the 1980s, one directly related to economic problems.

My understanding of the structure and working of the Indian economy had shown me that the policy of liberalisation launched by Indira Gandhi in the early years of that decade would not succeed in dealing with India's basic problem—the removal of poverty. In a paper I wrote in March 1983 (Kurien 1983) I visualised that the logical progression of a process of industrial growth based on import surplus was to get caught in a balance of payments crisis. In 1987, when the general consensus in the country, including among most economists, was that 'there is strong evidence that the Indian economy is now on a new growth path . . . made possible by a sound and responsive macro-economic policy environment' as the *Economic Survey* immediately preceding the famous Rajiv Gandhi budget of 1987–88 claimed, I was sharply critical of what was going on. I made use of the budget to expose the strategy behind the new policy as growth by and for the island of affluence and to insist that it would not be sustainable for long (Kurien 1987). However, I must say that I had not anticipated that the collapse would come in just two to three years.

XII

I now turn to my most ambitious work, *The Economy*. I worked on it continuously from 1988 to 1991, but the account of my earlier work given here would show that it was in the making for a much longer time. I may claim that it is the product of my professional involvements of four decades.

In *The Economy* I made a deliberate decision to shift attention from economics to the economy. The reasoning behind this was that if economics is a representation, exposition or interpretation of the economy (the relationship between the economy and economics is a contested issue and in a way the present book, especially the rest of the chapters, is a commentary on this problem), it is necessary to have an essentially descriptive account of the economy itself. I, therefore, described the economy as society's arrangement to provision the material needs of its members and spelt it out more elaborately as 'a structure of relationships among a group of people in terms of the manner in which they exercise control over resources, use resources and labour in the production of goods and services, and define and settle the claims of the members over what is produced'. Granted that the second part of the statement was couched in plain, everyday language, its novelty was the first part. I felt it necessary to emphasise right from the beginning that the economy is about *people* (and *not* merely about things, commodities or money), and about *relationships* among people. In this sense, the economy is similar to society itself but only a segment of all social relationships that constitute society as it is meant for a specific purpose, namely to provision the material needs. I pointed out that in this sense 'the economy' is not an independent entity but something that is mentally carved out for purposes of enquiry. The idea was to communicate that the economy is not an entity with well-defined boundaries, but always merging with other social spheres. If it is, thus, porous at the boundary, it is always in a state of flux within because it is the result of the interaction of diverse social forces, some complementary and others conflicting, and cannot but reflect the constant interplay of these forces which display a tendency to get solidified.

If the provisioning of the material needs of its members is the objective of the economy, then the primordial forces that shape it are two somewhat opposing ones, a sense of belonging and a sense of authority, which are held together in dynamic tension in the most primordial of social organisations, typically a tribe, or a clan for instance. I, therefore, felt that to understand the nature of the economy, it is necessary to start with an appreciation of the social formation that can be depicted as 'in the beginning' both in a conceptual and historical sense. I decided to accept a tribe for this purpose and in order, initially, not to become preoccupied by the boundary problems, isolated the tribe and set it in the midst of a forest with no 'other' to interact with. I designated the economy of such a group as the 'rudimentary economy' and the task was to study its internal structure. Since its internal structure and dynamics are closely related to its demographic features, I pressed into service Chayanov's analysis of the peasant economy. But Chayanov has no explicit recognition of the authority component which I found absolutely necessary for understanding a rudimentary economy. Through the combination of the sense of belonging and authority components I was able to examine the nature of the division of labour (in production) and transfer (for distribution) within the system. In relation to transfer I recognised two aspects: first a horizontal transfer or sharing related to the sense of belonging and, second, a vertical transfer related to authority and a basic transfer from the 'workers' to 'non-workers' (children, the aged and the infirm). By the combination of and interaction between the sense of belonging and authority, I was able to see in the rudimentary economy many of the issues that figure in political economy. At the same time by isolating the group from interaction with 'others', it was possible to exclude exchange which has become the centre of modern economics. Another aspect that was excluded from the rudimentary economy by isolating it from 'others' was ownership. While the rudimentary economy was being used mainly for analytical purposes, I pointed out that households in all contemporary economies retain the basic elements of the rudimentary economy, though certainly not in pure form. And in economies such as India's, I showed, the producer-households have a much closer resemblance to the rudimentary economy.

The next step was to examine a 'village economy' which, by construction, was seen as a collection of rudimentary economies as its constituent units. The introduction of 'others' gives rise to the notion of ownership which would remain hazy, and to exchange and markets which would stay limited. Thus the units of the economy must be thought of as subeconomies with internal arrangements of their own, but with some interactions with others. However, a village economy would show two distinct features of its own. First, a transfer of part of the produce from the producers to owners (a vertical transfer) and, the second, a differentiation of the units on the basis of endowments and demographic features. Two different kinds of units on these bases were recognised, the resource-rich but labour-scarce on the one hand and the labour-abundant but resource-scarce on the other. The basic asymmetry between the two was also noted and its implications dealt with. The vertical transfer from the producers to the (non-producer) owners was recognised as 'surplus' generated by the former, but appropriated by the latter. It was shown that on the basis of this transfer would arise an urban economy which would be complementary to the village economy to some extent, but its antithesis in another sense. The urban economy would lead to an expansion of exchange which, in turn, would lead to a transformation, over time, of the village economy itself.

What emerges from the transformation is the capitalist economy with exchange as its central feature. But the significance of the capitalist economy is not merely or mainly that exchange becomes ubiquitous, but that labour power itself gets commoditised and so the vertical transfer of the surplus from the producers to the non-producing owners appears as but part of the horizontal transfers which exchange is supposed to generalise. Unlike other economic formations, it becomes easier to mentally carve out the economy in this situation because the desire to accumulate profit (the vertically transferred surplus that accrues to the capitalists) emerges as the rationale of the system and a uniform valuation process resulting from generalised exchange appears as its unifying principle with the market emerging as the sole institution. But I pointed out that this was just a myth propagated for ideological reasons, that the market and the pricing principle have critical limitations and the capitalist economy cannot function without adequate support of a non-economic authority, the state.

Having thus demonstrated that 'the economy' (the capitalist economy to be more accurate) is not a self-regulating system and does not and cannot function on the basis of 'laws' or principles internal to it, I reviewed attempts to establish post-capitalist socialist economies as conscious efforts to bring the economy explicitly under social control. Critically appraising what these attempts were able to achieve since the Soviet Revolution of 1917, I went on to examine the systemic factors which were responsible for the collapse of several of them which, while I was drafting the concerned sections in 1990, were ongoing processes.

These accounts of 'ideal-type' economies and their transformation constituted the first part of *The Economy*. In the second part, I made an attempt to use these building blocks for an analytical description of the Indian economy. In Chapter 7, the central chapter of the book, I suggested that a national economy such as India's must be studied in terms of its constituent heterogeneous units (in particular, those that are essentially of household characteristics, those primarily geared to the market and the pricing principle, and those related to the state) and the variety of links that get established among them. Describing the combination of units and links as activity chains and suggesting that the functioning of a national economy at any given time could be observed through the activity chains, I went on to indicate that the changes that are experienced by the economy over time could be appraised in terms of:

1. Changes in the internal structure of the units.
2. Changes in the unit-mix of the system.
3. Changes in the activity chains, or in the pattern of interaction among the units.

This procedure of understanding a national economy, I designated as a 'micro-global approach'. In the two succeeding chapters I tried to apply this approach for evaluating the evolution of the Indian economy and its ongoing transformation both during the colonial period and since Independence. These were then supplemented by a macro view of growth and change. The penultimate chapter was devoted to an exposition of the phenomenon of the continuing poverty of the masses along with the growing affluence of a small segment of the population. By way of conclusion I entered into a discussion of the possibilities of shaping the economy, especially in an inclusive post-capitalist manner.

XIII

With the writing of *The Economy* I had assumed that my journey for discovering the Indian economy was finally over. In any case, I was not going to do any more major writing, or at least I was going on 'long leave'. This thought entered my mind partly because the completion of *The Economy* in July 1991 coincided with my formal retirement from the Institute and I wanted to be 'away from it all'. But this is not the way it actually happened. After the mid-term general elections in May–June 1991, a new Congress government under the leadership of P.V. Narasimha Rao had come to power with Manmohan Singh as the Finance Minister. The balance of payments crisis of the economy was formally acknowledged, the rupee was devalued and an agenda for reforming the Indian economy through globalisation, liberalisation and privatisation was announced while negotiating a loan from the International Monetary Fund.

All along, my study of the Indian economy was confined to its internal structure with but occasional reference to the external sector. My analysis was also of the 'real' economy. Now it became clear to me that I would have to look at the Indian economy in a global context and that consequently finance would have to figure prominently in all future analyses. Hence I responded positively to an invitation to give some lectures in the United States on 'global economic development'. During the five months I spent in the United States from January to May 1992, I tried to update myself on the global economy. For many people the new element in the global economy was the collapse of the socialist regimes of Eastern Europe, the break-up of the USSR and the global spread of triumphant capitalism that these seemed to presage. I was not convinced about the validity of such claims. It was very clear that even if capitalism was geographically triumphant, functionally it was proving to be a failure in handling real-life economic problems, especially in its home base. Several studies had appeared pointing out the consequences of 'Reaganomics' which was heralded in the 1980s as the surest way to stimulate the American economy. After a decade of reliance on the gospel of free enterprise, the American economy found itself in a prolonged recession, said to be the worst since the Great Depression of the 1930s, unemployment level was high and growing, America had become the largest debtor nation in the world, there were many instances of failure of banks and instability of the financial system, many small investors had been ruined and, in the midst of it all, a small percentage of population had reaped enormous benefits. A widely discussed study assessing Reaganomics by an author who was once a staunch Republican said:

> The 1980s were the triumph of upper America—an ostentatious celebration of wealth, the political ascendancy of the richest third of the population and the glorification of capitalism, free markets and finance [and that] most of the Reagan decade, to put it mildly, was a heyday for unearned incomes as rents, dividends, capital gains and interest, gained relative to wages and salaries (Phillips 1990: xvii, 11).

Nor were the troubles confined to the US. Most West European countries faced similar problems and, indeed, no part of the 'triumphant' capitalist world was able to present a picture of sane economic conditions. The World Bank's *World Economic Development* 1991 had summed up the 'global' economic situation at the beginning of the 1990s thus: 'A seven-year expansion in the world economy came almost to a halt in 1990. Signs of slowing economic activity in a number of large industrial countries became evident as monetary policies were tightened in response to production at near capacity levels and rising inflation . . .' (World Bank 1991: 19).

In developing countries, real GDP growth declined from 4.3 per cent in 1988 to 2.9 per cent in 1990, the lowest since 1980. The main reasons—in addition to continuing macroeconomic instability and domestic policy weaknesses—were falling non-oil commodity prices, high international (non-dollar) interest rates and slower growth in world trade. Several subsequent assessments of the global situation at the beginning of the 1990s confirmed this sombre picture of what 'triumphant capitalism' was in fact achieving. The irony of the situation was that even in the midst of such chaotic conditions and miserable performance, shrill and powerful 'theoretical' voices were asserting that capitalism always promotes growth and ensures efficiency. There was something wrong with the theory or with those who were propagating the theory contrary to what anyone familiar with the real conditions could see.

My second observation was that the global economy of the 1980s and 1990s was not exactly the international economy of the early nineteenth century when Ricardo put forward his theory of comparative advantage and whose neo-classical version had become *the* theory of international economic relationships. This theory was still a theory of international *trade* while the international movement of capital had become the real issue in the 1980s. This theory was an analysis in real terms whereas the central problem currently was the emergence of global finance. And perhaps most important of all, this theory had assumed countries or national economies as the basic units of analysis while in the emerging global economy the new element has been a set of units, non-governmental and transnational—the multinational corporations (MNCs). This, in itself, was not much of a discovery. But from my perspective the pertinent finding was that the emerging global economy was not just the international economy of economic theory of the past which envisaged national economies alone as its primary units. Rather, the global economy must be viewed as the interaction among primary units with different agenda—the national economies primarily concerned with real economic issues subject to financial constraints and the MNCs with financial profits as the main, if not sole, aim and everything else as means to it. I felt that the conceptualisation I had done of a national economy, as consisting of the interaction of *heterogeneous* units or subeconomies, could be modified to represent the global economy as the interaction among *overlapping* heterogeneous subeconomies.

Keeping these in mind I wrote a number of pieces on the emerging global economy and situating the Indian economic reforms since 1991 in that context. The most important among them was 'Indian Economic Reforms and the Emerging Global Economy' in the *Economic and Political Weekly* in which I pointed out that the implicit, and sometimes explicit, assumptions of the reform measures with the accent on 'opening up' the economy were in sharp contrast to the realities 'out there' (Kurien 1993b).

These studies also showed me that a segment of capital in all countries of the world had indeed become global in a sense in which it had never been before and that those who own and control such capital could take full advantage of its complete homogeneity (as the most abstract form of economic power) and superfast mobility to subjugate most aspects of the real economy practically everywhere in the world. From this perspective labour power is at a disadvantage because it is intrinsically specific (the skills and abilities of particular human beings) and far less mobile than 'quicksilver' capital. It occurred to me that under these circumstances the inherent conflict of interest between capital and labour would manifest itself in new forms within countries and across nations necessitating a re-examination of the role of the state as the expression of the political power of the people as against the economic power of capital. These thoughts have found expression in my latest work, *Global Capitalism and the Indian Economy* (Kurien 1994).

XIV

On the basis of the explorations of the past four decades, the following general observations can be made about economic theory in its relation to real-life economic problems.

(a) In order to have a proper appreciation of economic theories—theoretical systems—it is necessary to get down to their basic postulates and assumptions. They are of a substantive nature, but may lie hidden for a long time because their validity could have been taken for granted at the time and in the places where the theoretical systems initially took shape.[4] It is now generally conceded that neo-classical theory which reduces all economic activities into exchange-like categories reflects the dominance of small producers and their market activities in Europe and America during the second half of the nineteenth century. But the work of Arrow, Debreu, Koopmans and others more recently have brought out that the more basic postulate of that system, especially of its Walrasian general equilibrium version, is the second part of the survival condition which postulates that all participants in the system have enough initial endowments on the basis of which to survive and to enter into market transactions. The centrality of this postulate is brought out by the fact that the separability of the production and consumption decisions hinges critically on it. The division of the decision makers into 'consumers' and 'producers', and thereby also into 'buyers' and 'sellers' also arises from it. Hence it is the postulate on which exchange, as the central economic concept, is anchored. I have shown that if the survival condition does not obtain, the system collapses (not only in a formal mathematical sense, but in a substantive economic sense) failing to yield some of its celebrated inferences. It collapses in the sense that very different institutional arrangements would emerge as the survival mechanism: work-sharing and produce-sharing units in the alternate system that was seen to result. In turn, it will also affect the vocabulary of the system invalidating, for instance, the universal applicability of 'wages' and 'profits' and replacing them with composite entities.

Without going into details, it can be seen that the separability of the savings and investment decisions is the substantive economic postulate of the Keynesian system with corresponding links with the underlying institutional setup of the system and its vocabulary.

(b) If theoretical systems in economics are, thus, embedded in real-life economic conditions which are temporally and spatially specific, they cannot claim to be 'universal' if that expression is meant to convey applicability across time and space. This is not to say that theoretical systems with the *logical* property of universality cannot be constructed whose claim can only be that given the postulates, the conclusions universally follow. But as the basic economic postulates, involving the institutional set up in which theory is unavoidably embedded, are of necessity time and space specific, the plurality of theoretical systems must be conceded. Granted this, it follows that frequent reformulation of theoretical systems is also called for.

(c) The basis for such reformulations is the continuous quest for the substantive essentials of the economy, that is, those factors which permit the 'economy' to be carved out of 'society' for analytical purposes. However, since economy and society are evolving entities (rather than machines with repetitive operations) the manifestation of these essentials must be specifically located. Such manifestations constitute the social framework of the economy, i.e., its institutional structure (at any time and in any place) which, as mentioned earlier, is basic to the working out of theory.

(d) The tendency to homogenise and universalise these structures is fallacious and is done not because that leads to a proper understanding of the real-life economy, but because it provides determinateness of the theoretical system and predictive powers to the theorist as a derivative from it. The complexity of the economy embedded in a variety of 'units' with heterogeneous structures and agenda, and diverse patterns of their interaction must be accepted as the basic feature of contemporary economies and consequently as the basis of theories about them. The economy must be conceptualised as an evolving complex entity.

(e) Such a conceptualisation of the economy, whose units have different agenda, makes the economy an open system, constantly under the influence of 'non-economic' factors which are part of the agenda of the units. However, the interaction between the economic and non-economic will vary over time.

(f) The agenda of the units must be taken serious note of by economic theory. They supply the 'behavioural postulates' in decision making. Once this is done, some of the standard procedures in theoretical analysis, such as the neat separation between micro and macro views of the economy, will have to be re-examined. It will become necessary to probe the economy at different levels (different levels of aggregation and disaggregation, for instance) and from different perspectives (different kinds of sectoral classifications) without providing a priori significance to any, but making each of them relative to the structural characteristics of the economy and to the problems to be examined. A major implication of such a procedure will be to call into question the sanctity of the evaluation of all economic activities via a single maximand.

(g) If, thus, theoretical analysis becomes inevitably purposive, theory itself cannot escape from some goal orientation. While that may shatter all pretenses of theory to the value neutral, it will certainly make it easier for economic theory to be more meaningfully related to economic problems and for the dialogue between the two worlds to proceed more fruitfully.

These statements may appear to be rather cryptic and abstract. But they have been derived from my encounters described in the earlier parts of this chapter. The chapters that follow attempt to explicate and develop them further.

Notes

1. Schumpeter points out in the text that even where there is a unique solution to the Walrasian system, it need not be economically meaningful in the sense that an actual system might work with it and then says in

the footnote: 'The occurrence of such a case, eg. of the inability of some participants in the market to secure a 'maximum of satisfaction' above starvation point, might be treated as a special form of economic, if not of mathematical, breakdown of the system (Schumpeter 1954: 1006, fn 20).

2. Malenbaum (1962) was of special help in formulating these hypotheses.
3. Published in Japanese and included in Kurien 1974.
4. Maurice Dobb points out: 'It is possible to characterise and to classify economic theories, even the most abstract, according to the manner in which they depict the structure and roots of economic society, and according to the significance of so depicting it for historical judgement and contemporary social practice' (1973: 36).

3

ECONOMICS: FORMAL AND SUBSTANTIVE

Formal and Substantive

I

In this chapter I propose to make a selective survey of economic theory to comment on the relationship between its formal and substantive aspects.

At first it may appear that the formal and substantive are clearly distinct, possibly even antithetical. In terms of the two 'worlds' referred to in Chapter 1, the formal may seem to be the attribute of the world of theory and the substantive that of the world of problems. Karl Polanyi's thought is the leading example of this polarisation between the formal and the substantive. In his essay, 'The Economy as an Instituted Process', Polanyi draws a distinction between the substantive and formal meanings of the term 'economic', and says:

> The substantive meaning of economic derives from man's dependence for his living upon nature and his fellows. It refers to the interaction with his material and social environment, in so far as it results in supplying him with the means of material want satisfaction. The formal meaning of economic derives from such words as 'economical' or 'economizing'. It refers to a definite situation of choice, namely, that between the different uses of means induced by an insufficiency of those means (1957: 243).

The thesis that Polanyi puts forward is that the two meanings of 'economic' that he designates have little in common and that only the substantive meaning is capable of identifying the economic phenomena in all societies, past and present. Polanyi also identifies the formal meaning of economic with Robbins' 'scarcity' definition of the subject. His criticism is not so much against the attempt to provide a formal definition of the subject as against the manner in which it is projected to be 'universal' because, he argues, the formal definition of 'economic' is simply a formulation of the logic of the market system where price, as the indicator of the economic significance of goods, reveals their relative scarcities and thus becomes the signal in the determination of choice. Polanyi implies that the accent on logic in the formal approach empties economics of its substantive elements, which he identifies as an instituted process of interaction between man and his environment resulting in a continuous supply of want satisfying material means. These processes, he claims, are embedded and enmeshed in social institutions, some of which have a definite economic orientation, but others are distinctly non-economic.

It is this 'embeddedness' of the economy that is central to Polanyi's argument. In the subsequent chapters I shall try to establish that this aspect has to be considerably reinforced to enter meaningfully into the relationship between economic theory and economic problems. However, I believe that Polanyi's distinction between the substantive and the formal is neither sound nor tenable.

Part of the problem is that Polanyi identifies *the* formal with *a* formal definition of economics. It is true that the 'scarcity definition' of economics is widely held—mainly because its pedagogic simplicity and apparent universality have rendered it to become the first lesson in academic training in economics, as many textbooks testify. Consequently it is almost second nature for economists to say that economics *is about* scarcity, reifying the formal into the substantive, an issue, to which I shall return later in the chapter.

The false opposition between the formal and the substantive arises because Polanyi identifies the formal with one of the formal approaches that he does not agree with. He asserts:

> The two root meanings of 'economic', the substantive and the formal, have nothing in common. The latter derives from logic, the former from fact. The formal meaning implies a set of rules referring to choice between the alternative uses of insufficient means.

The substantive meaning implies neither choice nor insufficiency of means; indeed some of the most important physical and social conditions of livelihood such as the availability of air and water or a loving mother's devotion to her infant are not, as a rule, so limiting. The cogency that is in play in the one case and in the other differs as the power of syllogism differs from the force of gravitation. The laws of the one are those of the mind; the laws of the other are those of nature. *The two meanings could not be farther apart; semantically they lie in opposite directions of the compass* (Polanyi 1957: 243–44, emphasis added).

The passage illustrates the identification of the formal in economics with scarcity and choice, as well as the consequent view that the formal and the substantive 'have nothing in common', and that they are polar opposites. However, it is one thing to say that *semantically* they lie in opposite directions of the compass, and something ·different to argue that in a field of study they should be kept apart. Polanyi's own work shows that the twain meet and *have* to meet in any worthwhile discussions of problems and analyses of facts. Polanyi has to admit that 'the study of shifting place occupied by the economy in society is therefore no other than the manner in which the economic process is instituted at different times and places. This requires a special tool box' (Polanyi 1957: 250). Surely, a toolbox of this kind is not a fact: it is a mental construct! And, as designed by Polanyi, it consists of the core concept of 'integrative mechanisms' and its derivatives, reciprocity, redistribution and exchange. Aren't these terms similar to scarcity and choice arising from 'the laws of the mind' rather than the laws of nature?

The fact of the matter is that both the substantive and the formal are necessary to delineate a field of study, and economics is no exception to this general proposition. The discussion in the previous chapter has shown how the substantive forms the basis of even the most formal treatments. And the formal—whether in the elementary form of a classification or in the form of a mathematical model—is essential for dealing with specific and concrete issues. Often it is even impossible to 'see' a concrete problem till material that lies scattered is brought together, cleaned up, ordered, set in juxtaposition with other material, etc., all of which are exercises of a formal nature. The real issue is how to hold the formal and the substantive together while retaining the conceptual distinction between the two.

The Classical Tradition

II

The distinguishing feature of the early literature in economics is the manner in which the substantive and the formal are interwoven. The substantive component is not a matter of surprise because, almost till recently, concrete problems arising from real-life situations were the raw material that formed the basis of economic studies. What is surprising is that even before economics (or political economy) came to be recognised as a separate field of enquiry, the formal element was quite discernible—whether it was the distinction between use value and exchange value which goes back to Aristotle or the concept of the just price that was the concern of medieval scholastics.

It will be useful, from this perspective, to look at the *Wealth of Nations* because it is generally considered that, as against the essentially substantive discussions of the mercantilists or even the physiocratic attempts to represent the economy in the form of a numerical chart or tableau (which, therefore, is analytical in nature), it is Adam Smith's work that is the beginning of theoretical work in economics.[1] How are the substantive and formal brought together in the *Wealth of Nations?* Announcing the substantive thrust of the work, unambiguously and unapologetically, is the title itself—*An Inquiry into the Nature and Causes of the Wealth of Nations*, a practical question which both the mercantilists and the physiocrats had raised, and one which was everybody's concern at that time. Smith explicitly linked up the individual's desire to improve his condition and the possibility to enhance the wealth and prosperity of society.

The natural effort of every individual to better his own condition, when suffered to exert itself with freedom and security, is so powerful a principle, that it is alone, and without any assistance, not only capable of carrying on the society to wealth and prosperity, but of surmounting a hundred impertinent obstructions with which the folly of human laws too often incumbers its operations (Bk IV, Ch V–II: 40).[2]

The social embeddedness of the economy is explicitly recognised: the primary agents are the social classes, noticeable even to the untutored persons, of the day-labourers, landlords, merchants and masters. And, if more descriptive accounts are needed, the menial servants, bakers, butchers, brewers, masters, workmen, apprentices, farmers, smiths, carpenters, wheelwrights, ploughwrights, masons, bricklayers, tanners, physicians, men of letters, players, buffoons, musicians, opera singers and dancers, and the sovereign are all there— 'real people within the constraints of existing institutions' (Deane 1978: 10). Real-life activities are described in rich detail. In a pin manufactory 'one man draws out the wire, another straights it, a third cuts it, a fourth points it, a fifth grinds it . . . the important business of making [a] pin is, in this manner, divided into about eighteen distinct operations' (Bk I, Ch I–I: 5). The woollen coat, which the day-labourer wears, is the produce of the joint labour of a great multitude of workmen, 'the shepherd, the sorter of the wool, the wool-comber or carder, the dyer, the scribbler, the spinner, the weaver, the fuller, the dresser' (Bk I, Ch I – I: 10). Also, the merchants, the shipbuilders and sailors, those who produce the tools for these variety of persons. These descriptions are, of course, time and space specific. Capital, for instance, is 'a stockpile of food and implements accumulated *before* the process of production began and subsequently *advanced* to labourers in anticipation of the returns from the final output' (Coats 1962: 38).

> We rarely hear, it has been said, of the combinations of masters, though frequently, of those of workmen. But whoever imagines, upon this account, that masters rarely combine, is as ignorant of the world as of the subject. Masters are always and everywhere in a sort of tacit, but constant and uniform combination not to raise the wages of labour above their actual rate (Bk I, Ch VIII–I: 59).

There is also this original statement of the 'trickle down' mechanism: 'The houses, the furniture, the clothing of the rich, in a little time, become useful to the inferior and middling ranks of people. They are able to purchase them, and the general accommodation of the whole people is thus gradually improved, when this mode of expense becomes universal among men of fortune' (Bk II, Ch III–I: 311).

It is not necessary to labour the point further: practically every page of the first treatise in economics is filled with descriptive, substantial stuff. In fact, J.B. Say (1841) considered the *Wealth of Nations an* 'immethodological assemblage of the soundest principles of political economy, supported by luminous illustrations . . . an irregular mass of curious and original speculations, and of known and demonstrated truths'. Something of the Anglo-French academic rivalry is certainly reflected in this view. But even Maurice Dobb has stated that 'a characteristic of the *Wealth of Nations* was its unsystematic character so far as theory was concerned, adding that 'some have even regarded this perhaps as among its leading virtues: that it was able to illuminate so much because it was concerned so largely with history and with particular situations and did not strain after conceptual unity' (1973: 66).

III

Overall assessments of the *Wealth of Nations* have continued and will go on. I will confine myself to the limited task of searching for the formal strains in it. It is possible to identify at least three ways in which the formal element can be traced in the work.

The first consists of drawing out generalisations or substantive (rather than logical) principles from the descriptive material and illustrations. These can be seen throughout the book. For instance:

> This great increase of the quantity of work which, in consequence of the division of labour, the same number of people are capable of performing is owing to three different circumstances; first, to the increase of dexterity in every particular workman; secondly, to the saving of time which is commonly lost in passing from one species of work to another; and lastly, to the invention of a great number of machines which facilitate and abridge labour, and enable one man to do the work of many (Bk I, Ch I–I: 7).

There is, then, the oft-quoted passage indicating the principle underlying exchange.

> Give me that which I want, and you shall have this which you want is the meaning of every such offer; and it is in this manner that we obtain from one another the far greater part of those good offices which we stand in need of. It is not from the benevolence of the butcher, the brewer, or the baker that we expect our dinner, but from their regard to their own interest. We address ourselves, not to their humanity but to their self-love (Bk I, Ch II–I: 13).

There is also the seldom-noticed passage, on the very next page, which provides another basic principle relating to exchange.

> The certainty of being able to exchange all that surplus part of the produce of his own labour, which is over and above his own consumption, for such parts of the produce of other men's labour as he may have occasion for, encourages every man to apply himself to a particular occupation (Bk I, Ch II–I: 14).

Many more instances of this kind can be cited dealing with the relationship between exchange and money, surplus and employment, wage level and prosperity and so on. Let me refer to two more. The first is the passage that leads to the conclusion that rent is not a compensation for the improvement brought about on land, but a monopoly price:

> Kelp is a species of sea-weed, which, when burnt, yields an alkaline salt, useful for making glass, soap, and for several other purposes. It grows in several parts of Great Britain, particularly in Scotland, upon such rocks only as lie within the high water mark, which are twice every day covered with the sea, and of which the produce, therefore, was never augmented by human industry. The landlord, however, whose estate is bounded by a kelp shore of this kind, demands a rent for it as much as for his corn fields (Bk I, Ch XI–I: 131).

The second is about the relationship between town and country:

> As subsistence is, in the nature of things, prior to conveniency and luxury, so the industry which procures the former must necessarily be prior to that which ministers to the latter. The cultivation and improvement of the country, therefore, which affords subsistence, must, necessarily, be prior to the increase of the town, which furnishes only the means of conveniency and luxury (Bk III, Ch I–I: 337).

What is the nature of these statements? They are, clearly, logical derivations, but they are not mere exercises in logic. The derivations are from substantive premises which are observations from 'the nature of things'. Second, they are in the nature of generalisations, but not generalisations derived by the inductive process based on the frequency of occurrence. In most cases, they are drawn from a single concrete instance. They make no claims to 'universality' and are, indeed, bounded by the specificity of the real. Adam Smith's substantive principles, thus, are logical inferences from descriptive understandings of specific real-life instances. They may, therefore, be considered *analytical descriptions*: they combine substance and form. The lesson to be learned from the *Wealth of Nations* is that analytical description is the foundation of meaningful formalisation about real-life conditions.

There is a sense in which the entire book may be considered as an exposition of analytical description. The first proposition is that the annual labour of every nation is the fund which originally supplies it with the necessaries and conveniences of life. The productivity of labour depends on the division of labour. The division of labour is limited by the extent of the market. When the market spreads, it generates a commercial society where prices regulate economic activity. Prices of commodities consist of the wages, rent and profit which must be paid to produce it. The demand for those who live by wages increases with the increase of revenue and stock of the country. The demand for men, like that for any other commodity, necessarily regulates the production of men: quickens it when it goes too slowly and stops it when it advances too fast. The profit of stock also depends on the wealth of the society. But the increases of stock which raises wages, tends to lower profit. Rent is a monopoly price. Whenever a person saves from his revenue, he adds to his capital. Capitals are increased by parsimony, and diminished by prodigality and misconduct. The greater part of capital of every growing society is, first, directed to agriculture, afterwards to manufactures, and last of all to foreign commerce.

This, of course, is no summary of the great work or even of the first three Books from which the statements listed above have been gathered. But they illustrate the method of working out the contents of a field of study, especially the study of an aspect of society—logical inferences drawn from the rudiments of social life, each inference then becoming the premise for a further inference, cumulatively producing a corpus of substantive understanding of the working of a complex economic system.

IV

It is not suggested that this is *the* method underlying the *Wealth of Nations* or even of relating substance and form in it. Indeed, the formal element in the work must be traced at least at two more levels.

The first is in relation to 'value'. Much has been written on this, a lot of it quite controversial. I shall only consider how far the treatment of value in the *Wealth of Nations* can be seen as part of its formal element. Subsequent developments in economic theory have made value one of the most formally treated subjects. Certainly, there is none of this in the *Wealth of Nations*. I am inclined to accept Schumpeter's verdict that Smith was not primarily interested in the causal explanation of the phenomenon of value, and that what he wanted was essentially 'a price theory by which to establish certain propositions that do not require going into the background of the value phenomenon at all' (Schumpeter 1954: 309).[3] For this purpose he drew the well-known distinction between 'value in use' and 'value in exchange' indicating that his intention was to investigate the principles which regulate the exchangeable value of commodities. Exchange value was very much under discussion in those days. The Physiocrats had already brought the system of market exchanges to the fore and had made an attempt to establish that it was subject to certain objective economic laws. Smith might have also felt that with the markets rapidly spreading exchange value, prices might yield some clues to the understanding of the working of the system as a whole. In Chapter V of Book I, there are confusing statements about 'the real price' ('The real price of everything ... is the toil and trouble of acquiring it' (p.26). 'Labour alone, therefore, never varying in its own value, is alone the ultimate and real standard by which the value of all commodities can at all times and places be estimated and compared. It is their real price' (p.29), etc.), but in Chapter VI there is a more coherent discussion of the component parts of the price of commodities. It is first established that the price of any commodity must finally resolve itself into wages, rent and profit. Then there is the passage which establishes the identity that the sum of the exchangeable value of all commodities is equal to the sum of the shares of the three classes:

> As the price or exchangeable value of every particular commodity, taken separately, resolves itself into some one or other or all of those three parts; so that of all the commodities which compose the whole annual produce of the labour of every country, taken completely, must resolve itself into the same three parts, and be parcelled out

among different inhabitants of the country, either as the wages of their labour, the profits of their stock, or the rent of their land. The whole of what is annually either collected or produced by the labour of every society, or what comes to the same thing, the whole price of it, is in this manner originally distributed among some of its different members. Wages, profits, and rent, are the three original sources of all revenue as well as of all exchangeable value (Bk I, Ch VI–I: 46).

This can be thought of as a mere 'adding-up theory' of prices, as later writers described it. But, from our point of view, it can also be considered as formal analysis at a different level than was seen earlier.

The third level of formal treatment in the *Wealth of Nations* is yet another way of seeing the economy as a whole. It takes off from the observation that the annual revenue of every society is always precisely equal to the exchangeable value of the whole annual produce. Then it brings out a further aspect of the relationship between the whole and its parts, which is, perhaps, the most quoted passage from the *Wealth of Nations*:

As every individual, therefore, endeavours as much as he can both to employ his capital in support of domestic industry, and so to direct that industry that its produce may be of greatest value; every individual necessarily labours to render the annual revenue of the society as great as he can. He generally, indeed, neither intends to promote the public interest, nor knows how much he is promoting it. By preferring the support of domestic to that of foreign industry, he intends only his own security; and by directing that industry in such a manner as its produce may be of the greatest value, he intends only his own gain, and he is in this, as in many other cases, led by an invisible hand to promote an end which was no part of his intention. . . . By pursuing his own interest he frequently promotes that of the society more effectually than when he really intends to promote it (Bk IV, Ch II–I: 400).

Several comments are necessary about this key passage. It must certainly be recognised as the summing up of the logical arguments of the earlier sections of the work which, according to Smith himself, was an attempt 'to explain in what has consisted the revenue of the great body of the people' (Introduction, p.3) and a prelude to the discussion of the policy issues taken up in the Fifth and Sixth Books (mainly Volume II). Hence it is the highest level of formal treatment that Smith reaches where, following the chain of reasoning based on substantive issues, he tries to show the economy as an entity in which the great body of people, pursuing its own interest, promotes the interest of society as a whole.

Having said this, it is important to point out that in recent years this single reference to the invisible hand in the entire *Wealth of Nations* has been given a significance that Smith did not appear to have intended. Those who now frequently refer to the invisible hand imply that Smith meant by it the invisible forces of the market as against the visible hand of the state, and that it is the magic of the market that ensures that when individuals try to increase their own revenues, the revenue of society as a whole also becomes as large as it can be.

It is doubtful whether Adam Smith himself attached much significance to the invisible hand. It certainly is not a frequently recurring expression in his writings—taking into account his philosophical writings also. It occurs only once even in *The Theory of Moral Sentiments*. There, it appears in a passage where Smith has some disparaging comments about 'the natural selfishness and rapacity' of the rich landlords who, in order to gratify their own vain and insatiable desires, employ people of inferior rank, but in so doing 'they divide with the poor the produce of all their improvements'. (Raphael and Macfie 1976: 184–85). That is what the invisible hand achieves in the context. Is it the working of some economic principle, or some other supernatural power? In a footnote to the passage, Raphael and Macfie point out that in Smith's first reference to the invisible hand in *The History of Astronomy*, the invisible hand is that of Jupiter: 'Fire burns, and water refreshes; heavy bodies descend, and lighter substances fly upwards, by the necessity of their own nature; nor was the invisible hand of Jupiter ever apprehended to be employed in those matters.'[4]

Since the invisible hand has such different meanings in the writings of Smith, which in one context refers to a natural outcome and in another a supernatural intervention, it seems best not to make tall claims about it.

There is, however, a related question. What role does Smith assign to self-interest in economic matters? Is it the one unifying principle of the economy which holds together its diverse activities? There is no doubt that self-interest as a human motivation has a privileged position in the *Wealth of Nations*. However, the role that Smith assigns to self-interest must be situated in a larger context which is very clearly stated in *Moral Sentiments*. The opening sentence of *Moral Sentiments* states: 'How selfish soever man may be supposed, there are some principles in his nature, which interest him in the fortune of others, and render their happiness necessary to him, though he derives nothing from it except the pleasure of seeing it' (Raphael and Macfie 1976: 9). Smith insists also that this sentiment, which he refers to as compassion and sympathy, 'like all other original passions of human nature, is by no means confined to the virtuous and humane', but is also present in 'the greatest ruffian, the most hardened violator of the laws of society'. Human beings have other innate sentiments too, justice and beneficence being the other prominent ones.

Which of these can be said to be crucial from the point of view of society? For this question too, Smith has a clear answer. 'Society may subsist, though not in the most comfortable state without beneficence, but the prevalence of injustice must utterly destroy it... [beneficence] is the ornament which embellishes, not the foundation that supports the building. . . . Justice upholds the edifice. If it is removed, the great, the immense fabric of society ... must in a moment crumble into atoms' (Raphael and Macfie 1976: 86).

In *Moral Sentiments*, self-interest is situated within such a larger system of virtues consisting of sympathy, beneficence and justice. The role assigned to self-interest in this context bears close resemblance to ambition or duty.

> We should despise a prince who was not anxious about conquering or defending a province. We should have little respect for a private gentleman who did not exert himself to gain an estate, or even a considerable office, when he could acquire them without either meanness or injustice. A member of parliament who shows no keenness about his own election, is abandoned by his friends, as altogether unworthy of their attachment. Even a tradesman is thought a poor-spirited fellow among his neighbours, who does not bestir himself to get what they call an extraordinary job, or some uncommon advantage (Raphael and Macfie 1976: 173).

Such passages may be paraphrased to say that self-interest in economic matters is the prescribed role for members of a society who are governed by a sense of sympathy and justice.

V

This connection helps us to move on to a further issue—the 'embeddedness' of the economy. The social embeddedness of the economy is indicated quite explicitly in the *Wealth of Nations* itself. The economy functions within a social order whose head is the sovereign and who must provide the preconditions for the working of the economy. These are set out in Book V (Volume Two) as the 'duties of the sovereign'. The first is that of protecting the society from violence and invasion of other independent societies. The second is that of protecting the members of society from the injustice and oppressions from within— the administration of justice. And the third is

> that of erecting and maintaining those public institutions and works, which though they may be in the highest degree advantageous to a great society, are, however, of such a nature that the profit could never repay expenses to any individual or small number of individuals, and which it therefore cannot be expected that any individual or small number of individuals should erect or maintain (Bk V, Ch I–II: 210-11).

The private economy which aims at enabling people to provide a revenue or subsistence for themselves is, thus, set within a commonwealth or the state of which the sovereign is the visible symbol. To put it differently, the economy of exchange or of mutual horizontal transfers is possible only if there is a vertical transfer of resources from the people to the sovereign. The expenses and the sources of revenue for the sovereign, the treatment of which constitutes the major portion of Volume Two, is, therefore, an integral and basic part of Smith's treatment of economics. This has to be emphasised because a century later a group of theorists jettisoned this 'public finance' part to construct a model of the 'entire' economy as consisting of exchange relationships, and those who tried to perfect this model during the current century claimed that they were the direct inheritors of Adam Smith's economy based on the innate human propensity to truck, barter and exchange.

But in the *Wealth of Nations* the economy is set within society and under the sovereign. In the *Moral Sentiments* society itself is shown to be subject to a 'divine Being', 'the great Director of the universe', 'the all-wise Author of Nature', to obey whose will is considered the first rule of duty. The economy, therefore, is not an autonomous entity subject solely to its internal arrangements. The economy is subject to society, and society is subject to the will of the Divine. Hence, it is reasonable to consider that the social harmony that Smith's passage on the coincidence of self-interest and social interest implies is not the result of the working arrangements of the economy (market, competitions, etc.), but is brought about by the invisible hand of the divine Being. Smith who was known to be greatly influenced by stoic philosophy wrote:

> The ancient stoics were of opinion that as the world was governed by the all-ruling providence of a wise, powerful, and good God, every single event ought to be regarded, as making a necessary part of the plan of the universe, and as tending to promote the general order and happiness of the whole (Raphael and Macfie 1976: 36).

Smith had clear views as to how social and economic harmony is brought about, though they were not explicitly stated in the *Wealth of Nations*. There is no reason to think that in writing the treatise on political economy he had given up his broader philosophical positions expressed in *Moral Sentiments*.[5]

VI

The *Wealth of Nations*, considered to be the first theoretical work on political economy, is primarily on substantive issues concentrating on two policy problems which were real to the times: how does the national product grow, and how does it get distributed among the different claimants, landlords, capitalists and workers. There is no attempt in the work to problematise the 'nation' which is treated as the basic unit of analysis or the 'classes'. They are simply accepted as self-evident social realities. The formal aspect of the work consists mainly of the attempt to draw out a chain of substantive principles from a rich descriptive narrative of the ways in which people make a living and some make profits—two primary activities that constitute the 'raw material' of the distinctive discipline of political economy. In the formal sphere Smith's success consisted of interrelating a wide range of disparate activities by locating their logical interconnections. In his attempt to provide a theory of value, Smith was not particularly successful. And, in his effort to establish the principle of harmony between the self-interest of individuals and the interest of society as a whole, he relied very heavily on a set of philosophic presuppositions spelt out in *Moral Sentiments* which included acknowledging a Supreme Being—at once the all-wise Author of Nature, and the inmate of the human breast—whose invisible hand it is that establishes a social order informed by sympathy and justice within which individuals have the responsibility to look after themselves.

In the evolution of economic theory since the days of Adam Smith the relative roles of the formal and substantive aspects have continued to be discussed and debated. It will be recalled that this question was one of the main debating points between Ricardo and Malthus, the former emphasising the formal and the latter the substantive approaches. Later in the nineteenth century and through much of the twentieth, it became evident that Ricardo had the upper hand. Keynes was to remark that Ricardo had 'constrained the subject for a full hundred years in an artificial groove' and that 'If only Malthus, instead of Ricardo, had been the parent stem from which nineteenth century economics proceeded, what a much wiser and richer place the world would be today' (Deane 1978: 83).[6]

I shall not go into details of Ricardo's formalism but simply touch upon his role as the one from whom (and, indeed, *against* whom) the neo-classical tradition perfected its formalism.

Since the accent is to be on Ricardo's contributions to the formalisation of economics, it is worth noting that, in a sense, he too was a substantivist. What later became the celebrated treatise, *The Principles of Political Economy and Taxation* (1818), was based on his first work, *Essay on the Influence of a Low Price of Corn on the Profits of Stock* (1815), thus indicating that Ricardo took off from a much discussed policy issue, whether or not British agriculture was to be protected against the importation of corn from the continent. Second, like Adam Smith, Ricardo also made it clear that the central problem of economics was to decide how 'the produce of the earth' is divided among 'the three classes of the community, namely, the proprietor of the land, the owner of the stock or capital necessary for its cultivation, and the labourers by whose industry it is cultivated' (Ricardo 1911: 1). Much of Ricardo's work was in relation to land and agriculture using corn as the basic unit which led Blaug to observe: 'The bare outline of Ricardo's system can be grasped by supposing that the whole economy consists of a giant farm engaged in producing wheat by applying homogeneous doses of 'capital-and-labour' to a fixed supply of land subject to diminishing returns' (Blaug 1962: 81).

Third, throughout the analysis there is a (socially determined) subsistence wage which is accepted as a datum.

However, even through these substantive aspects, the formal element begins to emerge. Ricardo's interest was not merely to find out how the produce gets distributed among the agents; he was trying to 'determine the laws which regulate' the distribution. It is this search for laws and their determinateness that is the hallmark of Ricardo's work, and which gives it a formal character. The procedure adopted is graphically narrated by Schumpeter:

> His interest was in the clear-cut result of direct, practical significance. In order to get this he cut that general system to pieces, bundled up as large parts of it as possible, and put them in cold storage—so that as many things as possible should be frozen and 'given'. He then piled one simplifying assumption upon another until, having really settled everything by those assumptions, he was left with only a few aggregative variables between which, given these assumptions, he set up simple one-way relation so that, in the end, the desired results emerged almost as tautologies (Schumpeter 1954: 472–73).

All this cutting, chopping and freezing (and twisting and turning too?), according to Schumpeter, was to produce an 'engine' which 'grinds out results, within wide limits, no matter what the concrete problem is that is fed into it', and which 'works the same way, formally, whether the problem is the effect of a tax or of wage policy, or of a piece of regulation, or of protection and what not' (Schumpeter 1954: 474). The advantage of constructing such an engine is that it will be available, and can be used, for an infinite variety of purposes.

Schumpeter felt that the *particular* engine that Ricardo constructed was defective and led economics on to a wrong track, but seemed to approve of the general method of constructing an all purpose engine which welds together into a systematic unit the individual elements that make up general economics. Anyway, since the days of Ricardo, the central problematic of the leading tradition in economics, which I have elsewhere designated as the 'Anglo-American tradition', has been to arrive at a theoretical system which can analyse and explain anything and everything that can be described as an economic problem. Lionel Robbins' statement that economics is the science which studies human behaviour as a relationship between ends and scarce means which have alternative uses was, perhaps, the logical end product of the quest whereby *all* economic problems were shown to be manifestations of scarcity. Certainly the movement was towards enhanced precision and rigour of analysis. 'The cutting knives of economic discussion became sharper', says Maurice Dobb, but 'whether they are used to cut so deeply is another matter' (1973: 176). In what follows, I shall take up this question for more detailed analysis.

Neo-classical Formalism

VII

In ushering in the revolution associated with his name, Jevons had claimed that the 'true system of Economics' he was building up was the necessary correction to the distortion that Ricardo had made.

> When at length the true system of Economics comes to be established, it will be seen that the able but wrong-headed man, David Ricardo, shunted the car of Economic Science on to a wrong line—a line, however, on which it was further urged towards confusion by his equally able and wrong-headed admirer, John Stuart Mill. There were economists such as Malthus and Senior, who had a far better comprehension of the true doctrines (though not from the Ricardian errors) but they were driven out of the field by the unity and influence of the Ricardo–Mill school. It will be a work of labour to pick up the fragments of a shattered science and to start anew, but it is a work from which they must not shrink who wish to see any advance of Economic Science (Jevons 1970: Preface).

However, we may note that the 'wrong-headed' Ricardo had provided a great deal of inspiration to the Jevonsonian revolution. First, there was the 'engine' that he had invented which Jevons, Menger, Walras and others responsible for the marginalist revolution perfected further. Second, although Adam Smith had attempted to produce a system of political economy, it was Ricardo who really succeeded in carving out a self-contained economic system, and in that process he 'started and finished with the economic problem and refused to be side-tracked by philosophical, sociological or historical considerations' (Deane 1978: 75). Deane points out further that

'Ricardo's technique of abstract reasoning from *a priori* postulates, his propensity for logical–mathematical rather than philosophical–historical theories had important implications for the methodology of orthodox economics away from the real world by encouraging the theorist to depend on a type of theory which called for logical refutation rather than empirical verifications (Deane 1978: 93).

It is this procedure of 'simplification and generalisation' which Malthus found so objectionable in Ricardo that became the hallmark of the marginalists or the neo-classical economists later on. Through his process of abstraction, Ricardo also restricted the scope of economics to the determination of value. His successors did not find his theory of the long-run relative exchange values of reproducible goods general enough, but they took the cue from him and decided that a self-contained theory of exchange value of *all* goods could be projected as the basic universal law of the science of economics. And, finally, Ricardo gifted to his more 'scientific' successors the procedure of applying to the solution of practical problems theories derived from abstract postulates. Schumpeter had named it the 'Ricardian Vice', but those who accused Ricardo of being wrong-headed made it their greatest virtue.

If the classical school derived the substance of its political economy from the ground, the neo-classical school turned to the realm of thought to work out a formalised version of economics. Jevons, Menger and Walras made their scientific intentions quite explicit. According to Jevons:

As all the physical sciences have their basis more or less obviously in the general principles of mechanics, so all branches and divisions of economic science must be pervaded by certain general principles. It is to the investigation of such principles—to the tracing out of the mechanics of self-interest and utility, that this essay has been devoted (Jevons 1970: 50).[7]

In the preface to the fourth edition of *Elements of Pure Economics*, Walras compared economics to astronomy and mechanics, and claimed:

It took from a hundred to a hundred and fifty or two hundred years for the astronomy of Kepler to become the astronomy of Newton

and Laplace, and for the mechanics of Galileo to become the
mechanics of d'Alembert and Lagrange. On the other hand, less
than a century has elapsed between the publication of Adam Smith's
work and the contribution of Cournot, Gossen, Jevons, and myself.
We are, therefore, at our post, and have performed our duty (Walras
1954: 47–48).

Walras, the engineer, was quite clear that the aim should be to
convert economics into a 'physico-mathematical science'.

As the accent on the scientific character of economics became
quite pronounced since then, it is worth exploring what Walras and
others meant by 'science'.

Science, according to Walras, had been demonstrated as a search
for universals of which corporeal entities are manifestations. Corporeal entities come and go, but universals remain for ever. Universals,
their relations, and their laws, are the object of all scientific study.
Walras then draws a distinction between applied economics and the
pure theory of economics, and states that the latter 'is a science which
resembles the physico-mathematical sciences in every respect'. A feature of the physico-mathematical sciences is that they go beyond experience as soon as they have drawn their type concepts from it.

From real-type concepts, these sciences abstract ideal-type concepts which they define, and then on the basis of these definitions
they construct *a priori* the whole framework of their theories and
proofs. After that they go back to experience not to confirm but to
apply their conclusions. Everyone who has studied any geometry at
all knows perfectly well that only in an abstract, ideal circumfer-
ence are the radii all equal to each other and that only in an
abstract, ideal triangle is the sum of the angles equal to the sum of
two right angles. Reality confirms these definitions and demonstra-
tions only approximately, and yet reality admits of a very wide and
fruitful application of these propositions. Following this same procedure, the pure theory of economics ought to take over from
experience certain type concepts, like those of exchange, supply,
demand, market, capital, income, productive services and products.
From these real-type concepts the pure science of economics
should then abstract and define ideal-type concepts in terms of
which it carries on its reasoning. The return to reality should not

take place until the science is completed and then only with a view to practical applications (Walras 1954: 71).

In this sense neo-classical economics is a constructed system removed from the real-type situation through abstraction. One should not expect a strict correspondence between the constructed system and the real system, although the concepts of the former may appear to be drawn from real life. If, for instance, the constructed system had not used expressions like exchange and markets in wide currency in day-to-day life, but had used other expressions instead, the language of formal theory and everyday life would have been completely different. But Walras points out that even the physical sciences share this problem: words like velocity in mechanics, and heat in physics, are used in the respective sciences after giving them special meanings.

In a scientific discourse key terms derive their meaning in relation to other terms used in the discourse. Walras, indeed sets up a system of this kind thereby also showing both the link and the distinction between the constructed system and what it purports to represent. Thus *social wealth* is defined as all things that are *scarce*. Scarce things are those that are *useful* and in *limited quantity*. Things limited in quantity are *appropriable*. Useful things limited in quantity are *valuable* and *exchangeable*, and so on (Walras 1954: Lesson 3).

In all these procedures there was very close adherence to Newtonian physics.[8] Two aspects of this adherence to, or imitation of, Newtonian physics should be noted. First, as Capra points out, Newton's universe consisted of homogeneous particles of matter, atoms, which became the basic building block of the system. Neo-classical economics accepted homogeneous individuals as its primary units (Capra 1983: 51). Second, as gravity became the unifying principle in Newton's physics, marginal utility became the integrating principle in neo-classical economics. In what follows, I shall confine myself to two related aspects of the formalism of neo-classical economics: certain formal problems relating to the approach and the relation of the theoretical system to real-life economic conditions.

VIII

To enter into the formal structure of neo-classical economics, we may consider three features which Bharadwaj (1978) indicates as common to Jevons, Menger, and Walras. The first is the assumption of symmetry among the distributive classes, particularly labour and capital. As a matter of fact, the problem is a much deeper one. As already indicated, neo-classical economics has little use for class as an analytical category because its primary units are individuals who, for functional purposes, are regrouped as consumers, producers etc. Because of the underlying assumption of the homogeneity of the primary units, they may be grouped together in any manner that facilitates the analysis and no particular grouping carries any deeper significance. The second feature is closely related to this aspect. The homogeneity of individuals is achieved through reliance on the Benthamite depiction of the rational pursuit of self-interest as the innate characteristics of all individuals. The primary units of the system thus become free, decision-making individuals attempting to maximise their own self-interest—identified as utility. Given such individuals, all economic activities are shown to be exchanges among them or exchange-like activities in which they are involved. This is the third aspect.

The three are brought together by establishing a link between utility-maximising individuals and the concept of 'equilibrium'. Walras is the most systematic in exposition and so we shall follow him.

Walras' basic model is one of barter where 'the buyer of a thing is the seller of that which he gives in exchange', and, correspondingly, 'the seller of a thing is the buyer of that which he takes in exchange' (Walras 1954: 83), thereby removing the arbitrary identification of one of them as seller and the other as buyer, and also establishing their basic similarity. Defining *value in exchange* as the property that certain things possess—of not being given or taken freely, *commodities* as things that are valuable and exchangeable, and the *market* as a place where commodities are exchanged, Walras moves to his first general proposition:

> Given two commodities in a market, each holder attains maximum satisfaction of wants, or maximum effective utility, when the ratio of intensities of the last wants satisfied is equal to the prices. Until this equality has been reached, a party to the exchange will find. it to his advantage to sell the commodity the rareté of which is smaller than its price multiplied by the rareté of the other commodity and to buy the other commodity the rareté of which is greater than its price multiplied by the rareté of the first commodity (Walras 1954: 125).

And then introducing competition also, the further generalisation is arrived at:

The exchange of two commodities for each other in a perfectly competitive market is an operation by which all holders of either one, or of both, of the two commodities can obtain the greatest possible satisfaction of their wants consistent with the conditions that the two commodities are bought and sold at one and the same rate of exchange throughout the market (Walras 1954: 143).

Then,

The main object of the theory of social wealth is to generalize this proposition by showing, first, that it applies to the exchange of several commodities, for one another as well as to the exchange of two commodities for each other, and secondly, that, under perfect competition, it applies to production as well as to exchange. The main object of the theory of production of social wealth is to show how the principle of organization of agriculture, industry and commerce can be deduced as a logical consequence of the above proposition. We may say, therefore, that this proposition embraces the whole of pure and applied economics (Walras 1954: 143).

So universal is this analysis, based on the same principle, that Walras claimed that 'the whole world may be looked upon as a vast general market made up of diverse special markets' (Walras 1954: 84).

That prices—exchange values established through competitive markets—are the index of the economic significance of commodities, is the principle that was established. In spite of the differences in approach of the leaders of the neo-classical school, it is this basic principle that they all hold, with the marginal utilities of satisfaction-maximising rational decision-making individuals as the underlying condition. Menger, for instance, first established that marginal utility could explain the prices of goods and services for which there was demand from consumers, which, therefore, were directly related to their wants or preferences. But then he went on to argue that means of production—or 'goods of higher order', as he called them—also came within the concept of economic goods because they too yielded consumers' satisfaction, though indirectly, through helping to produce things that do satisfy consumers' wants directly. Thus they acquired their indices of economic significance (and hence of exchange values) from the same marginal utility principle. Hence, prices, established through the forces of demand via marginal utility, also governed the determination of costs (prices of the means of production) on the supply side. But since costs to the producers or firms are incomes to households, the same marginal principle also automatically covers the phenomenon of income distribution. Production (or allocation of resources) and distribution, thus, are seen to be two sides of the same coin. Commenting on this, Schumpeter remarks: 'The whole of the organon of pure economics thus finds itself unified in the light of a single principle—in a sense in which it had never been before' (1954: 913). Walras was the one who brought this out most clearly and systematically which Schumpeter described as his 'revolutionary creativeness'.

IX

A formal model of the economy unified by a single principle has, certainly, some major advantages. Among them the most important is the manner in which it demonstrates the interconnectedness of markets pertaining to a diversity of goods and services, of goods for consumption and goods for production, and, as has been demonstrated subsequently, the markets for labour, commodities, bonds and money. We now take it for granted, but when it was first demonstrated it was simply dismissed as an unintelligible proposition. Important too is the demonstration of the simultaneous determination of allocation and income generation which, later on, has come to be celebrated as the duality theorem. A third is that scarcity has been seen as one of the central issues in economics, although on that aspect some clarifications and corrections are necessary as we shall soon see.

But is it true that all economic processes can be reduced to the pricing principle? And how valid is it to claim that principle itself is based on the subjective valuations of independent and autonomous individuals? How is it that the societal dimension, indeed the social embeddedness, of the economy which was the cardinal principle of the classical writers, gets jettisoned so completely?

As was sharply pointed out by Jevons, the neo-classical economists were not merely trying to formalise the economic traditions that they had inherited, but to correct it and put it on the right course. This was achieved in two different ways. In the first place, the concept of value was completely changed. The classical economists were trying to arrive at an objective notion of the value of commodities by locating the commodity and its values in the production process. The neoclassicals shifted value to the subjective realm, arising from the innate preferences of independent and autonomous individuals, and arrived at when such individuals confront one another through exchange. Second, the classical writers giving priority to production visualised the economy as a process through time, while the neo-classicals, concentrating on exchange, conceptualised the economy in equilibrium or a state of rest at a given time, thereby also setting aside the need to consider time as a determining factor in comprehending the economy.

The major issue to be examined is the extent to which these different conceptualisations help in coming to grips with real-life economic problems. Jevons and Menger were of the view that the analysis they had developed was directly applicable to concrete situations. Towards the end of his major work, Jevons wrote:

> The problem of economics may, as it seems to me be stated thus: Given a certain population, with various needs and powers of production, in possession of certain lands and resources of material required, the mode of employing their labour which will maximize the utility of the produce (1970: 254).

Nothing could be more concrete than this! And, of course, the great success and popularity of Marshall's *Principles* was the manner in which it demonstrated how the tools of economic analysis could be applied to problems of everyday life. It can certainly be conceded that whether at the level of the individual, the household or the enterprise where the objectives and means are *given*, the marginal analysis can be effectively put to use to solve problems. Whether the same is true at the level of the economy as a whole is a different matter and will have to be scrutinised.

As has already been noted, Walras was of the view that the stylised version of the economy, especially its individual components, should not be expected to be realistic. Hence, to begin with, we may concentrate on some formal problems arising from the frozen equilibrium view of the economy that is common to neo-classical analysis in general.

Using a system of simultaneous equations, Walras depicted the economy as a network of inter-related markets in equilibrium. He did not establish the uniqueness of the equilibrium or the conditions for its stability and simply assumed its existence on the ground that there were enough equations to solve for the specified unknowns. Subsequent work has shown that this is not a sufficient condition for the existence of equilibrium.

But even granting that an equilibrium exists, some crucial problems arise from the analysis. In the case of barter (with which Walras begins), equilibrium, the equality of the quantity supplied and demanded, is reached because, starting from a position which is not equilibrium, the participants make the necessary adjustments. This is possible because both the parties are free to make the adjustments as they do not have to take prices or quantities as given. In fact the ratio of prices is established through the quantity adjustment process. When the barter case is generalised, however, the participants are still free to make the quantity adjustment, but must treat the price as given because that is what competition implies. In this situation (and unlike in the case of barter) the participants get regrouped separately, as buyers and sellers. The buyers' demand for goods is considered to be a negative function and the sellers' supply a positive function of price, and the equilibrium is arrived at where supply and demand are equal. Arrow (1959), has raised the question how that equality is arrived at if both buyers and sellers must take price as given.[9] In equilibrium, of course, the equality of supply and demand is also 'given' and nothing really happens. But if prices do not have to be taken as given, then one is dealing with a situation of disequilibrium where the parties must be assumed to be free to make both price and quantity adjustments. Hence, in disequilibrium, the market will consist of a number of monopolists facing a number of monopsonists, each trying to protect his own interest. Recalling that barter is a case of bilateral monopoly, generalised exchange can only be considered as a 'large number of barters', though that expression appears rather awkward. The point simply is that if generalised exchange is considered to be a wider version of barter (as Walras maintains), it can only be thought of as the confrontation between a number of monopsonists and monopolists. There is nothing in the analysis to show how such a situation gets converted into equilibrium, and a competitive one at that.

Walras does not address this question directly. But indirectly, this is the problem that he deals with via the concept of 'tatonnement' and the introduction of the auctioneer who has the power to annul all contracts till equilibrium is reached. Whatever the procedure, the fact remains that there is no proof that the self-interest of utility maximising and profit maximising participants *automatically* leads to competitive equilibrium. What is basically a situation of conflict among monopolists and monopsonists can be converted into the harmony of competitive equilibrium only by an invisible or a visible hand.[10]

The underlying problem here is the nature of the relationship between the individual participants in the system and its systemic features, and, in one form or another, it manifests itself in neo-classical analysis, old and new. I shall refer to two such cases, one old and the other relatively new.

The first is Menger's attempt to establish the logic of exchange. The realist that he was, Menger starts with 'the simplest case'—two farmers, A and B, who are carrying on isolated household economies, i.e., they are isolated self-sufficient producers–consumers like Robinson Crusoe. But at the end of the year, each finds that he has a surplus of what he produces.

> The farmer with the surplus of grain must completely forgo consumption of wine since he has no vineyards at all, and the farmer with a surplus of wine has no foodstuffs. Farmer A can permit bushels of grain to spoil on his fields when a peg of wine would afford him considerable pleasure. Farmer B is about to destroy not merely one but several kegs of wine when he could very well use a few bushels of grain in his household.[11]

Under these circumstances what would be more natural for these two pleasure maximising farmers than to enter into exchange?

However, some nagging issues remain. Is exchange then based on scarcity or on surplus? More important, if there are not markets and production for sale in the markets (neither of which is shown to come from the desires or activities of the two isolated farmers), how can one of them be with only grain and no wine at all, and the other with only wine and no foodstuffs?

The second example comes from Koopmans—who deals with 'the classical and time honored example of a man by whom production and consumption decisions are made in combination: Robinson Crusoe' (1957: 17). After demonstrating that 'there exists a price system with the help of which Robinson the producer can separate his decisions from those of Robinson the consumer and laborer' (1957: 20), Koopmans goes on to say:

We are not interested at this stage in the question whether or how, by some process of trial and error, Robinson can obtain knowledge of a price ratio that will do this trick. We are even less interested in the question whether a single person who operates simultaneously as supplier and consumer should even want to resort to implicit prices for decentralized decision making. The principal point to be derived from our discussion is that if a line of separation exists it defines a price system that makes such a decentralization possible. This conclusion, seemingly artificial when related to a single decision maker, is part of the logical and mathematical basis for an understanding of the operations of competitive markets (1957: 20–21).

The question of how the line of separation, so crucial for the understanding of the competitive model, gets established through individual decision making is simply avoided. The argument, then, is that if (somehow!) competitive prices are established, and if all participants accept them, there will be a competitive market! Something far different and far less than the usual claim that individuals through their maximising behaviour achieve their own self interest and bring about the competitive system of social harmony. As Shackle aptly puts it, the procedure adopted was not so much a *route* to knowledge, as an inference from it (1972: 104).

There is a further point to be noted in relation to the generalisation of exchange. The generalised exchange system is considered to be an activity involving consumers and producers (definitely and explicitly in Walras, and implicitly at least in those who follow the Walrasian tradition). But how valid is it to assume that when exchange gets generalised and trade consequently expands, it can be carried out without traders? This may appear to be more a factual than a logical issue, and so it is up to a point. I shall argue later that a neat separation between logic and facts which is derived from the postulational method is not tenable in economics (see the final chapter). But the recognition of the role of intermediaries in the system is more than a factual matter. It also affects the logic of the system. If it is granted that the intermediaries—in this case, the traders—are not directly interested in either consumption or production, and that as legitimate participants in the system they must also be treated as maximisers, it will have to be conceded that they will do what they can to achieve their own objective. One of the consequences of this is that the informational symmetry, which is a basic assumption in generalised competitive exchange, may not be tenable as traders derive their profits to a large extent by generating and taking advantage of the informational asymmetry between the different 'real' participants of the system.

X

Holding up a more detailed discussion of this aspect till the next chapter, let me now turn to the relationship between exchange and production in the Walrasian general equilibrium model and in neo-classical theory in general. The similarity between exchange and production in neo-classical theory is based on the notion that they are both ways of generating utility through the transformation of goods (or of goods and services), and that, therefore, both are governed by the marginal rate of transformation or substitution and, hence, are not different in essence. But this view arises from a lack of appreciation of the nature of exchange and of production as economic activities. If exchange takes place not only because goods are valuable, but also because they are appropriated, as Walras rightly recognised, then it is more than a transformation of goods; it must also be seen as a change in ownership. Exchange, as an activity, is a transaction between two parties only to the extent that they are both owners of the goods (or services) they wish to transact. Whether it is the subjective or the objective and social ('institutional') aspect of ownership that is dominant in exchange can be debated, but at least the latter cannot be ignored. Now, production, viewed again as an activity, is, in the ultimate analysis, human interaction with nature and so is not, and cannot, be viewed as 'transaction between owners'. However, production, for this reason, does not become a mere technical activity: it too is a social activity based on division of labour and a variety of social organisations arising from it and facilitating it (of which exchange is a part). Neo-classical economics, by underplaying the appropriation aspect of exchange, locates it in individual subjectivity; by totally ignoring the social aspects of production, it is converted into a physical operation. Emptying the social content of both these activities, neo-classical economics converts the economy into a 'world of objects upon which individuals are let loose' (Levine 1977: 183). In so doing it also makes production a mere replication of, and sequel to, exchange, a feature that Marx had pointed out as one of the characteristics of vulgar economics.

Exchange and production as activities differ in at least one more crucial aspect. Conceptually, exchange can be viewed as an atemporal activity not only in the sense that the buying and selling take place simultaneously but, more importantly, also in the sense that what is done at one moment of time can be reversed at another future occasion. On the other hand, production as an activity is carried out *through* time and, what is once done, cannot be reversed. The irreversibility of historical time, thus, is the distinguishing feature of production as an activity. To take time away, and to treat production and exchange as similar in logic, is to do violence to what constitutes the essence of production.

General equilibrium analysis is not guilty of this procedure. It only circumvents it by working with a *given* bundle of goods which, therefore, avoids all questions of how the goods happen to be there. The givenness of goods, however, is not only a matter of analytical convenience. It is very closely linked to what neo-classical economics has come to treat as the central problematic of economics itself, viz., scarcity. In neo-classical writing scarcity is related to utility and the limited quantity of goods. In the absence of production the givenness of goods is absolute while the desire for them is limitless. Hence, scarcity rests on an unexamined assumption of unlimited wants and an assertion of the givenness of goods. If these two premises are granted, then scarcity can be deduced or 'generated' as a consequence. Scarcity, then, is a construct, *not* a fact. It may be stated that neo-classical economics is so constructed as to feature scarcity as its central problematic. That, certainly, is a permissible logical procedure, but converting a mere construct into a fact and projecting it as the central fact of any economy is patently illogical.

It can be shown also that the attempt to establish that scarcity arises from unlimited wants and limited means is a subtle way to isolate scarcity from one of its major correlates, if not determinants, namely, appropriation. Logically it can be argued that scarcity arises not because useful things are limited in any natural sense, but because limits are put on them through appropriation. Such was the classical position. I have already quoted Adam Smith's treatment of kelp which can be interpreted to say that an estate which is bounded by a kelp shore comes to have rent not only because kelp is useful, but also because a landlord has already appropriated it. This is not a forced interpretation either. Adam Smith goes on to say, 'The rent of land, therefore, considered as the price paid for use of land is naturally a monopoly price' (Bk I, Ch IX–I: 131). Kelp and the rocks on which it grows come to have price (index of scarcity) because they are made scarce by restricting supply through appropriation. Obviously not all prices are monopoly prices if monopoly is taken to mean, literally, control over supply by one person or agent. But the price system works via the exclusion principle which relates prices more closely with appropriation than with scarcity as such. Or, if it is logically valid to argue (as Walras does) that useful things which are scarce are appropriated, it is equally valid to say that useful things which are appropriated *become* scarce.

The problem of appropriation in neo-classical theory is, in fact, more involved. Walras was eager to show that the question of property was completely extraneous to his analysis, and, following him, neo-classical economics is generally silent on matters relating to property and ownership. But if exchange is based on appropriation or ownership, it enters very much into the analysis. What neo-classical economics does is to accept a given pattern of ownership and to sanctify that 'giveness' by generating a concept of efficiency associated with it. There is a more subtle issue too. In a market system, exchange based on appropriation becomes the indicator of the scarcity index; it is also the recognised mode of appropriation. The system, therefore, provides an incentive to individuals to generate scarcity via its own functioning. In real-life situations it is quite common to come across attempts by individuals using the market mechanism in this manner to generate scarcities in their favour. But neo-classical theory does not provide for this possibility of the participants thus taking advantage of the system. It is somewhat surprising that a theory based on the self-interest of individuals does not deal with this possibility.

The explanation is twofold. The first is that through an assumption not always adequately spelled out, neo-classical theory rules out this possibility. This assumption relates to the 'initial' distribution of goods (resources) among the participants where it is considered that the distribution is such that no participant has enough resources to be able to 'subvert' the system. This is more an empirical statement than a logical premise. The fact is that the logic of the system is crucially dependent on this substantive condition. The beautiful neo-classical system anchored in individual preferences derives its logical properties from an objective condition regarding the distribution of property rights which arises neither from individual preferences nor from technological factors but from a social arrangement.

The second explanation is even more pertinent. The 'individuals' in the theory are not real active beings in their concrete social surroundings, but agents specially created to play a carefully designed role in the theoretical schema—mere 'clothelines on which to hang propositions of economic logic' as Schumpeter, the great admirer of the marginalist revolution, frankly admitted (1954: 886-87). This treatment of individuals is no accident: it is the manifestation of the utilitarian philosophy on which neo-classical economics so heavily depends. As has been pointed out:

> Utilitarianism sees persons as locations of their respective utilities—as the sites at which such activities as desiring and having pleasure and pain take place. Once note has been taken of the person's utility, utilitarianism has no further direct interest in any information about him. . . . Persons do not count as individuals in this any more than individual petrol tanks do in the national consumption of petroleum (Sen and Williams 1982: 4).

Or, as Rawls points out, the agents considered by utilitarian philosophy and neo-classical economics are not a 'plurality of distinct persons with separate systems of ends' (Rawls 1972: 29) but simply dummies with certain prescribed attributes, chiefly, 'rationality'. To put it differently, individuals, the primary units in neo-classical theory, are not people who exercise free choice; they are creatures who behave exactly as the theorists want them to behave.

It is on the basis of the 'preferences' of such individuals that neo-classical theory celebrates the concept of efficiency via the correspondence between competitive equilibrium and Pareto optimality. Pareto optimality is usually defined as a situation where no one can be made better off without making someone else worse off. It, therefore, comes to have an air of objectivity based on which the emotive notion of efficiency is also projected as an objective criterion. But this is a wrong, though convenient, interpretation. Strictly speaking, Pareto optimality is a situation where no one can be made better off *in terms of his preferences* without making someone else worse off *in terms of his*.[12] Thus, it is a highly subjective position to which the theorist provides a garb of objectivity, and even verifiability, because though the participants themselves do not know the preferences of other participants, the theorist knows the preferences of *all* participants as he is the author of all the preferences and, indeed, of all the participants too!

It is not only the participants that the theorist fashions according to his will, the world of technology too is subordinate to it. Like individual preferences, production functions are also a 'given' to the theorist—but given on his own terms. Corresponding to all individuals facing the same prices and, therefore, the same relative prices, theory requires that all firms also have the same marginal rates of technical substitution, provided they too respond to given prices. In order to achieve this, every production function must be locally linear-homogeneous. This imposed condition of 'given' production functions is more than a technological requirement. Its significance, as Koopmans brings out (1957: First essay), is that it comes in handy to show that if any given number of independent profit maximising firms are price-takers, then the maximisation of aggregate profit implies maximisation of individual profits, and the converse. One can, and must, go a step further. It will be recalled that according to Walras the firm (strictly speaking, the entrepreneur) makes neither profits nor losses. One of its implications is that if, thus, equilibrium is a situation of no excess profits, then profit maximisation yields an income distribution with no room for social disharmony—a very useful and powerful conclusion, indeed. Further, as Boland sums up:

> In any assumed linear world, everything adds up: the aggregates can never differ from their atomistic parts; nothing is left over to be accounted for by any forbidden exogenous means; and, most important, there is nothing endogenous to upset the general equilibrium (Boland 1982: 88).

The elegance of the neo-classical theoretical stage, therefore, depends not so much on the characters themselves, but on the elaborate make up done in the green room!

XI

It must be conceded that all these features of neo-classical economics have been brought out in and through the attempts of Walras, Arrow–Debreu, Koopmans and many others, to formalise it. Formalisation, as such, is thus a two-edged sword; it brings out both strengths and weaknesses. Hence, it is not surprising that some of those who have contributed to its formalisation, and are considered to be its defenders, have also pointed out its major drawbacks.[13] Some attempts to make the theory conform to the basics of the real, social, world have also come from them. The 'survivor problem', dealt with by Arrow and Debreu, and annotated by Koopmans, is a good example. Commenting on the model of the competitive economy as worked out by Arrow and Debreu, Koopmans says: 'The hardest part in the specification of the model is to make sure that each consumer can both survive and participate in the market, without anticipating in the postulates what specific prices will prevail in an equilibrium' (1957: 59). Then he lists the two survivor conditions, which I have already cited in the previous chapter, viz., first, that the total output is more than required for total consumption and, second, that each consumer can, if necessary, survive on the basis of the resources he holds and the direct use of his own labour, without engaging in exchange, and still have something to spare of some type of labour which is sure to meet with a positive price in any equilibrium. Converting the two necessary conditions into a real-life situation, Koopmans also observes that the model 'would be found best suited for describing a society of self-sufficient farmers who do a little trading on the side' (ibid: 62). This looks intuitively appealing as an example of an economy of decentralised decision makers. However, it seems to me that it poses more problems than it solves. What the model purports to depict is not an economy where most goods are produced *within* self-sufficient households which can also take up trade as a kind of extra: it is not meant to be a model in which the participants occasionally turn to trade, but one in which the participants *live* by buying and selling, i.e., where exchange is generalised. More pertinently, if most economic activity is presumed to be done by self-sufficient farmers, the economy must be considered to have a large segment which is not necessarily responsive to market signals. This condition may be closer to reality, but then, again, it restricts the model's claim to arrive at a principle of allocation in the economy as a whole.

A more appropriate analogy for the general equilibrium model, therefore, would appear to be the parable of the prisoner-of-war (POW) camp originally proposed by R.A. Radford, and made popular by Joan Robinson (1971: 4–5). The men are kept alive (more or less) by official rations, and they receive parcels from the Red Cross once a month. The contents of the parcels are not tailored to the tastes of the individual recipients. It is, therefore, possible for each one to gain and for the camp to reach a state of Pareto optimality by swapping what each values less for what he values more. The Warder, of course, functions as the Walrasian auctioneer, ensuring that no contract is binding till all markets are in equilibrium. There is, therefore, peace, harmony and welfare within the camp, all that is claimed to be achieved by self-interested individuals responding to the laws of the market.

In terms of the initial endowment of the participants, the process of tatonnement and the pressure of an auctioneer, the POW camp example may be closer to the market model, certainly of the Walrasian kind than the one suggested by Koopmans, and yet there are problems. The fact is that although Jevons, Menger and the early pioneers of the neo-classical school might have been trying to model some real-life economy they were familiar with, neo-classical economics as it was perfected subsequently does not represent, nor does it purport to represent, any real-life situation. Whatever might have been the intentions of the early writers, as the models have been worked upon by those who came after them and in that process became increasingly formalised, they have also become increasingly removed from real-life situations. This is not the result of formalisation as such, though increase in formalisation has the built-in danger of emptying the content. The distancing of the neo-classical basic models from reality may be attributed to something else. It is possible to think of them as dealing with a paradox. Arrow and Hahn in a joint work on competitive analysis present the paradox thus:

> The immediate 'commonsense' answer to the question 'What will an economy motivated by individual greed and controlled by a very large number of different agents look like?' is probably: There will be chaos. That quite a different answer has long been claimed true and has indeed permeated the economic thinking of a large number of people who are in no way economists is itself sufficient ground for investigating it seriously (Arrow and Hahn 1971: vii).

From Adam Smith to the present, economists have tried to deal with the paradox of harmony prevailing or at least chaos not resulting in an economy in which individuals motivated by self-interest interact with one another. What conditions are required to show that the decentralised decisions and actions of such agents can result in a coherent disposition of resources which can be claimed to be superior to some other dispositions, such as that by a centralised agency? If this is considered to be the question (and about the *only* question) that economics as a field of study is to be concerned with, then the competitive model put forward by Walras and others, and reinforced by leading economists of our own time, provides an answer. If this is the question, it can be argued that whether or not Adam Smith set out to design an economic order, based solely on self-interest, the question is still worth pursuing. In pursuit of this question, there is no harm in ignoring an answer given by a distinguished member of the profession who said: 'The working of self-interest is generally beneficient, not because of some natural coincidence between self-interest and the good of all, but because human institutions are arranged so as to compel self-interest to work in directions in which it will be beneficient'.[14] The answers to the question, say Arrow and Hahn, can be found if one is willing to accept, as agents those who have been programmed to discharge some responsibilities, technology as satisfying some strict conditions, resources as fairly equally distributed, information as freely and uniformly available, and a host of other conditions. Not only will this elaborate intellectual equipment provide an answer to the riddle; with a little more effort, the elegant formulation that results can even be shown to have some features of an economy! The agents can be clubbed together as decision makers and can then be partitioned into consumers, producers and resource holders, each performing an assigned task; a bundle of commodities can be taken as given; exchange and production, and all other economic activities can be simulated—and a stage-managed economic system emerges with some very desirable properties. Since these properties are institutionally neutral they may be claimed to be universal, and if real-life economies do not correspond to them, it can be claimed that they should. The theory thus derived, says Shackle,

> satisfied to an extraordinary degree some canons of conceptual beauty. It answered a list of questions which seem to form a closed circle to achieve a self-subsistent completeness. It involves very few ultimate principles. It achieved a unified simplicity·which powerfully commands assent. On its own terms it explained everything (Shackle 1972: 105).

XII

In this brief and selective survey of economic theory I have devoted what may appear to be disproportionately long sections to neo-classical economics. This is partly because neo-classical economics is about the most formalised theoretical system which, therefore, lends itself to a critical appraisal of the connection between the formal and the substantive in economics. The somewhat detailed examination of neo-classical economics also reflects the fact that in the Indian context at least, and possibly elsewhere too, neo-classical theory is *the* economic theory and hence an exposition of its structural aspects, it is hoped, serves the purpose of an in-depth understanding of what is taught and learned as economic theory. So strong has been the influence of neo-classical economics in India that there are those who hold the view even today that there is only one economic theory and that neo-classical economics is its revelation.

Hence it may be useful to examine why neo-classical economics has such a hold on the minds of professional economists. Its universalising logic—its ability to explain 'everything'—is of intuitive appeal. It is not only a logical structure, it is also a closed system. It is the closed structure that gives it explanatory power over 'everything', i.e., that which it has chosen to include within its closed boundary. Its tight boundary enables it to specify quite sharply what constitutes an economic problem and what does not, and then to provide a logical explanation to what is within. A tight structure of this kind can also be made determinate. It, therefore, provides the professionals the skill and power to arrive at definitive conclusions through reasoning, and the ability to make 'predictions' on that basis especially if assumptions can be made 'to let theorems emerge, all neat and provable', as has been remarked.[15] This is what has enabled economics to emerge as the most 'scientific' among disciplines dealing with human and social problems. If its votaries cling on to this feature of the discipline and make it the most important aspect too, it is hardly surprising.

Closely associated are the pedagogical advantages of the structure. Since economics, in this approach, becomes primarily logic, its 'principles' can be rigorously spelt out, neatly packaged and easily communicated. Those who have skills in logic and mathematics can build on it, demonstrating their creative potentials; the humble ones can learn it by rote. Thus it becomes all things to all men, to each according to his ability. Among the pioneers of the neo-classical tradition, Marshall it was who contributed most to its immense pedagogical popularity. But Marshall generated his own version of the new economics. What Deane refers to as his mature neo-classical school 'replaced the fragmented, often vaguely defined, philosophically oriented analysis of the classical school with an integrated theory of value-in-use and value-in-exchange in which market price was mathematically determined by the intersection of the schedules of supply and demand' (1978: 107). Somewhat surprisingly this integration was achieved by disintegration elsewhere. By the skilled use of the *ceteris paribus* assumption and partial equilibrium analysis, Marshall taught generations of students to think of each market in isolation where prices were determined by the forces of supply and demand alone, their relative contributions depending on the 'time' available for the adjustment of the quantity supplied. By so doing Marshall strongly brought economics much closer to day-to-day problems. He further reinforced this sense of realism by going back to Adam Smith's style of drawing analytical principles from real-life situations.

But this sense of realism was partly illusory. Marshall's demand and supply curves, the former downward sloping and the latter upward sloping, have become so much a part of conventional wisdom and have also come to be accepted as real-life entities. But how 'real' are they? If one is discussing problems of buying and selling in real life, it must be conceded that in most instances the buyer is dealing with a trader and not a producer. A producer's supply curve may be upward sloping in the sense that he will be able to supply more at a *higher* price. But a trader is usually willing to supply a larger quantity at a *lower* price. His supply curve, therefore, is in fact downward sloping posing problems to the determination and stability of equilibrium. The point here is not so much the shape of the supply curve as the question of who are the agents to be taken into account in any given situation and is related to the recognition of intermediaries that I have already referred to.

The illusory realism of neo-classical economics is more pervasive than this instance though. Its basis is the clever use of the 'givenness' of which Marshall's *ceteris paribus* is only a visible recognition. But the preferences of the individuals are given and not subject to the influences of the economic system. The initial endowment of the participants is given—in such a way—that no one can dominate over another. Information is given. Even equilibrium prices are given, and it is given too that all participants are price takers. With so much treated as 'given', though much of it goes contrary to reality and common sense, economics is shown to be a matter of technology and, increasingly, of numerology. Its 'laws' are, therefore, projected as its own laws and tampering with them is proved to be dangerous. Economics was shown to be concerned only with prices and allocation on which it could dictate public policy as these dictates were based on 'science'. Everything else was considered to be questions of value, and hence subjective, from which science had to withdraw. And withdraw it did from questions of welfare and income distribution (except in the rare but distinguished works of a few like Pigou), of growth and development and most other economic problems of concern to ordinary mortals. In this sense, the tenacity and popularity of neo-classical economics have been based on its claims to scientism that enables it to ignore questions of power, justice and many other crucial social issues, and thus to become a powerful ally of the status quo. A discipline designed in this manner cannot be claimed to be science; it is an ideology whose purpose is to prevent an understanding of real-life issues.

Institutionalism

XIII

The formalism of the neo-classical school did not go unchallenged. The Historical School in Europe and the Institutionalists in America were constantly and vehemently raising their voices against the evaporation of the empirical element in the writings of the 'theorists' of their time. One of the protestors said:

> More and more did they turn into completely drab, abstract arm-chair scholars, interested in divisions and definitions: into socialist visionaries: into calculating mathematicians: into doctrinaire, all-embracing theorists of natural law and of Robinson Crusoe stories. . . . Only one remedy offered itself in this situation: the return to empirical reality.[16]

It is possible to gain a lot of insight from the writings of the Historical School and of the Institutionalists, especially Veblen. But in their quest for empirical reality the Institutionalists became mere critics of theory and the Historical School turned out to be opposed to theory. 'Fact finding' became their common professional vocation.

However, in more recent times, a new set of institutional economists have emerged who do not discard the formalism of theory, but try to locate institutions in suitable theoretical framework. In this and the next section I shall evaluate their effort paying special attention to the manner in which they deal with the formal and the substantive in economics. Their accent, undoubtedly, is on the substantive.

I shall first deal with Gunnar Myrdal, a reference to whose work has already been made in the previous chapter. In several of his writings Myrdal had expressed the view that an understanding of broader social and political factors was necessary to come to grips with economic issues and that neo-classical economists by trying to derive economic theory from the subjective theory of value had not really achieved anything very significant. 'Social life' he said, 'is the result of historical development and is anything but a logical system' (Myrdal 1953: 198). His criticism of neo-classical economics was rather harsh.

The practical results of the subjective theory are not particularly impressive either. It neither conveys knowledge of facts, nor does it solve practical problems. It is an abstract barren construction of great complexity for the uninitiated. It is one of those systems so common in the social sciences, which yield only pseudo-knowledge (Myrdal 1953: 96).

This assessment was made originally in the late 1920s. In the mid-1960s when Myrdal turned to a study of the poverty of Asian nations, the criticisms were directed against most western theories of economics which had come to treat economic problems purely as 'economic' abstracted from sociological, political, cultural and geographical aspects. He described his three-volume *Asian Drama,* with its subtitle, 'An Inquiry into the Poverty of Nations', as an 'out and out institutional' study. The central idea in the institutional approach, he pointed out in the preface, 'is that history and politics, theories and ideologies, economic structure and levels, social stratification, agriculture and industry, population developments, health and education, and so on must be studied not in isolation but in their mutual relationship' (Myrdal 1968: x). This may appear to be too tall an order, but Myrdal was equally eager to show that his institutional approach was not *anti*-theoretical, but that it called for a more general theory than modern economics had come to have. In this sense theory was to be understood as a 'logically correlated system of questions addressed to the material' (ibid: xii).

The main features of the 'institutional theory' were presented in Appendix 2 in Volume III of the *Asian Drama.* The procedure was to set up a 'social system' consisting of conditions that are usually inter-related in that a change in one would cause a change in the other. The conditions were classified into six broad categories: (*a*) output and incomes; (*b*) conditions of production; (*c*) levels of living; (*d*) attitude towards life and work; (*e*) institutions and (*f*) policies. Myrdal's contention was that what he described as the modern western approach, both western liberalism and Marxism, confined themselves to the first three or even the first two of these conditions. Institutions are tempo-rally and spatially specific and what Myrdal listed as the South Asian institutions of the mid-twentieth century were

> a land tenure system detrimental to agricultural advance; undevel-oped institutions for enterprise, employment, trade and credit; defi-ciencies of national consolidation; imperfections in the authority of government agencies; instability and low effectiveness in national policies; low standards of efficiency and integrity in public admin-istration; ineffective organs for provincial and local self-govern-ment; and a weak infrastructure of voluntary organisations (Myrdal 1968: 1863).

To get a further picture, these must be supplemented by a list of attitudes of the people of the areas towards life and work; low levels of work discipline, punctuality and orderliness; superstitious beliefs and irrational outlook; lack of alertness, adaptability, ambition, and general readiness for change and experiment; submissiveness to au-thority and exploitation; low attitude for cooperation and low stan-dards of personal hygiene (Myrdal 1968: 1862).

Without entering into any discussion about the veracity of the two lists we may examine how adequately and effectively these aspects have been put to use in the author's own analysis. It is possible to identify instances where Myrdal used his larger social system analysis effectively, other instances where he largely ignored his own analytical technique and still others where he was not sure how the technique was to be used. The best example of the first kind is the treatment of the problems of labour utilisation, especially the concepts of 'unemploy-ment' and 'underemployment'. In what Myrdal identified as the 'mod-ern approach' problems of unemployment and underemployment are seen as the result of resource endowment where a huge population is dependent on limited resources, land in particular. With the help of statistics Myrdal established that while the land–man ratios in the countries of South Asia might be low, they were not as low as in some advanced countries in the West or in Japan . On this basis he argued that the approach to the problems of South Asian economies, in terms of levels of income and factor combinations in production (i.e., conditions *a* and *b* of the social system), was inadequate. Bringing in the cultural and institutional factors, he maintained, instead, that in these countries, 'the bulk of the labour force is embedded in a climatic, social, cultural and institutional matrix that not only tends to perpetuate present low levels of labour utilisation, but also resists rapid and immediate adaptation to novel and unfamiliar ways of living and working' (Myrdal 1968: 999). Whether valid or not, Myrdal had an explanation of a set of problems in terms of his analytical structure.

In contrast, while dealing with the issue of corruption Myrdal's explanation was that

while it is, on the one hand, exceedingly difficult in South Asia to introduce profit motives and market behaviour into the sector of social life where they operate in the West—that is, the economic sphere—it is, on the other hand, difficult to eliminate mobilisations of private gain from the sector where they have been suppressed in the West—the sphere of public responsibility and power. In South Asia those vested with the official authority and power very often exploit their position in order to make a gain for themselves, their family or social group (Myrdal 1968: 948).

Again, we shall not enter into the substantive validity of these statements. But one part of Myrdal's analysis shows that where South Asians can make easy gains they do so, which does not agree with another part of the analysis which claims that South Asians are irresponsive to opportunities for betterment of their living conditions.

This ambiguity is seen in the treatment of some of the other aspects as well. For instance, the elaborate analysis of the comparative levels of labour utilisation in farm operations in West Bengal and Central Thailand offers two explanations for the component of hired labour being higher in the former. The first is a cultural–institutional one, that a high-caste farmer in Bengal, if he can possibly afford to do so, will limit his role to that of supervision. Large numbers of farmers belonging to the cultivating castes follow his example and hire farm servants or casual labourers to do most of the work (Myrdal 1968: 1088). But on the very next page there is a different kind of explanation.

The very low work participation of the Bengal farm families is not typical for other and less *densely settled parts of India*. Some of the farm studies conducted in other parts of India show members of farm families working more hours per year than do those in Thailand. On the other hand, the liberal use of hired labour, even on fairly small farms, is found also in other farm studies. This feature of Indian agriculture is clearly demonstrated by the existence of a large army of agricultural workers *drawn mainly from the landless class* (Myrdal 1968: 1089 emphasis added).

If the density of population and the existence of landless agricultural labourers explain the pattern of labour utilisations on farms, then it is very much a 'pure economic' explanation. The point to note is not Myrdal's ambivalence about the two alternative explanations, but that the 'social system' of mutual interactions seems to divide itself into two and explanations come to be offered *either* in terms of the first three conditions (representing purely economic factors) alone *or* solely in terms of the next two conditions (representing cultural factors). If in the course of analysis the social system is thus seen to disintegrate, it cannot be claimed to be of a robust theoretical nature and the institutional factors which are prominently projected can be quite conveniently utilised as the occasion demands.

I am, therefore, led to conclude that Myrdal's institutional *theory* is rather shaky. It is not surprising that while Myrdal came to have many ardent admirers because he brought in institutions, cultural aspects and value premises to the inquiry into the poverty of nations, hardly anybody has picked up his theoretical frame to be used as it is or to be modified further. In passing, one of Myrdal's substantive failures may be noted too: he failed to note that poverty is not *of* nations, but *in* nations—a very major distinction indeed.

XIV

There was a time, not long ago, when an institutional economist had the same standing among economists as a veterinarian among the medical profession. But thanks to the work of Douglass North or, more likely, thanks to the recognition that his work received from the Nobel Foundation, institutionalism, or at least the 'new institutional economics', is in fashion now. Unlike the old institutionalists for whom neoclassical economics was the target of attack, what the new institutional economics has been trying to do is to accept neo-classical economics as the most valuable among the theoretical traditions in economics, but to make it more realistic. In the late 1970s North wrote: 'Neo-classical theory has made economics the pre-eminent social science by providing it a disciplined, logical analytical framework. To abandon neo-classical theory is to abandon economics as a science' (1978: 974). But it is not surprising that North, the historian of economic events, cannot reconcile himself fully with the neo-classical theory that converts life into logic. He knows that institutions, 'humanly devised constraints that shape human interactions' and provide 'a structure to everyday life' (1990: 3) cannot altogether be left out of economic affairs. Hence, his recent attempts have been to devise an analytical framework to integrate institutional analysis into economic theory and economic history.

North provides three main reasons that necessitate the incorporation of institutions into economic analysis. First, the behavioural assumptions of traditional theory are too simplistic if not patently wrong. The assumption of rational choice on which traditional theory is based holds that individual decision makers in the system have true knowledge about the working of the system itself so that their decisions and actions are in conformity with the systemic requirements. But how can this be? 'Individuals make choices based on subjectively derived models that diverge among individuals and the information the actors receive is so incomplete that in most cases these divergent subjective models show no tendency to converge'(North 1990: 17). If one wishes to be realistic, one has to accept that motivation of participants is more complicated and their preferences less stable than what received theory postulates. Once this is accepted, it will not be difficult to see that institutions arise in the process of human interactions and that once they emerge, they greatly influence motivations and actions. Second, traditional theory's assumption about the nature of information and the flow of information in the system is also questionable. That all participants have full information about everything is the assumption that received theory makes. No institutions are necessary in a world of complete information and where, therefore, information is a free good. But if the more realistic situation of incomplete information is accepted, again, it will not be difficult to see that institutions necessarily evolve and become part of the system. Via the assumption of complete knowledge, theory also eliminates uncertainty—thereby, again, making the system institution proof because a major role of institutions in a social system is to reduce uncertainty by establishing a stable structure of human interactions.

North's case for institutions is strongest in his insightful analysis of exchange. Basic to his argument is the recognition that commodities that enter into exchange have different attributes, not all of them equally visible to the parties in the exchange. Viewing exchange in its broadest sense as transactions in *property rights*, it is therefore possible for parties to an exchange to generate ownership or property rights taking advantage of the differential perception of the attributes of the goods being transacted. Exchange then becomes not merely a bid for goods, as traditional theory views it, but also an attempt by the parties to become 'residual claimants' of the property rights generated in the process of transaction. North, thus, suggests that this problem, usually confined to the principal–agent transaction, is of wider significance. If this is granted, then it can be seen that the system is one of information asymmetries, the resulting transaction costs and the agencies required to enforce contracts. These aspects do not figure in traditional theory because of its simplistic notion of exchange.

> As long as we maintain the fiction of a unidimensional good trans-
> acted instantaneously, the problem of policing and enforcement are
> trivial. But when we add the cost of acquiring information and,
> specifically, of measuring, the problems become major ones. It is
> because we do not know the attributes of a good or service or all
> the characteristics of the performance of agents and because we
> have to devote costly resources to try to measure and monitor them
> that enforcement issues do arise (North 1990: 32).

North, therefore, takes into the realm of exchange the transaction costs problem, usually dealt with in the context of firms and production, and locates the case for institutions in that milieu. In his words:

> Institutions provide the structure for exchange that (together with
> the technology employed) determines the cost of transacting and the
> cost of information. ... The institutions necessary to accomplish
> economic exchange vary in their complexity, from those that solve
> simple exchange problems to ones that extend across space and time
> and numerous individuals. ... The greater the specialization and the
> number and variability of attributes, the more weight must be put on
> reliable institutions that allow individuals to engage in complex

contracting with a minimum uncertainty about whether the terms of the contract can be realized (North 1990: 34).

Because third-party agencies required for enforcement of contracts may have to have coercive power, North provides a place for the state also in this approach to institutions.

North's arguments providing for the existence and role of institutions in social and economic life are, certainly, convincing. But the issue is not the strength of arguments showing that institutions exist and perform—any one with common sense will have to grant that—but to see how compatible this real-life view of institutions is with the basic postulates of neo-classical theory which North does not want to abandon, though he is quite critical of some aspects of it. Even while vehemently asserting the role of institutions, there is an underlying tenor of methodological individualism in North's writing. His recent study (North 1990) on institutions (on which I have relied), it may be noted, is in the Cambridge Series in the Political Economy of Institutions and Decisions with the central question (as spelt out in the Series editor's preface): 'How do institutions evolve in response to individual incentive, strategies, and choices, and how do institutions affect the performance of political and economic systems?' (p.vi). The first of these questions, while recognising the existence and significance of institutions, amounts to what Boland calls 'reductive individualism' which treats institutions as mere epiphenomena.

> Institutions are to be analogous to pictures printed in the newspaper. What appears in any newspaper picture as a person's face is actually only a collection of black and white dots. One can explain the appearance of a face by explaining why the dots are where they are' (Boland 1982: 31).

That is also North's position on institutions. 'Institutions are a creation of human beings. They evolve and are altered by human beings; hence our theory must begin with the individual' (North 1990: 5). Further,

> Defining institutions as the constraints that human beings impose on themselves makes the definition complementary to the choice theoretic approach of neo-classical economic theory. Building a theory of institutions on the foundation of individual choices is a step

towards reconciling differences between economics and social sciences (North 1990: 5).

Institutions as arising from the decisions and actions of individuals are seen more prominently in Andrew Schotter's formal treatment of economic and social institutions which, incidentally, demonstrates that institutional analysis does not have to be thought of as the antithesis of the formal approach. Schotter (1981) draws attention to two distinct approaches to institutions which he identifies with John Commons and Karl Menger. Commons found traditional economic theory based on individual actions inadequate and tried to build institutional economics based on collective action, in all its variations. Menger, on the other hand, saw institutions arising out of the selfish interaction of individuals each pursuing his own self-interest. Schotter places himself in the latter 'school' along with Robert Nozick, who shows how the state as a social and economic institution can be shown to emerge from the uncoordinated decisions of self-interested individuals, and John Rawls who demonstrates that social institutions that form the basis of a just system can also be derived from the choice of free individuals. Whether Rawls will agree that he and Nozick have the same approach to individuals and society is a different matter. The point that Schotter makes is that Rawls, Nozick and he himself begin from what he calls 'a Lockean state of nature' in which 'there are no social institutions at all, only agents, their preferences and the technology they have at their disposal to transform inputs into outputs' (Schotter 1981: 20). One of the crucial issues here is the manner in which 'wholes' like the economy and society are to be conceptualised, and I shall take this up for more detailed examination in the succeeding chapters. For the moment, therefore, I continue with Schotter.

The problem with economics as it exists today, says Schotter, is that it is hampered by an institutional short-sightedness that greatly inhibits its analysis of social problems. The short-sightedness results from a fixation on the market which alone neo-classical economic theory recognises as an institution. Underlying it is the neo-classical theory's treatment of agents as mere automata responding to market signals as a thermostat responds to temperature. 'The neo-classical agents are bores who merely calculate optimal activities at fixed parametric prices. . . . No syndicates or coalitions are formed, no cheating or lying is done, no threats are made—merely truthful parametric behaviour' (Schotter 1981: 150). If this naive, unrealistic behavioural assumption is removed and if the agents are thought of as capable of strategic choices under different circumstances, then they will discover that in their own selfish interest it is necessary to evolve institutions that deal with problems of coordination, problems of the much discussed prisoners' dilemma type, problems of externalities and so on. The question that Schotter poses is: Which is a more fruitful theory—one that arrives at a determinate economic environment of the neo-classical variety starting from simplistic behavioural assumptions or one that can recognise a variety of economic environments with a plurality of institutions based on more realistic behavioural assumptions of the type that he shows to be possible.

But can the basic neo-classical theory be metamorphosed in this manner and still retain its theoretical niceties? Those institutionalists who are styled as 'the imperfect information school' confront this question. I take Joseph Stiglitz as a representative of this school particularly because he has dealt with institutions that are characteristic of the rural scenes in the 'less developed countries' (LDCs), tenancy in particular. Reflecting on his own work and those of scholars of his persuasion, Stiglitz admits that their dissatisfaction with received theory is that it is inadequate in explaining some central facts within its domain, 'the dramatically different standards of living of those who happen to live in different countries, and within different regions with the same country' (1989: 18). Differing from the widely prevalent views that poverty in such situations is the result of either the irrational behaviour of the agents or the inadequacy of resources, Stiglitz turns to an analysis of the institutional set up of the countries concerned to see whether an explanation can be found there. For instance, why is sharecropping so prevalent in the LDCs? Earlier views on sharecropping, going back to Marshall, had noted its dampening of incentives and hence the tendency has been to think of it as an inefficient institution. But then why would an inefficient institution persist? The answer that Stiglitz and others arrived at is that sharecropping clearly performs a role in sharing risks between landlords and tenants and that in the absence of insurance markets it performs an important economic function. In fact, sharecropping is a reflection not only of the absence of certain markets but also the absence of perfect information—the landlord cannot know how effectively a potential tenant will work if he is hired as a wage worker— the typical principal–agent problem. Hence, the rationale of apparently inefficient institutions like sharecropping is seen in the absence of markets and of complete information. From this Stiglitz moves to the conclusion:

The theorem that asserts that market resource allocations are Pareto-efficient is of very restricted validity. Not only does it require perfect competition, but it is valid only if there is a complete set of markets and perfect information, conditions that are clearly not satisfied (1989: 23).

The conflict between the formation of neo-classical theory and real-life situations in which context the new institutionalists locate institutions very clearly emerges here. But the procedure that these theorists adopt is far from satisfactory. They are unwilling or unable to get away from 'the Walras–Pareto fixation': first, rational behaviour gets identified with response to markets and, second, efficiency gets identified with competitive market equilibrium and Pareto optimality. Stiglitz says:

Sharecropping can be viewed in part as an institutional adaptation to the absence of certain risk (insurance) markets. But . . . the fact that institutions respond, that they perform certain economic functions, does not mean that they perform these functions 'optimally' that the resulting equilibrium is, in any meaningful sense, efficient (1989: 24).

But what is a meaningful sense of 'efficiency'? While Stiglitz the theorist works with the Paretian concept of efficiency, Stiglitz the developmental realist has to admit: 'A land reform that took land away from the landlords and gave it to the peasants would not be a Pareto improvement, since landlords would be worse off; but not only would such a reform reduce inequality, it might well increase national output substantially' (1989: 25). As I have already indicated, within the tight boundaries of the neo-classical economic theoretical system, concepts such as rationality and efficiency have their systems-related meanings. The dilemma of those, such as the new institutionalists, who try to make the system realistic is that it is not amenable to such treatments. Consequently, arguments for the recognition of a plurality of institutions which, however, identify rationality with responding to market signals and efficiency with competitive equilibrium will run into incompatibilities sooner or later. The explanation of a phenomenon, where imperfections or asymmetries of information are the crucial aspects, cannot be carried out in terms of a theory that has perfect and symmetric information as one of its basic postulates.

In this respect Schotter's position is much more tenable: he shows that with the rigid behavioural assumption of neo-classical theory, it is not possible to accommodate any institution other than the markets and hence he is asking for a different theoretical approach that is based on different notions of human behaviour. Bounded rationality and satisficing, as advocated by Herbert Simon and other behaviourists, become the central core of his system. The limitation of his analysis is the insistence on reductive individualism which is difficult to understand because he recognises that the individuals of neo-classical theory do not succeed in establishing the market economy through their own self-interested decisions but only through the introduction of an auctioneer, *deus ex machina*, who has the power to invalidate all contracted prices till equilibrium prices are arrived at in all markets. We must repeat that the neo-classical agents are not merely price takers, but takers of *equilibrium* price. And nobody has shown so far that the equilibrium prices are, or can be, established solely through the decisions and actions of self-interested individuals.

XV

In the light of the treatment of the formalism of neo-classical economics and the realism of the institutionalists we may consider again the relationship between the formal and substantive in economics. The problem with neo-classical economics is not that it is a formalised theory. I have already pointed out that it is through the process of formalisation that we have come to have a proper appreciation of the theory, including its many internal structural problems. But in the process of formalisation, neo-classical theory has also converted the substantial concrete into logical constructs through excessive abstraction. *That* is the problem. Marx had warned about this problem in one of his early writings.

> Is it surprising [he asked] that everything, in the final abstraction... presents itself as a logical category? If you let drop little by little all that constitutes the individuality of a house, leaving out first of all the materials of which it is composed, then the form that distinguishes it, you end up with nothing but a body; that if you leave out of account the limits of this body, you soon have nothing but a space—that if, finally, you leave out of account the dimensions of

this space, there is nothing left but pure quantity, the logical category? (Marx 1955: 92).

It is not the individuality of a house that neo-classical theory has emptied but, strangely enough, the individuality of the individual! This we have seen already. But why did this happen? After all, Adam Smith too had given a prominent place to individuals—self-interested individuals too—in his system. But Smith was dealing with real-life individuals with their specificities resulting from division of labour and brought into new bonds of interdependence with others through exchange. He found this to be the difference between *human* individuals and individuals of other animal species. In contrast, neo-classical theory begins with the individual defined in terms of strict behavioural axioms. The relations among such individuals, then, is seen as purely external to them. Unlike in Smith where individuals interact because they are different, in neo-classical theory they interact because they are all the same, mere repositories of preference functions. Neo-classical theory treats firms also in the same manner.[17] After all, what are firms other than repositories of production functions, and what is production other than a transformation of utilities? Neo-classical formalism, thus, takes away from its theory the essence of the human and the social, depriving the system of the possibilities of change over time. Once this is done economics becomes just a method, a procedure of maximising subject to constraints. From this it is only a small step to argue that it does not matter to theory (*economic* theory) as to whether 'the individual maximizes wealth, religious piety, the annihilation of crooners, or his waistline'.[18] The problem with neo-classical economics, thus, is that it uses a pseudo-universalising form to suppress and glide over all specificities of substance.

The old institutionalists protested against it; the new institutionalists are trying to put content into the form through a realistic representation of the firm, as the transaction-cost analysts from Coase to Williamson have been doing, or by an incorporation of institutions generally, as North has been proposing. But whether neo-classical theory will lend itself to that kind of grafting of the substantive to its deliberately designed logical frame is doubtful.

This does not mean that formal analysis of substantive problems is not possible. The real issue is the level of abstraction that will succeed in illuminating substantive problems without becoming substitutes for them. The procedure adopted by Keynes and earlier on by Marx are examples of that approach. Keynes was addressing himself to the substantive problems of intense, persistent, trade depression associated with widespread and exceptionally high levels of unemployment of the post-First World War period throughout Europe and America. The neo-classical explanation of these, especially unemployment, was that it was a result of the failure to adhere to the prescriptions of theory. Lionel Robbins wrote: 'It is a well-known generalisation of theoretical economics that a wage which is held above the equilibrium level necessarily involves unemployment. . . . The history of this country since the War is one long indication of its accuracy' (1935: 146). Convinced that this theoretical explanation of chronic unemployment was wrong and its corollary, that the way to solve the problem was to *reduce* wages, was counterproductive, Keynes set about to provide an alternative theoretical explanation to the same substantive problem. His explanation was not in terms of wage levels, but of the investment decisions of entrepreneurs based on expectations about the future and of the savings propensities of households dependent largely on the level of their income and their preference to hold part of their assets in liquid form for speculative purposes. Not only did he thus provide a different set of explanatory variables, but he included in his system a range of non-market and not easily quantifiable features as also the major institutional arrangements of an advanced capitalist economy. The formal aspect of Keynesian theory consisted of the weaving to-gether in a logical manner such diverse elements as the animal spirit of the entrepreneurs, the liquidity preference of the households, the insti-tutional arrangements for the supply of money and for the variety of options for holding wealth, and much more. The logic and the form were, thus, meant to illumine contemporary concrete problems of the economy in the short run, though their explanatory potential was not confined to them.

From this angle Marx's contribution was even more significant. Writing at a time when industrial capitalism was still emerging, his attempt was to capture its innate dynamics and to lay bare its essential characteristics. Marx's analysis was of a social order in which exchange relationships had already been well established, where the social rela-tion between men had assumed 'the fantastic form of a relation between things' and where two distinct classes were emerging as a result of the historical processes of the past, one class consisting of those who were coming to own all means of production and whose behaviour was guided by the principle: 'accumulate, accumulate', and another class, deprived of all productive means and having nothing other than their labour power to sell. Marx showed economic processes taking place within this social framework. Technology was shown to be a major driving force of the system, but technical progress was shown to arise from the behavioural motive of the real-life economic agents, the capitalist enterprises, to substitute machinery for labour in their quest for profits and accumulation. In turn, this was shown to result in a change in the commodity composition of the economy—the rising organic composition of capital—which led to a transformation of the enterprises on the one hand and the systemic problem of the falling rate of profit on the other. The picture is that of an economy evolving over time with both its primary units and its systemic features undergoing transformation through the process. As Deane aptly puts it:

> Marx offered a vision of an economy expanding under competitive pressure, increasing its fixed capital stock at the expense of the labour force, concentrating the nation's capital in fewer and fewer hands, steadily increasing the scope of the large-scale, capital intensive enterprise, running into successive crises as opportunities for technical progress accelerate the pace of capital formation, so that the resulting over-production drives prices down and the rate of capital formation then contracts; and so generating a situation of chronic under-employment punctuated by severe depressions. . . . For the first time economists were presented with a model which explained growth and fluctuations of the economy in terms of the reactions between and institutional environment and the technique of production, that emerged from the industrial revolution (1978: 139).

XVI

The discussion in this chapter has been about the language of economic theory concentrating on the most conscious and formal attempt to establish it as a deductive system. I shall be taking up some aspects of economics as a deductive or postulational system again in the concluding chapter. But before that it is necessary to provide a coherent discussion of the economy itself which is taken up in the next chapter.

Notes

1. This view does not go unchallenged. There are those (and Marx was one among them) who consider William Petty as 'the father of bourgeois classical political economy, which did not limit itself to the study and description of visible economic phenomena but proceeded to an analysis of the internal laws of the capitalist mode of production' (Anikin 1975: 55).

2. This procedure of reference to *The Wealth of Nations* is followed throughout giving the Book and Chapter where the passage occurs followed by Volume and page numbers in Everyman's Library edition (Introduction by Prof. E.R.A. Seligman) 1910 reprinted in 1964.

3. Dasgupta (1983: 12) points out that Kaldor held the view that economic theory went wrong right at the beginning when Adam Smith turned to the theory of value.

4. Footnote 7 (Raphael and Macfie 1976: 184–85).

5. Raphael and Macfie deal with this question quite explicitly in their Introduction to *The Theory of Moral Sentiments* (TMS) and state. 'The Stoic idea of nature and the natural form a major part of the philosophical foundations of TMS and WN alike. The Stoic doctrine went along with a view of nature as a cosmic harmony' (p. 7). Also, 'Anybody who reads TMS. . . will not have the slightest inclination to be puzzled that the same man wrote this book and WN, or to suppose that he underwent any radical change of view about human conduct' (p. 20).

6. *Collected Writings of J.M. Keynes* Vol X, *Essays in Biography* p. 87 quoted by Deane.

7. Jevons (1970), in the Preface to the Second Edition of *The Theory of Political Economy* (1871) suggested that, as Marshall had already done, the name of the subject should be changed from Political Economy to Economics, obviously to emphasise its scientific character.

8. A more detailed discussion of the impact of Newtonian science on neoclassical economics is taken up in Chapter 5.

9. Arrow (1959), examines the standard competitive market equations

$$D = f(p), \quad S = g(p) \tag{1}$$

and
$$S = D \tag{2}$$

where D is the demand for the commodity, S its supply, p its price, and the functions f(p) and g(p) represent the behaviour of consumers and producers, respectively. Under competitive conditions, it is assumed that both consumers and producers *take prices as given*. The question he raises relates to the rationale of (2), or the process that brings about the equality of supply and demand. The underlying assumption of (2) is the 'Law of Supply and Demand' which can be expressed as

$$dp/dt = h(S - D) \tag{3}$$

where
$$h' < 0, \quad h(0) = 0 \tag{4}$$

and h´ is the rate of change of the function h with respect to an increase in the excess supply. Equations (1) and (3) together define a dynamic process in which supply, demand and price vary over time till (2) is satisfied. But if consumers and producers must take prices as given, whose decision is it to change prices according to equation (3)? The standard assumption that under competitive conditions consumers and producers are price takers, therefore, takes away the possibility of adjustments required to *reach* equilibrium.

10. On the contrary, instances such as the familiar Prisoner's Dilemma show the limitations of self-interest as the basis of decision and action. Parfit (1984) examines the Self-interest Theory at the philosophical level to point out how it is self-defeating. See also the recent discussions on altruism in American Economic Association's *Papers and Proceedings*, May 1993.

11. Cited by Levine 1977: 194 where there is a fuller discussion on this issue.

12. In a discussion with Kaushik Basu in the *Economic and Political Weekly* (EPW) I have pointed out the significance of this observation. See EPW, Vol. XXIV, Number 42, Oct. 21, 1989 and Vol. XXV Numbers 18 and 19, May 5–13, 1990.

13. See Arrow 1981; Hahn 1981.

14. Edwin Cannan, quoted with approval by Pigou (1938: 128-29).

15. The phrase is Barbara Bergman's in Marr and Raj (1982: 339).

16. Gustav von Schmoller on Wilhelm Roscher in Spiegel (1952: 365).

17. Robbins, in fact, talks about the 'dreariness and mediocrity' of dealing with the organisation of production.

18. Stigler quoted by Lowe (1965: 204).

4

THE ECONOMY AS AN EVOLVING COMPLEX SYSTEM*

This chapter conceptualises the economy somewhat differently from what obtains in mainstream economics, particularly what underlies neo-classical economic theory. The argument is that the economy is an evolving entity and that the evolutionary process from the earliest to the present can be analysed in terms of the primary units in the economy and their interactions, with the units getting differentiated over time and the patterns of interaction undergoing change. The need for continuity of treatment has resulted in the chapter turning out to be longer than the others. Summary statements of the argument are given in italics at the beginning of each division. Some readers may find them helpful. Those who do not may skip them and concentrate on the text.

The 'Units Question'

Identifying the primary units of analysis is the first task. In neo-classical theory the primary units are individuals. However, it is an undeniable fact that individuals do not live in isolation, but as social beings they are always situated in groups interacting with other members of the group. After drawing attention to this fact in section I, sections II and III try to establish the rationale of accepting groups or organisations as the primary units of analysing the economy. The main argument is that while organisations consist of individuals they are more than the sum of the individuals and that the patterns of

*interaction among the individuals give them a distinct identity, struc-
ture and agenda. The relationship between the individual members of
a group and the group itself gets codified, informally and formally, as
institutions. Section IV emphasises the need, in real-life situations, to
visualise individuals, groups (organisations) and institutions in their
unavoidable interconnections.*

I

'The general perfectly competitive equilibrium is about economics
rather than about [the] economy', a scholar has recently remarked
(Gustafsson, in Maki et al. 1993: x). This is another way of expressing
the 'language' problem that I have dealt with in Chapter 1 and has a
bearing on the issues touched upon in Chapter 3 as well. Economics as
a field of study can be a way of conceptualising the real-life economy:
but it need not be. Instead, it can become the conceptualising of an
interesting logical problem which may have or appear to have some
bearing on the real-life economy. I have tried to show that such, indeed,
is the status of the general equilibrium model. But can the real-life
economy be conceptualised in some other manner? That is the question
to be examined in this chapter.

Consider for a moment the Indian economy. What is the significance
of the adjective 'Indian'? Principally it refers to the fact that the entity
concerned is that of the Indian people. Real-life economies are always
about people and about an aspect of their social interaction. They
are *not* about individuals (Robinson Crusoe) and their introspection.
In this sense the economy is rather like language, an expression of
human interaction. An individual trained in the *social* process of communication may use language to express his own personal feelings
and thoughts, and may even talk to himself, which, however, does not
make language an individual's personal capacity. So is the economy: it
is essentially an expression of *social* processes although an individual
trained in them may convert them into introspective imputations.

This societal dimension, the social embeddedness of the economy,
is further reinforced by the fact that real-life economies are closely
related to *groups* of people. The 'Indian' in the Indian economy refers
to the people grouped together as the Indian nation. The 'Chinese
economy', the 'Canadian economy', the 'Nigerian economy', the 'Bra-
zilian economy', etc., also refer to similar national groupings of

people. From the time of Adam Smith, at least, the nation has been accepted as the most obvious, if not the most natural, grouping of people from the point of economic analysis. A major fall-out of the acceptance of neo-classical economics as theory par excellence has been the tendency to take the economy away from this and all other groupings of people. It is to some extent the consequence of the methodological, reductive individualism underlying that theoretical system which also permits it to *re*group people solely on the basis of analytical convenience (as consumers, producers, etc.). But if, as I have tried to establish in the preceding chapter, even the individuals of neo-classical economics are mere analytical constructs, the problem is indeed much deeper. It is basically the reflection of the effort of neo-classical economics to detach the economy from its societal substantive base and to take it to the realm of the formal universality of pure logic. Be that as it may, we have today the incongruous situation where economic analysis is strongly embedded in the nation as the grouping of people and thus the unit of analysis (economic performance is measured in terms of *national* income) while economic theory pretends to be beyond all such societal groupings.

Whatever may be the pretentions and predilections of *economics* in this regard, the *economy* cannot be envisaged apart from groupings of people if the basic premise is accepted that the real-life economy is an aspect of social relationships. What groups of people should be accepted for probing into the economy is a question to be settled and I shall take it up subsequently. I refer to it as the 'units question' because the social groupings accepted will become the primary units for examining the economy.

One thing, however, appears fairly obvious—a multiplicity of units may have to be recognised. That was the classical pattern. Within the nation the classical writers recognised other social units, 'classes', which also appeared to them as natural units of society. In neither Smith nor Ricardo there was an attempt to problematise class (or the nation for that matter). That task was taken up by Marx who used class both as a unit of analysis and as an abstract category. An issue to be taken up seriously, in any attempt to understand the economy in our own times, is that both intranational and transnational units have to be taken into account—units of economic activity within a country and units of economic activity whose operations go beyond national boundaries.

It follows too that in order to understand the economy, it has to be seen in terms of its evolution. For, 'in the beginning' the economy could only have been an inseparable (even conceptually) component of the most primordial of the social groups—a tribe or clan or similar units remaining as isolated self-contained ones. When contacts are established with other similar groups, economic activities of all of them could undergo change. In due course units which are dissimilar could, and would, emerge, their interactions also would undergo changes. The factors and processes that bring about these changes have to be examined, but to perceive the economy without this element of change built into it would be to miss one of its innate characteristics.

If the economy, therefore, has to be viewed as consisting of units that emerge and change over time, it is also necessary to recognise that the multiplicity of units which are its constituents may be heterogeneous ones with differing agenda of their own even in relation to their economic objectives and activities.[1] Classical economists recognised that the social groups that they worked with had different economic objectives, orientations and constraints. It is neo-classical economics that homogenised all economic agents via the single maximisation objective that theorists assigned to them identifying it also with what they considered to be rationality. If that perverse theoretical detour is avoided it should not be difficult to accept that agents in an economy have differing goals.

Finally, if a multiplicity of heterogeneous units are recognised, it is necessary to concede that they may overlap as intranational, national and transnational units are bound to do. Hence the economy must also be considered as a multilayered complex entity. When all the characteristics identified earlier are brought together, it becomes necessary to conceptualise the economy as an evolving complex entity. Detailing this conceptualisation, providing its rationale and exploring its implications are taken up in what follows.

II

Neo-classical theory is based on individuals—of a sort—and their choices. Free choice by individuals forms both its analytical and ideological basis. Identifying methodological individualism as part of the 'hidden agenda' of neo-classical economics (invoking Samuelson and others to support this position), Boland defines it as 'the view that

allows *only* individuals to be decision-makers of social phenomena'
and goes on to say that 'methodological individualism does not allow
explanations which involve non-individualist decision-makers such as
institutions, weather or even historical destiny' (Boland 1982: 28). Two
comments are called for. The first is that nobody in his right mind will
claim that weather or historical destiny (or even the market for that
matter!) makes decisions. There should be no difficulty in conceding
that only individuals make decisions. But, and this is the second and
more pertinent comment, the inferences of neo-classical theory will not
follow on that basis alone. The assertion of neo-classical theory is
stronger than that. What neo-classical theory insists upon is that individuals, while making decisions, are guided solely by their own innate
preferences *independent of the decisions and actions of other individuals*. In fact, one can go a step further. As Koopmans points out in his
treatment of Robinson Crusoe, already referred to in the previous
chapter, neo-classical theory requires that Robinson Crusoe as consumer must make decisions independent of and uninfluenced by him as
producer. The problem with neo-classical theory in this sense, is that
it insists—*has to* insist—that the 'free' individuals who form its basic
units can only make those 'decisions' that the theory assigns to them. It
is for this reason that I have stated that the individuals of neo-classical
theory are only dummies, pieces in a game of chess, who have assigned
roles to perform.

Such 'individuals' cannot form the basis of an enquiry into real-life
economies. In real-life, decisions are all made by individuals, but in
making their decisions they are influenced by the decisions of others,
both of the present and the past, and are influenced also by considerations of the future. It is important to capture the nature of the influences that shape the decisions of individuals. This is because in real
life individuals are essentially *social* beings living amidst others and
constantly interacting with them. We need to recognise real human
beings in their concrete and social surroundings.

In such a context attention has to shift from decisions to actions
and to activity. This is because concentrating on decisions has the
built-in tendency to view everything from an individualist perspective. While decision may appear to be individualistic and introspective, activity has an external and societal connotation. And, if action
is taken as an expression of decision, it combines both the individual
and societal dimensions.

There can be little argument that economic activity takes place in and through different groupings of human beings.[2] It is difficult to think of production as anything other than a group activity. Even granting that it is consumption and not production that provides the rationale for the economy, how much of it takes place, *can* take place, apart from a group? How much of what I consume is entirely the result of my independent 'decision making'?

It does not seem necessary to argue that economic activity takes place in and through groupings of people, 'individuals'. What is necessary is to consider whether the rationale for the grouping of individuals for economic activity can be discussed. At one level the issue is the basis of society as such which has engaged the attention of great philosophers of all times. But I shall deal with the question at the operational level.

One of the obvious reasons for individuals to come together as groups is the fact that individuals are *different* in terms of natural endowments, capabilities, inclinations, expectations and so on. Human beings are male and female, young and old, and soon discover complementarities which can be put to use if they are together. Their differing natural endowments also open up possibilities of division of labour which enables every one within a group to be better off through mutual interdependence than through isolated independence. Further, grouping also enables the members to take advantage of economies of scale in different activities, gathering, processing, producing, protecting, etc. As Rawls puts it

Different persons with similar or complementary capacities may cooperate so to speak in realizing their common or matching nature.... It is through a social union founded upon the needs and potentialities of its members that each person can participate in the total sum of the realized natural assets of others (1972: 523).

Or, and more generally,

given the social nature of human kind, the fact that our potentialities and inclinations far surpass what can be expressed in any one life, we depend upon the cooperative endeavors of others not only for the means of well-being, but to bring to fruition our latent powers. And with a certain success all around, each enjoys the greater richness and diversity of the collective activity (Rawls 1972: 571).

That individuals stand to benefit through interaction and inter-dependence even when (hypothetically) they can be self-contained and independent is one aspect of the rationale of the grouping of people into various forms of 'collectives'—using the term in its literal meaning—or organisations.

III

The rationale of organisations can also be seen from another angle. Organisations can be thought of as information processing agencies. Neo-classical economics has made popular a notion of a world in which everything has a price except information which is considered to be totally free, readily and effortlessly available to anybody who wishes to have it 'as if it were a fluid to be passed into and out of the head of each individual', as Hodgson puts it (1988: 6). The glorification of the market in this theory is based on the supposition that the primary role of the market is as a carrier of information on the basis of which all agents are claimed to act. Within neo-classical economics, the transaction cost analysts have been trying to challenge (correct?) the unreality and untenability of such an approach to information.

But the cost of information is not the basic issue. Arrow, in his *The Limits of Organization* (1974), has made one of the clearest expositions of the nature of the information problem in economics. I shall follow it with one major difference. Arrow begins with the role of the market as an information carrier and treats organisations as a necessary supplement to the market because of the inability of the market to provide adequate information about some kind of goods (public goods) and some kinds of situations (decisions involving uncertainty and the future). But this 'in-the-beginning-the-market' approach is neither legitimate nor necessary as a careful reading of Arrow's writings on organisation shows. It is possible to begin with information itself and arrive at the rationale of organisations and markets. I shall, therefore, rely on Arrow's material, but re-route the argument.

The first thing to note is that contrary to the neo-classical view of information as clear and pure signal, it has to be treated at least as a signal accompanied by a great deal of what communciation theorists recognise as 'noise' that disturbs both its clarity and purity. Second, information is not all intelligible signals; it consists of codes, it is picked up from events and happenings; it may have to be inferred from a wide range of things, situations and people. Given this nature of information, it does not become effective, relevant or useful without a proper receiver that has to play an *active* role in receiving, decoding, assessing and interpreting what is received. An individual's brain usually performs these functions of receiving information. The individual is, thus, an *information channel* or, more accurately, has information channels, because channels can be created, abandoned, modified and so on in performing its function.

But the individual's capacity to develop information channels and to function as an information processor presupposes a group within which he functions. The reception of even the clearest of signals calls for the ability to distinguish one signal from another and an individual gains this ability from the group of which he is a member. This is to say that while individuals have the capacity to learn languages, no one learns a language except from others who already use it. The group is significant here because it is in possession of the information channels of those who are already its members. This can form the basis for another member to develop his own information channels. The group is, thus, the locus of the irreversible investments which accumulate over time and provide enormous economies of scale in the use of information. Almost always the group docs, and has to, carry more information than is currently required as a firm has to carry inventories, both necessitated primarily because of the presence of uncertainty. Granted that at any given time it is, therefore, unavoidable that some redundant information has to be carried, the group has the advantage of the pooling of information of its members.

The group, thus, will have a great deal of information that it has accumulated over time and information channels which are unique to it, not easily replicated or imitated by any other group. Because of the continuous interaction between the information that the group has accumulated and stores, and what it continues to receive, the group develops its own codes and comes to have an internal communication system of its own. This internal communication system that receives new information, decodes it and interprets it on the basis of what it has already acquired, also enables the group to make decisions about the present and involving the future, that is, to develop its *agenda*. All of this gives to the group an identity of its own which is different from the identity of its individual members and also from that of any other group. Each group has a distinct identity in view of its internal communicaion network and the agenda it develops.

It is for this reason that the group—whether it is a household, a tribe, a voluntary association of some kind, or a nation—cannot be thought of as an individual writ large or merely as an aggregation of individuals. A group is not like 'a sack of potatoes' because potatoes in a sack do not interact with one another whereas individuals in a group *do*. It is this *interaction* that gives the group characteristics which cannot easily be identified with any or all of its members. Consequently, from the point of view of the individuals that form the group, it is at once an enabler and a constraint. The group makes available to the individual information and opportunities that he cannot come to have all by himself. At the same time he has information channels of his own and his interpretations of new information may be quite different from what other members of the group give it. He may, therefore, find that the group stifles his initiative and blocks his opportunities. There may also be tendencies on the part of individuals to use the group to their own advantage, the problem of free-riding, which has received recognition in economics, but which will not make sense at all except in a group context.

Individuals and groups of individuals are aware of these problems. That is why codes of conduct are evolved in the smallest to the largest of groups and in the most intimate to the most formal of all groups. The codes could be simple or elaborate, informal or formal, ranging from customs and rituals to laws and regulations to statutes and constitutions. The collective name for these is 'institutions' and they are very much a part of the internal information and communication network of the group. They are 'internal' in the sense that often they make sense only to those who are within; even where those who are without may understand them, they will not be bound by them. Institutions are part of the information and communication set-up because they are meant both to facilitate and regulate the interaction of the members of the group. To the extent that the members of a group are held together, these institutions play a major role in their togetherness; when members quit a group it is often because they find its internal codes stifling.

Along with institutions, the cohesiveness of organisations or groups is ensured by the exercise of authority. Arrow says: 'Among the most widespread characteristics of organizations is the prevalence of authoritative allocations. Virtually universally, in organizations of any size, decisions are made by some individuals and carried out by others' (1974: 63). Authority, of course, involves some exercise of power.

Usually the exercise of power also includes the power to punish those who do not accept it or tend to defy it. But authority cannot be maintained solely by the power to punish: it must become acceptable to those over whom the power is exercised. 'In the deepest sense, coercion and consent combine and collude, albeit in different ways, to the same extent', says Godelier (1986: 13). Authority exists within the context of a strand of cooperation, of shared traditions, common involvement with current activities and expectations about the future which are the characteristics of a group. It may be noted too that just as a group has ways of imposing punishments on those who defy authority, it has procedures to reward those who accept it and go along with it. In general, therefore, as Arrow points out, 'authority is viable to the extent that it is the focus of convergent expectations. An individual obeys authority because he expects that others will obey it' (1974: 72). In this sense the general acceptance of authority considerably reduces uncertainty of behaviour and, hence, authority reinforces regularity and orderliness within the group, thus greatly facilitating the functioning of individuals—again up to a point beyond which it may turn out to be oppressive. Hence, authority, or acceptance of authority, may also be considered to be part of the institutional milieu of a group holding it together as well as forming the basis of its disruption or disintegration.

IV

In real-life situations, therefore, it is important to visualise individuals, groups (organisations) and institutions in their unavoidable interconnections: individuals exist in the context of groups and institutions; groups consist of individuals and institutions; and where individuals group themselves, institutions emerge. Only through illicit abstraction can the trio be separated. Separating them leads to conundrums of various sorts, the most important being the chicken-and-egg puzzle of 'which comes first'. Although it is clear that there can be no decisive answer to the puzzle, it is a favourite among some social theorists. Economists who are committed to the primacy of individuals and individual rationality, of course, strive hard to establish that institutions are the result of the exercise of individuals' rational decision making.

In passing, it may be pointed out that in the discussion of these issues, especially among economists, there is a great deal of ambiguity about the use of the term 'institution'. Often the term is used to include institutions as such *and* groups or organisations also. Thus, it is common to think of both marriage and the family as institutions, though the latter clearly is a group resulting from the coming together of individuals through the institution of marriage. In economics too this confusion was quite prevalent. For transaction cost analysts, the 'firm' is the institution. [3] But one of the contributions of the institutionalists, recently, is that they rightly insist on the distinction between institutions and groups or organisations. North, for instance, defines institutions as 'the rules of the game in a society or, more formally, ... the humanly devised constraints that shape human interaction (1990: 3) and claims that 'like institutions, organizations provide a structure to human interaction' (ibid: 4), but insists that a crucial distinction has to be made between institutions and organisations. He defines organisations as 'groups of individuals bound by some common purpose to achieve objectives' (ibid: 5) and identifies a wide variety of them, political parties, parliaments and city councils; clubs, schools universities and athletic associations; and in the economic realm specifically, firms, trade unions, family farms, cooperatives, etc. The relationship between the institutions and organisations is also recognised. 'Both what organization come into existence and how they evolve are fundamentally influenced by the institutional framework. In turn they influence how the institutional framework evolves' (ibid: 5).

But North's problem is that he cannot give up neo-classical individualism. 'Institutions are a creation of human beings. They evolve and are altered by human beings; hence our theory must begin with the individual'. And, 'defining institutions as the constraints that human beings impose on themselves makes the definition complementary to the choice theoretic approach of neo-classical economic theory, (1990: 5). North does not seem to realise that there is a distinction between real-life human beings and the individuals that neo-classical theory deals with, and that the 'choice' that the individuals of neo-classical theory make are different from what live human beings confront and make. However the real problem is that rooted in neo-classical individualism, North virtually abandons organisations after recognising their role in the evolution of institutions. This is because to take organisations seriously is not merely to recognise their existence as a matter of fact, but also to accept their *internal structure* as an analytical problematic. Neo-classical individualism forbids the recognition of groups or organisations with unique internal structures and agenda of their own. Hence while an institutional approach may appear to be compatible with the 'choice theoretic approach of neo-classical economic theory' up to a point, a genuinely organisational approach cannot even begin unless the adamant but untenable reductive individualism of neo-classical theory is given up.

However, it must be emphasised that to do so is *not* to give up the role of the individuals and their choices, but only to contextualise them in their natural societal milieu. I have, in sections II and III, provided the rationale for recognising the role of organisations even from an individualist perspective. The crucial question is whether it is possible to build up an analytical system recognising the internal structure of organisations as an unavoidable and important component because that is what the recognition of organisations implies.

Constituting the Economy

Accepting groups as the primary units for analysis underlines the essential social embeddedness of the economy and its institutional structure. But the economy does not encompass the whole of social relationships. Sections V and VI identify three 'substantive essentials' in terms of which groups constitute their economies. Section VII indicates the reasons for accepting the nation or the national economy as the main unit for analysis. But it is immediately pointed out that there are groups or subunits within the national economy, such as households, with their own economies, and that the national economy itself becomes a subeconomy within the global economy. The 'economy', therefore, is envisaged as a collection of overlapping units which may also be taken to be at different levels. Section VIII argues that different units have differing agenda and on that basis units are classified broadly as 'economically active' units on the one hand and 'economic organisations' on the other emphasising that the primary units of the economy are heterogeneous in nature. A third type of unit, a hybrid of the first two, recognised as the 'state' is also taken note of, reinforcing the heterogeneity of the primary units of the economy. Section IX draws out the main implications of visualising the economy as consisting of overlapping and interacting heterogeneous primary units. This division contains the essentials of the new conceptualistion of the economy.

V

The treatment so far has been about groups or organisations in general to indicate that from a real-life perspective individuals do not exist and function in isolation, but only along with other individuals, in groups, mutually interacting and influencing one another. Any such group will have elements of harmony and cooperation on the one hand and of conflict on the other, both arising from the unresolved, and ultimately unresolvable, problematic of person-in-society. All that can be stated is that individuals and their groups (or groups and their members) devise ways of 'holding together'—not for ever, because groups dissolve—but then other groups are formed. Stability and instability are built into the individuals-in-group situation.

If this is the characteristic of human beings, it must be presumed to be true also of their economy. What this means is that whatever may be the attributes of the 'economy', it must be seen first and foremost as a form of social relationship, primarily and essentially relating to groups (remembering that a group always consists of distinct and diverse individuals). One way to establish this is to point out that both the material and mental features of groups already mentioned—the material advantages of pooling the diverse capabilities of individuals and of an internal information and communication network constituting the mental component on the other—are also basic ingredients of the economy.

But to leave it at that will not be sufficiently specific to delineate the economy; its distinguishing features as a form of social organisation will have to be identified. What aspects of social relations constitute the economy? A clear cut answer is not easy because as a social organisation the economy has been evolving over time assuming different characteristics in that process. But if we trace it back to the beginnings and search for the basics, it can be seen that whatever is designated as economic relationships (if, indeed, a separation of the 'economic' from other social relationships is possible at that level) can be seen to be about the provisioning of the material needs for survival. It is assumed here—without argument or proof—that human beings are concerned about their survival and will always attempt individually and collectively to ensure it. In fact, the assumption is stronger, that survival is generally considered to be the primary concern of human beings, their basic need. In a sense, it is the desire for survival that forms the group activity also: individuals find it easier to survive when they are in the company of other individuals. One reason for this is that survival involves human interaction with nature and frequently this interaction is a group activity. If it is not necessarily so, it is at least advantageously so. And, if social unions are based on the recognition of needs, the most basic of all needs provides the rationale for such unions and the social unions make it easier for that need to be met. The social activity of providing substance for survival may, therefore, be considered as the first of the distinguishing features of the economy.

But, is it the most important feature of the real-life economy? This depends on certain factors. For humanity as a whole, provisioning the material means of survival—food, clothing and shelter—must have been the primary form of economic activity till just a few centuries ago. Certainly, for the vast majority of human beings even today, it is the attempt to survive that constitutes the economy.

It is, therefore, surprising that this experiential reality, this basic premise of any real-life economy, finds very little place in economic theory, ancient or modern. It is equally surprising that when it finds recognition, the tendency has been to dismiss it as a mere Marxist doctrine and an erroneous, if not dangerous, one at that because of the 'materialist' emphasis it seems to have. Marx and Engels, of course, stated in *The German Ideology* that 'life involves before everything else eating and drinking, clothing and various other things' and that 'the first historical act is thus the production of the means to satisfy these needs, the production of material life itself' (Marx and Engels 1976: 47). But this was not a specifically Marxist point of view. Long before Marx, William Robertson, distinguished friend and colleague of Adam Smith and David Hume, made the point that 'in every inquiry concerning the operations of men when united together in society, the first object of attention should be their mode of subsistence'.[4] The close link between the material and the social reflected in this statement is seen in *The German Ideology* too. According to Marx and Engels the production of the means of subsistence is but one 'moment' in a three-fold aspect of social activity, the other two being the production of new needs and 'the reproduction of men (the family), social intercourse'. These three aspects of social activity 'have existed simultaneously since the dawn of history and the first men, and ... still assert themselves in history today' (p. 48). Also, 'the production of life, both of one's own labour and of fresh life in procreation, now appears as a two-fold relation: on the one hand, as a natural, on the other a social relation—social in the sense that it denotes the cooperation of individuals, no matter under what conditions, in what manner and to what end' (ibid: 47–49).

I shall be returning to the interaction between the material and the social in economic processes. For the moment, let us consider why the crucial activity of provisioning survival—of making a living, in day-to-day language—does not find a place in standard economic theory. In a sense it is the result of what Schumpeter refers to as 'the Greek bequest'. Part of this bequest was to consider self-sufficient households as being responsible for catering to the basic needs of its members so that it became essentially a private activity. Transactions between the households, on the other hand, was activity of a public nature, particularly when it was mediated through money. What economic theory has tried to capture from its early days was this public activity. The emergence of economic theory is thus associated with the spread of exchange and markets, both taken up for systematic treatment by Adam Smith. It was on this foundation that standard economic theory has been built up. Seldom has it become necessary to look back and re-examine the basics. Occasionally, as when 'everything' in the system has to be priced as in the Arrow-Debreu attempt to expound the Walrasian general equilibrium, the boundary between the public and private disappears, but then, as has already been noted, the problem is overcome by *assuming* that what is being dealt with is 'a society of self-sufficient farmers who do a little trading on the side' (Koopmans 1957: 62)—an escape into the Greek bequest indeed! This escape route, however, is not available where the attempt is to deal with real-life economies—for, in them efforts to ensure survival form a major, if not central, activity. Whether that activity is a private or public one, or a mixture of the two, is a different issue which must be empirically examined and settled, and which, therefore, will also show how particular economies differ from one another. But on the significance of the activity and the need to bring it into the study of the economy there can be little doubt.

VI

Adam Smith, of course, was aware of the fact that a substantial part of economic activity was devoted to the production of 'the articles of subsistence' for which he gave the collective name 'necessaries'. The opening sentence of the *Wealth of Nations* is: 'The annual labour of every nation is the fund which originally supplies it with all the necessaries and conveniences of life which it annually consumes. . .' and later in the work (see Book V Ch. II, for instance) there is a detailed discussion of necessaries on the one hand, and, what is there referred to as, luxuries on the other. It is not necessary, at this point, to enter into the details of the discussion except to point out that while the provision of the articles of subsistence is an important part of any real-life economy, there was recognition from the early days that this certainly was not the only activity of real-life economies. Marx and Engels too expressed the same view. The second of the three aspects of social activity mentioned earlier is that 'the satisfaction of the first need, the action of satisfying and the instrument of satisfaction which has been acquired, leads to new needs' (Marx and Engels 1976: 48). Whether these new needs are referred to as conveniences, luxuries or anything else, the point is that real-life economies tend to rise above subsistence and generate a surplus. The generation of the surplus must, therefore, be considered to be as normal and natural in real-life economies as the provisioning of subsistence itself. To put it differently, human beings do not seem to be satisfied with mere subsistence, but would strive to rise above it if that were possible at all.

What determines whether it is possible to rise above subsistence? Adam Smith provides the answer right at the beginning of his work. Granted that society ('every nation') consists of 'those who are employed in useful labour' and 'those who are not so employed'—infants, old people and those afflicted with lingering diseases (Smith 1964: 1), whatever surplus that the former produces will go to provide for the subsistence of the latter. So, the possibility of society as a whole rising above subsistence will depend on the skill, dexterity and judgement with which labour is generally applied. 'Among the savage nations' of the past, there might have been little scope for such possibility and so they might have been reduced to the necessity of 'directly destroying, and sometimes abandoning' the dependents. 'Among civilized and thriving nations, on the contrary, though a great number of people do not work at all, many of whom consume the produce of ten times, frequently of a hundred times more labour than the greater part of those who work, yet the produce of the whole labour of society is so great that all are often abundantly supplied' (ibid: 1–2). The question, therefore, is how this increase in produce, this abundance, becomes possible, and the rest of the book is an attempt to provide the answer. In brief, the answer is that it depends on the improvement in the productive powers of labour which in turn depends on the quantity of capital stock which is employed in setting them to work on the one hand and the organisation of that work on the other. We may generalise and say that real-life economies find ways of increasing productivity through improved methods of production.

Three features of real-life economies have been identified so far: providing subsistence, generating surplus and finding ways of increasing productivity. Since the economy is basically a human enterprise we may rephrase them as follows: human beings strive to insure their survival; wherever possible they rise above mere subsistence; and, they devise ways to improve productivity. I shall refer to these as the substantive essentials of real-life economies. One may borrow the words of Lionel Robbins (1935) (from a different context, of course) and say that 'they are so much the stuff of our everyday experience that they have only to be stated to be recognised as obvious' (p 79). Robbins used this statement in relation to the postulates of economic theory such as that 'individuals can arrange their preferences in an order, and in fact do so' (ibid.). Whatever might have been the understanding about the nature of individual preferences when Robbins wrote these words in the early 1930s, later work has shown that 'arranging preferences in an order' is not such a simple, obvious and uncontested matter. In any case, the substantive essentials I have identified do not refer to economic theory or its postulates, but to real-life economies. Their validity, therefore, can be based only on real-life experience of the past and the present, and, hence, I do not propose any other procedure to validate them. It may be worth pointing out, though, that they are different from the fundamental conditions of human existence that Robbins spells out. 'The ends are various. The time and means for achieving these ends are limited and capable of alternative application. At the same time the ends have different importance' (1935: 12) from which the principle of 'economising' is derived. No principle is derived from the substantive essentials I have indicated. They will, however, be used to suggest how real-life economies function. Indeed, the significance of these facts of experience lies in whether or not they can enlighten the functioning of real-life economies and their evolution over time.

VII

The substantive essentials identified must be situated in the context of groups or units discussed in the previous section. That is, if the economy is a social entity and society consists of individuals in groups, the substantive essentials of the economy must be related to, and seen to be mediated through such groups.

What, then, are the groups relevant for the understanding of the economy? Here, again, Adam Smith had a clear answer: the group connected with the economy was the nation, undefined, but differentiated in terms of other nations. But the association of the economy with the nation goes to a much earlier period. According to Schumpeter, there were two sources through which economics acquired 'the status of a recognized field of tooled knowledge' by the eighteenth century: from the studies of the schoolmen and the philosophers of the natural law on the one hand and from the 'more boisterous stream that sprang from the forum where men of affairs, pamphleteers, and, later on, teachers debated the policies of their day' (1954: 143). Schumpeter identifies this second source as being related to the problems of the rising National State in Europe going back to the fifteenth century at least. In particular, he refers to the Italian writer, Diomede Carafa (1406–87), whom he considered to be 'the first to deal comprehensively with the economic problems of the nascent modern state' and who was followed by many writers in the next three centuries. Throughout this period, particularly during the mercantilist era of intense rivalries among the states, it became easy to identify the nation as a single unit, especially in terms of trade policy and military preparations. The national economy, as Schumpeter points out, came to be conceived 'as a sort of sublimated business unit, something that has a distinct existence and distinct interests of its own' (Schumpeter 1954: 163–64). This view was further strengthened in the eighteenth century by the writings of the 'systematic' literature represented, for instance, by the German professor, Justi, who

> dealt with economic problems from the stand point of a government that accepts responsibility for the moral and economic conditions of life... in particular for everyone's employment and livelihood, for the improvement of the methods and organization of production, for a sufficient supply of raw materials and foodstuffs, and so on through a long list of topics that include beautification of cities, fire insurance, education, sanitation and what not (Schumpeter 1954: 171).

The nation as *the* unit of economic analysis was, thus, fairly well established by the time the *Wealth of Nations* appeared. The identification of the economy and the nation has continued since then, and has been strengthened by macroeconomic analysis where the aggregates, especially of output, are all *national* aggregates. In the light of the 'globalisation' tendencies of the recent period some questions have been raised about the soundness of identifying the economy with the nation and I shall comment on these later. Suspending the problem of transnational economies for a while, I shall dwell on some intranational issues.

The nation, of course, is a 'group', as described earlier in this chapter—a collection of individuals with some common commitments and aspirations, but also with some conflicting interests, held together by their internal information and control devices, and by a variety of institutions—formal and informal, a structure of authority and an agenda of its own. We may take a look at the national agenda. Adam Smith had indicated three-fold duties of the sovereign which may be paraphrased as a partial statement of the national agenda: protecting the society from the violence and invasion of other societies; establishing an administration of justice to protect the members of the society from the injustice and oppression of other members; and, erecting and maintaining those public institutions and those public works which are advantageous to the society, but which individuals or small number of individuals may not find profitable to undertake. Now, it has been customary to suggest that the first two of these are 'non-economic', one relating to defence and the other to administration, while the third is considered to be clearly 'economic' though it may be noted that the public institutions suggested were 'those for facilitating the commerce of society' *and* 'those for promoting the institutions of the people'. But from another perspective, more in conformity with Adam Smith's own approach, all three of them involve 'the expenses of the sovereign', the use of resources, and hence could be legitimately considered as 'economic'. It is, therefore, not easy to differentiate a national agenda strictly into economic and non-economic. Second, using Smith's criterion of public expenditure as the basis, the three duties indicated may be regarded as a 'minimalist national agenda'. One interpretation has been that Smith was committed to and strongly endorsed such a minimalist national agenda (for the economy). But this is an interpretation which the text itself does not support. In terms of the first two duties Smith draws distinctions between the implications of these duties in different kinds of nations (hierarchically arranged with the 'nation of hunters' at the bottom, the 'nation of shepherds' above it and so on, with nations like his own as the most advanced; also the nations of Tartars, Arabs, Greeks and Romans, etc.). On the third duty, it is explicitly stated: 'The performance of this duty requires, too, very different degrees of expenses in the different periods of society' (Bk V, Ch I–II: 211). The best that can be said, then, is that the national agenda would vary a great deal, depending on time and circumstances, with no a priori criteria to validate them. From this perspective it may be worth taking a look at the national agenda spelt out in the Directive Principles section of the Indian Constitution.

There is a third, and from our point of view more important, comment to be made about the national agenda and, therefore, the nation as a group. Adam Smith's third duty implies that there are other groups *within* the nation which have agenda somewhat similar, in parts at least, to the national agenda. One set of such groups, obviously, are the households. Households too are collections of individuals with common bonds and even some conflict of interest, their internal communication arrangements, their traditions, conventions and pattern of authority, and their own agenda. Some striking parallels can be seen between the agenda of nations and households. Households too have the responsibility to protect their members from external aggression, to settle disputes among members and to carry out tasks which the members may not find advantageous to do individually. In terms of any criteria that can be designated as 'economic', the households too have the same ambiguities as the nation. Hence, if it is meaningful to talk about a national economy it is quite legitimate to speak of a household economy also, and this is frequently done. If the substantive essentials of the economy are pressed into service, the household as a group has greater responsibility in provisioning the articles of subsistence of its members than a nation has for *its* members. At the same time, though at one stage the household might have been *solely* responsible for this task, at other stages the household *by itself* may hardly be in a position to do so. In broader terms, household economies may turn out to be heavily dependent in many respects on the national economy of which they are a part.

A national economy usually has other constituent groups too, especially once it comes to have some surplus and the task of raising productivity becomes widespread. There will be units specialising in specific functions of trade, production, banking and similar activities.

Such units or organisations too have the group characteristics indicated earlier, but their agenda may be more clearly and formally stated.

Taking these variety of factors into account we arrive at the preliminary statement that a modern national economy is a group or collection of groups each with its own internal structure and distinct agenda, i.e., a collection of heterogeneous units. It is this heterogeneity of units that partly accounts for the complexity of the economy. We can now proceed to explicate this further.

VIII

Just as the individuals that constitute a group have their distinct characteristics and are different from one another, the groups too are distinctly different: even two households are never alike. However, taking into account their agenda with special reference to the substantive economic essentials, it is possible to classify them. I rely initially on a classification suggested by Max Weber. In *Economy and Society* (1978: Part I, Ch II), Weber divides organisations into those that are 'economically active' on the one hand and 'economic organizations' on the other. The former, households being the best example, engage in economic activities not as an end in themselves but because they are requirements of larger purposes. Weber also refers to them as being engaged in 'budgetary activities'. That is, the discharge of whatever it is that they consider to be their function necessitates economic activity, primarily working with a budget constraint. Apart from households, therefore, this category would include educational and cultural organisations, hospitals, a wide range of voluntary organisations, each one of which is a 'group' with its own specific agenda which is not an explicitly economic one, but which draws them into economic activity, and subjects them to economic discipline such as maintenance of accounts and balancing of budgets. The accounting legal expression 'non-profit organisations' may be an appropriate general characterisation of these groups or units.

They stand in sharp contrast to Weber's second set of organisations whose agenda is profit making and whose involvement in economic activities is a means to that end. In common parlance, of course, these are the business corporations, in trade, production, etc. They too are engaged in specific activities but their approach to these activities is different from that of the former group in the sense that the specificities themselves are not their main concern, but what they are expected to result in. They are different also in that their budget constraints are not as stringently binding as those of the economically active organisations.

Present day national economies consist of both these categories. National economies also have a third distinct unit, sometimes designated as government and sometimes as the state. It is the most amorphous of the three (types of) groups. In a sense, it has an agenda similar to those of the first group which, however, draws it into economic activity. In some instances it also takes on agenda similar to the second group. It, therefore, tends to be of a hybrid kind. But that is not its distinguishing feature. What gives it a unique role is that, frequently, it assumes a coordinating role of the entire national economy and thus exerts direct influence/authority over the other units.

We are quite used to thinking of the 'national economy' as a single integrated unit. But each one of its constituent units may also be thought of as an economy in its right. Such, indeed, was the case in Europe for a long time prior to the mercantilists. And then Adam Smith and followers, through their writings, started bringing together these disparate entities into the economy of the nation. It is, of course, well known that from the days of the Greek writers the household was considered to be an economy. In fact, the Greek word 'oikos' from which the term economy is derived, refers directly to the management of a household. As long as economic activity was basically the provisioning of the goods for survival and this task was undertaken by the household, there was a close identification between the household and the economy. The second constituent of the economy to be noticed was the state when certain 'economic' activities, especially those of a collective nature, emerged as the functions of the state. But since collective activities were thought of as part of 'polis' (and not of 'oikos'), these were considered to be 'political activities'—not economic ones. And, for long, the activities of the household and of the state were viewed as distinctly different (the former private and the latter public). When the common elements of some of the activities of the household and of the state came to be noticed, they were brought under the hybrid term 'political economy' ('polis' and 'oikos').[5]

During the period from the fifteenth to the eighteenth centuries separate corporate entities started appearing, initially to deal with long distant trade, with their agenda being almost exclusively 'economic activities' (buying and selling to make profits) unlike the households and the state whose agenda was not, and could not be, confined to economic activities however defined. They too had to be brought under the broad umbrella of political economy. It was during this period that the writings on political economy, as Schumpeter points out (1954: 156–60), dealt with these entities and their activities separately—relating to household management, principles of governance and commercial accounting.

There is no reason to think that households, enterprises and the state have ceased to be distinct entities, or their agenda, even economic agenda, have become similar. It can be granted, of course, that within a national economy these constituent units cannot be autonomous and self-contained entities. They interact with one another, but retain their internal structure resulting from their agenda and their own information network. A national economy must, therefore, be thought of as the *intersection* of (three kinds of) heterogeneous units and the units themselves be considered as subeconomies within the national economy interacting with one another, but retaining their separate identities. The national economies, in turn, become subeconomies within the global economy.

The interactions initially arise from the internal structure of the units and are, therefore, the derivatives of their agenda and their internal information processing procedures. They are also responses to perceived external opportunities. In a bilateral situation what is external to one unit is what is internal to the other, but evaluated by one's own internal structure. Hence the communication established between the two will have a very high subjective element in it from both sides. The communications may result in some agreement, a transaction, for instance. But even then it need not become objective in the sense that both parties would want a transaction based on similar terms to be repeated. It may turn out that the transaction is a one-time event with the negotiations (communications) and transaction becoming part of the history of both parties. But the history may get differently interpreted by the two parties and so if another transaction of the same kind were to take place again, it may well be on different terms. Where there are many units, multilateral communications may reduce the subjective elements to some extent. But if each unit sends out its signal based on its own considerations, if these signals get cluttered by other signals and if the receiving units decode the signals in terms of their own internal information channels, only under exceptionally stringent and highly arbitrary conditions can one expect standardisation of inter-unit information and terms of transactions. Hence, even where there are large number of units and multilateral communications are possible, there is no reason to expect inter-unit interactions to become standardised. Asymmetry of information, variety of interpretation of signals and tentativeness of transactions based on them must be taken as the normal features of the system reflecting a perpetual state of flux.

IX

This is not to say that the state of affairs will be unavoidably chaotic. For one thing, through their interactions the units influence one another and through that process often the internal structure of some of the units get altered, including their agenda. Hence the units, in their own interest may arrive at some working arrangements reducing but not totally eliminating the uncertainties and variations. It must be noted too that the interactions among the units which are subeconomies become part of the *internal* information and communication network of the larger unit, the economy. As in the case of any other unit, this larger unit too is held together by a wide range of institutions and an accepted procedure for the exercise of authority. Hence many of the *inter*-subeconomy interactions get institutionalised as *internal* arrangement of the economy. Horizontal interactions such as exchange and markets, and vertical interactions such as taxations, are typical examples.

We are now in a position to provide a further description of a national economy as an entity consisting of a number of heterogeneous units with their variety of interactions and in the process of constant change because of such interactions.

We thus have different descriptions of 'the economy': it can be viewed as a single unit; it can be represented as consisting of a number of units; it can be thought of as a number of heterogeneous units interacting among themselves. Nor are these the only possible ways of perceiving the economy. For instance, another commonly held perception of the economy is in terms of what Adam Smith and other classical writers described as 'the different ranks of the people' or classes. These different perceptions of the economy cannot all be reduced to a single comprehensive view of what the economy is: its innate complexity and inherently evolving nature precludes the possibility of any reductive simplification. The different perceptions are ways of understanding some aspect of that evolving complex entity and have to be judiciously made use of. The procedure suggested here has some important methodological implications which I shall take up for consideration in the next chapter. But to anticipate that discussion, it may simply be pointed out here that this is a problem that other fields of study are also grappling with.

Two direct implications of looking at the economy in this manner may, however, be indicated immediately. The first is that perceiving the economy as the intersection of real-life groups or units (such as households, firms or enterprises, and the state for instance) in terms of what has been described as substantive essentials brings out the social embeddedness of the economy. The economy, in this sense, is both a set of real-life activities (the attempt of real-life human beings to make a living or to make use of their surpluses) as well as a mentally carved out segment of real-life social processes. As a mentally carved out segment, its external boundary is porous and diffused, not rigid and well defined. This fact is best expressed in the words of Professor Cannan, whom Pigou quoted with approval:

> We must face, and face boldly, the fact that there is no precise line between economic and non-economic satisfactions, and, therefore, the province of economics cannot be marked out by a row of posts and fences, like a political territory or a landed property. We can proceed from the undoubtedly economic at one end of the scale to the undoubtedly non-economic at the other end without finding anywhere a fence to climb or a ditch to cross (Pigou 1938: 11).

In fact, one may go a step further and state that not only at its external boundaries but within it also, the economy must be thought of as being open to other influences. That is, since the household and the state are constituents of the economy, their 'non-economic' considerations will seep into the functioning of the economy, just as the 'economic' calculations of the firms may seep into the household and state also. In other words, there is no economy 'pure and simple'.

Second, there is little that is static and stable about the economy. Its constituents are constantly undergoing change from within because of the nature of the relationship between the members and their groups, and from without because of the interactions with other units. The economy must, therefore, be envisaged primarily in terms of its perpetual state of flux and change. To attempt to feature its 'givens' and to represent it as at rest is to miss its essential characteristics.

Now it can be seen why neo-classical theory with all its logical rigour and refinement is a poor if not distorted representation of the real-life economy. Three specific reasons may be pointed out. First, by taking the individual out of the group context, and by converting him into the 'economic man' behaving as theory expects him to behave, the neo-classical approach robs the economy of its innate ruggedness and heterogeneity and imposes upon it a smoothness that it does not and cannot have. In this process it also undermines the significance of what I have referred to as the 'units' question'. The economy, according to neo-classical theory is a collection of identical individuals doing essentially the same thing (performing the hedonistic calculus) and therefore an entity without external boundaries or internal divisions. It can, of course, be partitioned in any manner that is required, but that is a requirement of theory to achieve what it wants and not a property of the economy as such. Second, however, neo-classical theory slices off the economy completely from the rest of the social processes and confers on it an autonomy which it does not have. This contrived autonomy is then used to derive its independent principles and 'laws' over which the rest of the social processes have no influence and in which other social processes should not intervene. Third, by the manner in which it is constructed, neo-classical theory excludes historical time as a necessary and crucial factor in economic processes themselves. The economy is represented as a machine which has its internal movements but which in its totality is invariant over time. Thus, by insisting on symmetries, regularities and uniformities as the essential logical properties of theory, neo-classical economics provides a conceptualisation of the economy devoid of its essential features. Neo-classical economics can only be thought of as an attempt to set up a pseudo economy, not as a way of illumining or interpreting the real-life economy.

Evolution of a Multi-unit System

How has a modern national economy emerged as a multi-unit system of the kind described in the previous division? An answer to this question is attempted in this division. Sections X, XI and XII deal with a single unit economy embedded in a specific social group. Referred to as the 'rudimentary economy' it is a symbol of an isolated tribal economy. It is shown how this miniature economy has all the crucial aspects of a more developed or advanced one and how they are dealt with. However, it does not have two aspects that assume great significance in other economies, viz., the notion of ownership and issues relating to it and exchange. Section XIII shows the changes that come about when the economy takes a multi-unit composite form and outlines the types of interactions that emerge. Section XIV deals with exchange and its transformation over time. Section XV introduces intermediation as an aspect of the economy arising from the transformation and generalisation of exchange, and the emergence of merchants as a group of intermediaries. It is pointed out that intermediation introduces a qualitative difference to the structure and functioning of the economy.

X

So far I have tried to provide in the barest outline a conceptualisation of the economy distinctly different from what standard economic theory provides. I did this by accepting the national economy as the unit of discussion. The reason for doing so was partly because most of the time the concept of the economy is associated with the national economy, but also because it is at that level that the difference between the standard conceptualisation and what I have attempted can be seen fairly clearly. But the analysis is applicable at other levels too, especially at the global level as I shall try to establish later in the chapter.[6]

Prior to that, however, it is necessary to have some more understanding about the units themselves and of the nature of their interactions. But if the economy is constantly in a state of flux and change, as has already been indicated, because the units and their interactions are constantly undergoing change, the units themselves can be understood only in the context of an evolutionary process. However, except under the assumption that there has been and continues to be a unique and linear process of evolution which can be discerned in the case of all (national) economies, it will be difficult, if not impossible, to say much that is meaningful about the evolutionary process as such. I am not willing to make such a heroic assumption because even a casual look at the history of national economies shows very different patterns of the past. At the same time, I have also insisted that there are some common features that all economies, past and present share—what I have designated as the substantive essentials. It is worth making the effort to see whether some profiles of the metamorphosis of economies can be deduced from them. If that is possible, such an exercise can be supplemented with the knowledge of what actually happened to arrive at a logically meaningful and factually supportable notion of the evolutionary process. I believe this is how Marx tried to interpret the past and that Hicks' *A Theory of Economic History* (1969) is also based on a procedure of this kind.

In what follows I shall adopt a similar, though much simpler, method. It should be noted that my focus will be on the evolution and differentiation of the units of a (national) economy and that the exercise is geared, ultimately, to the understanding of the current reality of real-life economy—the Indian economy.[7]

Since the emphasis is going to be on the differentiation that an economy comes to have over time, the benchmark has to be an undifferentiated unit, that is, a unit that performs all economic activities without units or subeconomies within it. A self-contained household is such a natural primary unit.[8] But if the unit's self-sufficiency is to be taken seriously, it cannot be too small. That is why exercises of this kind take a somewhat larger entity, a tribe or a clan, as the primary unit. Marx provides the rationale for taking the tribe as the primordial primary unit of human society (and hence of the economy).

> The spontaneously evolved tribal community—or if you will the horde—the common ties of a blood, language, custom etc., is the first precondition of the objective conditions of life, and the activities which reproduces and gives material expression to, or objectifies . . . it (activity as herdsmen, hunters, agriculturalists, etc.) (1964: 68–69).

In order to emphasise the self sufficiency of the tribal community, we shall think of it as being set in the midst of a forest totally isolated from all 'others'. What can be said about the 'economy' of such a community? The first thing to note is that it is difficult to carve out the tribal economy from the tribal community. The tribal economy, in other words, is so completely embedded in the tribal community that only by a *tour de force* can the two be separated. Keeping this in mind, we may try to see how the economic functions get performed, starting with how the subsistence of the members is provided for. To simplify further, let us assume that the goods required for survival are all available in the forest—the fruits, roots and berries for food, the leaves and barks for clothing, the branches used for shelter, the twigs for fire, etc. Even so, they do not fall into the laps of people, but have to be gathered. The gathering of these provisions may be thought of as the community's basic activity and, for reasons already discussed, it may be considered as an economic activity. How will this be attended to?

The tribal community, obviously, consists of its individual members, not all alike. There are men and women, young and old—to feature only the natural differences among them. It is possible that there is some division of labour also among the members. A sexual division of labour is most likely because of the biological fact that women have an additional responsibility to the community that men do not have—that of bearing children (the third 'moment' specified by Marx and Engels). However, it is important to note that in the context of a tribal community, a sexual division of labour does not form the basis for dividing activities into work (that which men do outside the home) and non-work (which women attend to at home) as some other communities are prone to do. For instance, if hunting done by men is necessary for subsistence, the cooking done by women also has the same role. The characterisation of activity undertaken outside the home and for payment as 'work', and the rest of the activities as 'non-work' which is so easily made in economics belongs to a very different social and institutional milieu.

But there is a permissible and necessary distinction to be made in the tribal community, between those who directly provide for their sustenance and those who do not. If the total population of the community is designated by P, and those who directly provide for sustenance is designated by W (for 'workers'), then, of course $P > W$ or $P/W > 1$. Though this is rather elementary, the distinction and the ratio can be put to use to understand some important aspects of the (economic) workings of early communities.

It means, first of all, that the W members of the community have to provide (by gathering or producing) more than what is required for their own survival. The fact that such a 'surplus' has to be generated and that it will then have to be distributed among the non-W members constitutes one of the basic economic functions of the community. The non-W members, it may be noted, will consist of infants, the aged, the infirm and so on. Their support is part of the agenda of the community and the procedure for attending to their needs is an important aspect of the ordering of the community whether it is considered an economic function (as it concerns the distribution of goods for subsistence) or a political or social function (as it refers to support for a segment of the community). Second, the larger the value of P/W ratio, the greater is the effort that the W members have to put in to keep the community intact.

If, as mentioned earlier, the goods for the sustenance of the community are available in the forest (i.e., provided by nature), the provisioning of the material needs of the community is the result of expending such effort on nature. What it implies is that the community's economic functions will be determined, to a large extent, by its demographic features, in particular what, at a later period, would come to be designated as the 'dependency ratio'.[9]

It is, of course, not possible to specify the actual extent of effort to be expended or the extent of nature to be utilised without getting a lot more specifications about the community—its requirements, the nature of effort, the 'yield' of nature, etc. However, even with the information already available some broad, but important, relationships that link up the community's requirements or needs, the efforts of the W members and the extent of nature to be used can be indicated. As a preliminary step, let us note that under the conditions already specified, the community is not constrained by any consideration of ownership. Nature exists (let us say as forest or as cultivable land) and can be used without having to be owned. The community can take on any extent of forest or land that it cares to. Ownership will become an issue only if there is another community also, bringing about a distinction between 'us' and 'them'. Ownership, in other words, is a relationship between persons (about things or nature), not merely a relationship between persons and things: it is a *social* relationship which will have to be defined in terms of conventions, institutions, etc., once 'others' have to be taken into account in using nature (or things).

XI

So the issue that the community must decide is how much of nature or land to take on for its purpose, given its total membership (P), its W members and its requirements on the one hand, and the yield of nature or land on the other. It is easy to see that a minimum can be prescribed which will be related to the survival requirements of the community and its total number (P). But is there a maximum that the community can take even when land is freely available? The answer, is, of course, that there is, and it is related to the W members (actually the P/W ratio) and the maximum effort that they are able to put in. We may rephrase it and say that the community has two binding constraints, the one set by the minimum land it requires for the survival of its members and the other set by the extent of effort its W members are able to expend. Since these two constraints can be made use of in subsequent analyses also, it may be useful to identify them in terms of more general categories: we shall designate the former as *the resource constraint* and the latter as *the labour constraint*.

These two set the lower and upper limits of the economic activities of the tribal community. But is it possible to say something about their normal or usual level of activity? An empirical observation has been that tribal communities stick fairly close to the low level indicated by the resource constraint, that they do not move beyond the basic necessities of life. The basic necessities of life are not objectively determined and each community has its own standards for them. That the tribal communities still remain at a *low* level of material goods is not a judgement that they make but an observation made by those who study them, and reflects certain outside standards which may be purely arbitrary. The relevant question is whether the normal level of living of the tribals which outsiders may consider to be low is a matter of necessity or one of choice. This question has been debated and both possibilities have received support by those who are acquainted with the empirical situation. One view is that the tribals have severe limits on resources available to them and hence cannot but be at the subsistence level. This would amount to asserting that the tribal economy is always subject to the resource constraint. The opposite view is that the tribals remain close to what may appear to be the subsistence level out of choice and that they must be considered to be 'the original affluent societies' in the sense that they have more resources at their disposal than required to meet what they consider to be their needs. Those who support this view bring up as empirical evidence the fact that significant variations have been observed in the level of production and productivity of such communities over a period of time indicating that they can indeed go beyond what they themselves consider to be normal.[10]

In a sense the debate is futile because both positions are *empirically* possible and hence the issue cannot be settled at that level. But a broader issue of principle is involved which has got clouded because of the polarisation of views. The principle is that, in the kind of economy under consideration, the normal level of economic activity is determined by what the community considers to be its requirements or needs. A tribal economy may, therefore, be considered to be a need-based economy. If this general principle is accepted, it can be seen that both the interpretations given above can be accepted as empirical possibilities depending on specific circumstances. If the major parameter is what the community accepts as its need (by custom, consensus or whatever), the level of activity defined by it will be very close to survival if in terms of the size of the community, the resources accessible to it are low and it is, thus, forced to be near the lower limit discussed above: that is, the community is absolutely bound by the resource constraint. But if it is not making full use of the resources accessible to it, then the level of activity it normally undertakes, however low it may appear, should be considered to be a matter of choice.

Once again we come to the position that the key determinants of the level of economic activity in a tribal community are its size, the W members of the community, the resources accessible to it and its views on what the community's needs are. These determinants may interact in different ways. Consider the case where the community is pushed to the lower limit (the resource constraint). This may happen because of some calamity like a sudden flood or a severe drought or some other natural phenomena which deprive the members of the resources they were counting on. If this is just a local phenomenon, the members of the community have the option to migrate and to replicate their economy in some other location. A second possibility is for the community to 'tighten belts' for a while, an option available if previously the members were well above the survival level. A third response could be for the W members to put in more effort than they were doing earlier, or to devise some method (inventing some tools, for example) which will revise their productivity. The system may permit one or more of these possibilities which will also indicate the extent of slack it usually has and the elasticities it is capable of. If such possibilities do not exist, the only way out is, what is sometimes referred to as the *hard boiled solution*—some members (the non-W members, that is) will have to die. Except in that extreme situation, it must be presumed that a tribal economy will usually have within it some unused production potential, both of physical resources and of human effort because the community has decided to use less than it is capable of. Hence the economy may be thought to have some sort of demand constraint too, resources and efforts remaining unutilised because the 'demand' for goods is low. But strictly speaking that kind of terminology is not legitimate in the situation we are dealing with.

XII

Let us, therefore, turn to another aspect of the working of the tribal economy, that of the manner in which economic activity is organised. Productive activity in the tribal economy, it has been noted already, consists of human interaction with nature. It is organised on the basis of the community's recognition of its needs. The activity to satisfy the needs will be highly task-specific and some form of social division of labour for task sharing may get established. Beyond this it is not possible to say anything in general about productive activity. On the side of distribution too there is an underlying principle of sharing necessitated by the very composition of the community where there are some who are not engaged in productive activity, but who have a claim, recognised by the community, to what is produced. Even apart from this, the general principle of distribution in the community has to be one of sharing. A tribal economy may be said to be a redistributory system from this point of view.[11] It is as though the products of the economy are 'centrally' pooled after which they are distributed among all members. Different principles are possible for such distribution. 'To each according to his/her need; from each according to his/her capacity' is one of them. There is, however, nothing to guarantee that such a noble principle will necessarily get accepted or sustained. Another possibility is what has come to be known as the 'life boat' principle— that of considering the needs of the infirm and the aged as less important in relation to the needs of those who are likely to survive and continue to assist in the survival of others.[12]

Since these different possibilities exist, the crucial issue to be considered is how decisions on these matters are made. Who decides how tasks will be assigned among the members and how the produce will be distributed? There is no doubt that in a group of the kind we have been dealing with, most of these decisions are made according to custom which means that the community has internal working principles—its agenda and its information channels—accepted and followed generation after generation. History, therefore, is a major factor in the decision making process. A second observation that can be made is that the decision making process is likely to be heavily communitarian with most members having very few rights of their own because the members need a group for their survival and there is no other group to turn to, and the prospects of a few 'rebels' breaking off are also slim.

And yet, as in any other group, within a tribal community of the kind we are considering also, there are bound to be tensions between its members and the group as a whole. For instance, even if the 'ideal' distributive principle of 'to each according to his needs and from each according to his ability' is accepted, there can be differences of opinion about how needs and abilities come to be assessed. Some members are bound to feel that their needs have not been adequately recognised, but that too much is being demanded of them. There may also be individual members who would look for and take advantage of any possibility that may exist for free riding. In general terms, such communities can easily come to have incentive problems of different kinds.

There is one more aspect that can accentuate the inherent elements of conflict in the system. To say that decisions and actions in the community are largely decided by custom is somewhat illusory for the simple reason that only human beings, and not institutions or history, can make decisions. In a community that attaches crucial importance to customs the effective decision makers are those who have the right and the power to *interpret* the customs. That is why every tribe comes to have a chief who is seen as the community's custodian, interpreting and enforcing its customs. In this situation custom-oriented economies almost naturally turn out to be what Hicks calls 'command economies'. Within the community there will be a few who are close to the custodian and will become beneficiaries of his power to issue commands, and the many who cannot be in the inner circle and resent that fact.

However, as we have already noted, an important and unavoidable feature of a group is the component of authority which is necessary to keep the group together and which is beneficial even to individual members. It is this role that the chief discharges. In the broadest sense, therefore, the function of the chief is to hold the group together because in view of the inherent tension between individual members and the group at large, no group can be held together without a sense of authority and without conventions, customs, etc.,—institutions, in short.

The need for an authority in the tribe (the group) makes a major difference to its economy. A tribal economy is one of transfers of goods from one person to another and of services too in that manner. These are usually of a horizontal nature describing what Hicks calls its 'belowness'. Transfers at this level are the ones that readily get established as customary and come to be widely accepted. But because of authority the economy also comes to have an 'aboveness' with vertical transfers. These too get institutionalised and will be generally accepted. However, there is a difference. Under unusual circumstances (when the community's existence is threatened, for instance) additional transfers from 'below' to 'above' may be demanded or extracted. When that happens the distinction between the belowness and the aboveness which remained submerged in custom will become very pronounced.

This may appear to be a rather unimportant matter. Its significance lies in the fact that later on these two components will get separated into a household economy that will retain the elements of belowness and a state economy that functions on the basis of aboveness. Indeed, the more usual distinction between the horizontal transfers via exchange and the vertical transfers via taxation also is a further development from the primordial distinction between the below and the above.

On that note we may try to see why an account of the tribal economy constitutes a proper benchmark for a study of economic evolution and differentiation. The tribal economy is, in many ways, a miniature economy, or a rudimentary economy, as I have indicated elsewhere (Kurien 1992b: Ch 2). Its basis is the fact that a group of people have to exert themselves—thinking, deciding and acting—for their survival. It involves decision about their material requirements, devising ways of interacting with nature to provision them and implementing a principle to distribute the means of material satisfaction among the members. These activities constitute a major item on the agenda of the group and are carried out through working arrangements that they design for the purpose. The tribal economy reflects both social cohesion and social conflict, and is held together by the recognition of a centre of authority. In all these respects it is inextricably embedded in the community providing only the barest contours even to demarcate it mentally as a separate entity. Economies of the future emerge from such hazy beginnings and continue to carry within them the genes of their early formations.

XIII

Through the discussion of an isolated unit such as a tribal community set in the midst of a forest it has been possible to concentrate attention on the *internal* structure and agenda of the unit and to see how a unit *constitutes* its economy, and what the considerations relevant to it are. By accepting individuals, rather than groups, as the primary units, this is an issue that standard economic theory avoids or evades.

There is no doubt that isolated tribal communities that fully constitute their economies still exist within many national economies, including the Indian economy. It is equally true that the general tendency has been to ignore them and to bring into the analysis of national economies only those units that are thought to be *integrated* into the national economy, an expression which is not sufficiently examined because of the convenient assumption that integration of units happens where the market operates. Leaving out units that are known to exist makes the notion of the national economy incomplete, which is bad enough. There is also a more serious problem. By making the assumption that the market fully integrates the primary units into the national economy and by ignoring those units that are not thus linked with others, economic analysis sanctifies an unexamined concept of integration and by assigning the task of that integration to the market, distorts the function of the market as well. All these are matters that need to be re-examined.

To do this let us first examine the features of a multi-unit composite economy. Not surprisingly it will have some features that a single unit economy did not have. For each of the units within a composite economy, a distinction between what is 'ours' and what is 'theirs' arises. It will apply to the human beings (those who are members of our community and those who are not) as well as to physical resources (those over which we have rights and those over which we do not). The latter is the basis of ownership, but the notion of ownership need not get established immediately or fully. Initially only one aspect may get emphasised, the right of exclusive access (to a fairly well-defined segment of the forest, land or the waters). Second, the composite economy provides to the units the possibilities of inter-unit interactions. Whatever may be the nature of these interactions, they are external information channels which may influence and modify the units' internal information channels and may even affect their agenda. A unit can be said to be fully integrated into the composite economy only if its internal information network merges into that of the rest of the economy and its agenda too disappears. This is not likely to happen. But, of course, units may get linked with others and in the process may change their character.

In a composite economy, therefore, an examination of the links is just as important as an understanding of the constituent units. A composite economy is not only a multi-unit entity, but a units-and-links entity. But the nature of the links must be established on the basis of evidence and reasoning and not simply assumed or asserted as is frequently done.

If the units are all alike and self-sufficient, there is hardly any need for them to interact. Adam Smith recognised this, and in order to study inter-unit interaction, differentiated the primary units into deer hunters and beaver hunters. It is clear that Smith was trying to lay the basis for one form of inter-unit interactions, namely, exchange. Exchange, of course, is an important form of link between units and · if it is taken to be a natural thing to happen, it is not surprising. But there is no reason to think that it is the only natural mode of interaction between units, nor necessarily the earliest. In fact, a case can be made out that the most natural and earliest inter-unit link may be something different.

It may be recalled that a great deal of the economy of an isolated unit depends on its P/W ratio and the extent of forest or land (or physical resources in general) accessible to it and that in terms of these two, a lower and an upper limit can be recognised, identified respectively as the resource constraint and the labour constraint. Consider two neighbouring primary units which are similar in all respects except that one is close to the resource constraint and the other close to the labour constraint. To push the analysis further, let us consider that these are two farming households producing corn, and the physical resource under consideration is land. Let the two households be identified respectively as *Ha* and *Hb*. *Ha* may be driven to the resource constraint either because the land accessible to it is low or the P/W ratio is high. In either case, some adjustment is possible because the *W* members may be able to exert themselves more, but there is a limit to that too. If that limit is also reached and still the survival of the members cannot be assured, what is to be done?

There are two possible options. If the problem is a temporary one and perceived to be such by both, especially *Hb*, *Ha* may be able to borrow some corn from *Hb* (on the assumption that it has some ready surplus to spare) to be returned later. *Hb* may lend either out of consideration for a neighbour or because of the possibility of getting more corn from *Ha* when the corn is returned. The second possibility is for some *W* members of *Ha* to offer to work on the *Hb* land because *Hb* has land remaining unutilised as it is subject to the labour constraint. The *Hb* unit may permit the *Ha* members to use the land but claim a share of the additional corn produced on its land. These two possibilities will be referred to as borrowing and leasing. They are both transactions involving time, and forms of contract, however informal they may be.

Neither of these activities is exchange (though the latter may be given an exchange-like interpretation) but if they are also natural possibilities, they may well be the earliest forms of inter-unit links, transfer or transactions. As noted already, exchange is also one of the natural inter-unit transactions. Adam Smith attributed it to the innate propensity of human beings to truck and barter, while Marx provided a more objective (that is, empirically verifiable) rationale. According to him:

> Different communities find different means of production, and different means of subsistence in their natural environment. Hence their modes of production and of living, and their products are different. It is this spontaneously developed difference which, when different communities come into contact, calls forth the mutual exchange of products (Marx 1971: I–322).

Of these three different modes of inter-unit interactions it is not easy to decide which is or are likely to materialise and to get established. It will depend very much on the actual circumstances and conditions. The first two are, in some sense, simpler compared to the third, because in the first the interactions or transactions are solely in terms of the common good, corn, and the second, though involving land and labour also, gets mediated through corn. The conditions for exchange are more stringent as it calls for units producing different goods (deer and beaver, for instance) and will take place only if there is a double coincidence of needs or a third good that is commonly acceptable. It is possible that exchange is more likely in a composite economy of hunters while the other two are more likely in a composite economy of farmers. It is not very fruitful to speculate about this aspect. What is important to note is that early interaction among units need not have been or need not be, exchange; it could have been borrowing or leasing: a great deal depends on the nature of the economic activity of the units and the good(s) for survival.

Already a composite economy's potential for differentiation has emerged. Differentiation of units and diversification of links go together. The differentiation of units may arise due to demographic factors, resource endowments, nature of activities, the basic good for survival, etc. These are not necessarily independent; they frequently interact. It means also that there is a close connection between the internal conditions of the units and the (external) links that they come to have. The links that they are able to establish may bring about changes in their internal conditions as well. Most clearly they impinge on the information channels that the units have. The links, in fact get established because units send signals to one another which are extensions of their internal information channels. This does not mean that they reveal themselves fully to outsiders; there is bound to be some 'strategic' considerations in such signalling. Hence the signals sent out will be interpreted in different ways by the receiving units. Not all signals sent out and received will be acted upon and result in links getting established. The receiving units will first have to decode the signals and consider how their own internal conditions will get altered if they act on them.

It can now be seen that a composite economy is not merely an aggregation of its constituent units: taking the units and their links together, the composite economy becomes an entity with some characteristics different from its units. That is, a composite economy, even if it consists of only households as its constituent units, is not, and cannot be, 'a household writ large'; it will come to have distinct features of its own. The 'whole', in this case, is not merely the sum of its parts. Further, it is unreasonable to imagine that the information that flows within a composite economy will be uniform, smooth or undistorted. On the contrary, the presumption should be that it will be biased, cluttered and in many ways incoherent—a lot of noise floating about. If so, it is also very unlikely that the units will be similarly situated in respect of information that is available within the system. Asymmetry of information, imperfect information and the uncertainties associated with them must be considered to be the normal feature of a composite economy. The units may try to reduce the uncertainties by arriving at negotiated contracts with selected other units or by forming 'blocks' within the system. These too must be accepted as part of the internal structure of the economy along with its units and their interactions.

Even the simplest of a composite economy of interacting units will soon become an entity with characteristics not easy to anticipate. These aspects will be developed further after a discussion of exchange in the next section.

XIV

We have set exchange in a larger context of interactions within a composite economy. Such an approach is necessary to gain a proper understanding of exchange as *one* of the many possible interactions within an economy. Exchange, of course, is an important form of inter-unit transactions in any real-life economy. Within standard economic theory the emphasis is on the logic of exchange. That is important too. But even the logic can be better appreciated by first viewing exchange as an activity, a real-life activity which, unlike the logic that is claimed to be universal, is both spatially and, more so, temporally specific. Hence, as in other matters relating to the economy, we need to have an understanding of exchange also as an activity that undergoes transformation over time when conditions associated with it change. Within mainstream economics it is Hicks (1969 and 1989) who has alerted the profession about the need to take such a view of exchange. Others who had done so before him, but whose work he largely ignores, were Polanyi (1944 and 1957) and Marx (1971).[13] I shall draw on all three, but shall pay special attention to Marx's seminal contributions.

There are two aspects that distinguish exchange as a form of inter-unit transaction from other forms. The first is what both Marx and Hicks emphasise: as exchange is a transaction between two owners, it is between two parties 'at the same level' as Hicks puts it, unlike a transaction between a landlord and a tenant, for instance, who should be considered to be at two different levels. And, to the extent that both parties to exchange may be thought of as entering into the transaction voluntarily, it can also be considered to be beneficial to both parties. The second distinguishing feature of exchange is that, unlike borrowing and leasing where the full transactions are spread over time, exchange, strictly speaking, is a timeless and simultaneous transaction involving two parties and two goods. This aspect of exchange is most clearly seen in (primitive) barter where exchange can be said to take place only if the goods change hands at the same time. This is important because when two goods are simultaneously exchanged they mutually determine the 'prices' of the goods (the price of one in terms of the other).[14]

This is why barter is the real prototype of exchange. It manifests a form of 'reciprocal independence' of two parties arising from the right they have to alienate to mutual advantage that which they own. In this form each act of exchange gets 'extinguished' when the transaction between two parties and two goods is over. This is true even if the same parties are to enter into exchange again and even if the transaction is in relation to the same two goods because the terms of the transaction need not be the same again though there is nothing to prevent the parties from entering into a transaction which repeats the terms of a previous one.

There is another feature of barter that is significant. Unlike in other forms of exchange, in barter each party is at once a buyer *and* a seller. It is this feature of exchange that gets altered when exchange gets transformed from an unmediated to a mediated transaction, from the barter form of *C–C* (directly involving two commodities) to the *C–M–C* form with money, the universal equivalent, coming in between. The introduction of money, or, more accurately, the recognition of something as money, is a matter of great significance in economic evolution. With mediation introduced, exchange as a transaction turns out to be a two-stage process, the sale of a commodity for money and the purchase of another commodity with money, thus constituting two distinct circuits and introducing the distinction between seller and buyer, though it may be the same party involved in both, one after the other. The implications of this change are best expressed in Marx's words. When exchange comes to be mediated through money, he says, 'it breaks through all local and personal bonds inseparable from direct barter . . . and develops a whole network of social relations spontaneous in their growth and *entirely beyond the controls of the actors*' (1971: I–115, emphasis added). By bringing in processes which are beyond the control of the actors, mediated exchange further changes the character of a composite economy. Economic activities which remained largely confined to within the primary units begin to become greatly influenced by the transactions taking place between them. The stage is being set for the links to appear to be more significant than the units if the economy is viewed in its totality.

Before passing on to the further transformation of exchange into its *M–C–M* form, it may be useful to examine how exchange of the *C–C* form and of the *C–M–C* form affect the primary units in the composite economy we are considering, still consisting only of households.

Whatever may be the appearance, let us note that the units are still supreme because all of them retain the essential activities that the single unit economy was responsible for—they produce the (bulk of the) goods they require to meet the needs of their members, exercise control over resources needed for the purpose, now including the rights of ownership, and decide how the goods produced will be divided or shared among the members. In this sense their internal structure, including their agenda and the information channels are still significant. There are some differences though. To the extent that the units enter into exchange, they do not have to produce all their requirements; some of their needs can be met by procuring what others produce. Provisioning becomes a matter of production *and* purchase. By the same token, they do not have to use all that they produce; part of it can be sold to other units. To the extent that they decide to take advantage of this possibility, their resources and labour can be put to greater use, particularly if they were in a state of demand constraint (as noted in an earlier section). But they must still decide how much more to produce. Thus their internal activities may get altered. Some changes may also come about in their internal distribution patterns.

With the *C–M–C* form of exchange the households may come to have some differential advantages. As selling and buying are separated into two processes, and as exchange becomes more common, goods come to have a valuation apart from their use values with money taking on the role as the indicator of the value of goods. It also becomes the store of that value. Hence, households that are in a position to sell many goods and can store the value of goods sold in the form of money will come to have greater possibilities in exchange. A household which has only one good to sell and has many goods to buy will clearly be at a disadvantage compared with one which has money to buy the things it wants. It can be seen that *Ha* households are likely to be of the former kinds and *Hb* households of the latter kind. If so, *C–M–C* exchange will make the asymmetry between them more pronounced.

Although *M–C–M* exchange and *C–M–C* exchange both involve money, the difference between them is more significant than the difference between *C–M–C* and *C–C* forms. Even in the *C–M–C* form the exchange process still remains bounded to the producers' need to acquire goods that they do not produce. That is, the economy is still one of households that produce the bulk of their requirements with the role of money limited to that of a facilitator in what is essentially a goods economy. There is exchange and trade but these are peripheral activities. In other words, *C–M–C* exchange belongs to the feudal period about which Marc Bloch says: 'The society of this age was certainly not unacquainted with either buying or selling. But it did not, like our own *live* by buying and selling' (1965: I–67, emphasis added).

The *M–C–M* form of exchange must be associated with this fundamental difference between trade as an occasional activity in an economy primarily concerned with production, to trade as the all-pervading activity which sets the pace for everything else. It marks the transition from a traditional economy to a modern economy. Many aspects of this transition must be noted.

The most obvious, but not the most important, is the change in the nature of exchange itself. In the *C–M–C* form of exchange, exchange begins with goods and ends in goods: in the *M–C–M* form it begins with money and leads to money. The former was a limited quest for goods, the latter a limitless quest for money. So, exchange as an activity increases manifold. Second, this rapid expansion of exchange will also lead to some increase in production, readily to the extent that the primary units are characterised by slack. Till all slack is removed, and the resources and labour in the economy may be thought of as fully utilised, exchange and production can reinforce one another, thus substantially augmenting the performance of the units and of the economy as a whole. It is in such a context that the classical writers, Adam Smith particularly, put forward the case for removing all restrictions on trade and production and for leaving the economy to the forces of the market.

XV

But the most significant, though not adequately recognised implication of the *M–C–M* form of exchange is that it leads to trade as a specialisation and to the emergence of traders or merchants as a new group in the economy. Referring to the Rise of the Market, Hicks draws the following contrast between the (pre-market) customary economy and what comes after. The customary economy, he says,

> already practises agriculture; it has government, which may be of a simple form, but may be quite sophisticated; it has industry, at least in the sense of handicraft. What it does not have, and what is going to be so important, is trade. There are farmers, and soldiers, and

administrators, and craftsmen; but there are no traders, no one who is specialised upon trade. I would emphasize that it is specialization upon trade which is the beginning of the new world (1969: 25).

Earlier on, Marx had indicated the same. 'The splitting of exchange into purchase and sale makes it possible to buy without selling and sell without buying. It thus leads to speculation and gives rise to the merchant estate' (1973: 200).

The emergence of merchants who specialise in buying and selling marks a crucial stage in the evolution of a composite economy. They bring into the economy an activity that it did not have before, not that of trade, because it did exist even earlier, but that of *intermediation* that was unknown earlier. It is the process of intermediation that differentiates between buyers and sellers although the distinction between buying and selling gets established even with the *C–M–C* form of exchange. Its significance lies in the fact that households which so far *had to be* producer–consumers can be split into producers and consumers, thus affecting the homogeneity of the primary units that existed and turning them into heterogeneous units of producers, consumers and intermediaries. This transformation, of course, does not take place suddenly and fully, but can be seen to be of a fundamental nature.

For a while let us concentrate on the new group, the intermediaries or merchants. What is it that motivates them? The units that existed so far, the households, had their specific objectives and tasks to be done. The intermediation process, on the other hand, is motivated by a single objective—that of making profits because profits, the difference between the buying price and the selling price is the reward of intermediation. The emergence of merchants, specialising in intermediation, therefore, marks the beginning of 'economic' organisation as against 'economically active' organisations in Max Weber's classification that has been referred to. How do the merchants come to be able to make profits? When the selling and buying functions get separated, those who wish to sell a good will have to search for those who are willing to buy them and vice versa. A typical household that produces corn, for instance, must first find someone to buy it and then must look for those ready to sell the oil, salt and clothes, and the many other things it wishes to buy. There is no reason to imagine that all this information will be readily available. An important role that merchants as intermediaries play is as carriers of information as to who has what to sell and who wishes what to buy, thus reducing the cost of searching. For the services that the merchants render in this manner, the parties should be willing to pay. The merchants also play a more positive role. They can buy from those who wish to sell and *store* the goods till someone appears to buy them. By buying from those who wish to sell and selling to those who wish to buy, both sides are helped and both processes are facilitated. In a very meaningful sense, therefore, exchange increases and tends to get generalised not because money appears to mediate between buying and selling, but because through intermediation the merchants actively promote both buying and selling.[15] If this is right, then economic theories, such as the Walrasian general equilibrium theory, which try to bring out the conditions required for generalised exchange and draw implications from them without involving money and merchants, cannot be valid guides to understanding real-life economic processes whatever may be their validity from the point of view of logic alone.

The nature and rationale of the involvement of merchants in exchange also implies that exchange, from their point of view, is a very different activity. Households turn to exchange because they want goods that they do not produce: they are motivated by considerations of use values. But merchants who enter into exchange with money do so in order to have more money. Hence, as Marx points out, the $M–C–M$ form of exchange, strictly speaking, has to be seen as the $M–C–M'$ form where $M' > M$, equal to $M + \Delta M$. The aim of merchants in exchange is to make ΔM, profit, and make as much of it as possible. This becomes possible because unlike all other goods in the economy which have qualitative attributes, money is a pure quantity. And so maximising of profits by those whose motivation is the making of profits is an eminently reasonable objective or agenda. In fact, merchants can be considered to be the first group in the economy with a single-point agenda, maximisation of profits. In this respect too they are different from the other units in the system, the households. Households cannot have a single-point agenda. They have many specific tasks to attend to. If they are also said to have a single-point agenda of maximisation (unless it is that they are maximising whatever they want to maximise) it can only be considered to be an unjustified and arbitrary imposition from outside.

But let us continue with merchants, their motives and activities. A major role of merchants, it has been noted already, is to provide information to those who are eager to enter into exchange either as buyer or as seller and that this service is very valuable to these parties.

Merchants, however, do this not as a matter of social service. For them it is a part, a very important one, of their effort to make profits, a means to the end. Hence it must be presumed that they will use it as effectively as they can. How do they do it? A very natural way is to provide different kinds of information to the parties concerned. To someone who is eager to sell a good, but does not immediately find a buyer, a merchant can provide the information that hardly anybody would be interested in buying it, and use this information to beat down the price. Once the merchant buys it, he can change his tune and give a different kind of information to potential buyers. If the good concerned has different attributes, the merchant is in a better position to give different versions about it to the seller and the buyer. Where there are substitutes, again, the merchant intermediary is in a position to generate and take advantage of information asymmetries. In all of this he is taking some risk, but that is very much a part of the job of an intermediary. Buyers and sellers may be aware of the fact that they cannot rely completely on a single intermediary and turn to others. But the fact remains that exchange can be extended and generalised only with intermediation and that information asymmetry is something that is closely associated with it. That being the case, information asymmetry must be accepted as a built-in feature of the kind of an economy we are dealing with.

As agents who enter into buying and selling with money, merchants already have the advantages of that situation. Their objective is to go on adding ΔM through trading. It means that soon there will be several units in the economy characterised by pronounced money power, because money *is* purchasing power.

The accumulation of money in this manner marks the beginning of capital. As Marx points out, 'the circulation of commodities is the starting point of capital. The production of commodities, their circulation, and the more developed form of their circulation called commerce, these form the historical groundwork from which it rises' (1971: I–145). Thus merchants become merchant capitalists. Marx goes on to say:

> The restless never-ending process of profit-making alone is what he (the capitalist) aims at. This boundless greed after riches, this passionate chase after exchange-value, is common to the capitalist and the miser; but while the miser is merely a capitalist gone mad, the capitalist is a rational miser. The never-ending augmentation of

exchange-value, which the miser strives after, by seeking to save his money from circulation, is attained by the more acute capitalist, by constantly throwing it afresh into circulation (1971: I–151).

This interdependence of capital and circulation that reflects the activity of merchants also has a tendency to change the process of exchange primarily from a way of transacting goods into a means for accumulating capital.

Evolution as Differentiation

The theme of differentiation started in the previous division is continued here. Section XVI deals with the differentiation of household units and section XVII that of merchant units. Section XVII also shows how and why a new unit as the locus of authority in the system also emerges and describes the characteristics of an economic system with such variety of units. The sort of economy depicted in this section can be thought of as the representation of a feudal economy or of the economy of the rural areas in contemporary India and possibly many other countries also. In section XVIII the discussion moves over to a capitalist economy. The attempt is to see the capitalist economy also in terms of the units-and-links approach. The emergence of capitalist production units ('firms') and their characteristics are dealt with in section XIX. The differences that these units and the growing monetisation bring about in the economy are taken up in section XX.

XVI

Having dealt with exchange as one of the inter-unit links and examined the manner in which it gets transformed over time, we are now in a position to take an overall view of the kind of multi-unit composite economy that we have been considering. The focus now will have to be on the differentiation that takes place within it as a result of the activity of the units, including the variety of their interactions.

What may be referred to as the basic differentiation between the units (initially all households) arising from the P/W ratio in relation to physical resources has been touched upon in section XIII. On the basis of these two factors, households were divided into two categories, Ha, subject to the resource constraint and Hb to the labour constraint. As the *Ha* units are getting pushed to the level of survival, they will become increasingly dependent on the *Hb* units. This dependency has an appearance of complementarity—'the *Hb* units need the *Ha* units just as much as the *Ha* units need the *Ha* units'. But the *Ha* units have to depend upon the *Hb* units for their necessities while the dependence of the *Hb* units on the *Ha* units is for their conveniences, to use the criterion that Adam Smith made the basis of the division of goods. There is, therefore, a basic asymmetry in the relationship between the two types. Through the relationship the *Ha* units may manage to survive, but the *Hb* units have the opportunity to increase their conveniences. Thus, there is a good chance that over time the gap between the two will increase and the differentiation between the two will become sharper.

The asymmetry between the two types will affect their links. As already noted, the *Ha* will have to approach the *Hb* either for a loan or to lease out some of the *Hb* land. In their condition, the *Ha* units are in no position to lay down the terms of these transactions. It must be presumed that the *Hb* units will take advantage of the situation. In the case of a loan for instance, (usually given and to be repaid as corn) the *Ha* units will have to pledge labour services as collateral and in the not unlikely event of not being able to repay, the services may have to continue for long periods. This practice, repeated frequently, may get institutionalised as the workers of *Ha* units (why not even the non-workers like children also?) getting 'attached' to the *Hb* units. The attachment may go on for generations also. In the case of leasing, payment may be indicated as a fixed quantity of corn or, more likely, as a share of the produce. Over time, these arrangements may also get institutionalised in terms of the obligations of the owners of the land and of the lessee or tenant. Often a part of the arrangement will be that apart from the corn payment, the tenants will have to put in some work for the owners' cultivation. These arrangements which existed with regional variations in most parts of the world in the past, and continue in many parts even now, had been dismissed by standard exchange-centred economic theory for long as being either 'irrational' or at best being 'institutional' which simply reflected that theory's peculiar notion of rationality and of institutions. Of late, however, there have been many attempts to show that such practices are eminently rational in their contexts and to bring these institutional arrangements into appropriate theoretical formulations. (Azariadis and Stiglitz 1983, Braverman and Stiglitz 1982).

The *Ha* units may tend to get impoverished and the *Hb* units enriched. How will the *Hb* units make use of their additional wealth? There are different possibilities. The *Hb* members may eat and drink and make merry. In that process they may neglect the work that they should do and over time the affluence of some of the units may disappear and some of them at least will turn out to be *Ha* units. A second possibility is that they may come to have a large retinue—those who are responsible to defend them and their wealth, those whose duty is to entertain them and flatter them, those who devote their time to 'the nobler things of life' such as the arts and literature, and so on. A third possibility is that they may take on some work of construction of fortresses, monuments and temples that last for a long time. These different possibilities, it may be noticed, are ways of making use of the economy's surplus if an overall view of the situation is taken. But it is important to notice also that the surplus is not that of the economy in the abstract, but owned by some units in the system whether generated by them or by somebody else.

We may, therefore, pay some attention to this aspect. We have noted already that even a rudimentary economy has an element of surplus, generated by the workers (in cooperation with nature) and used for the sustenance of those who are not workers. There is, thus, a transfer of the surplus from those who generate it to others. In the rudimentary economy, the transfer is an intra-unit phenomenon. In a multi-unit system, in addition to it being intra-unit, it may also become inter-unit. The inter-unit transfer of surplus is closely associated with the notion of ownership that emerges in a multi-unit system. As already mentioned, the notion of ownership with all its implications may not be fully developed in an economy of the kind we have been considering. However, in a primarily land based economy, the right to have a share of what is produced on land by those who claim to be its owners gets established fairly early. This too happens basically because of the asymmetry between the *Ha* and *Hb* type of households. *Hb* households which claim the land as belonging to them (by heredity, conquest, possession or whatever) would want a share of the produce if they let *Ha* households use it. This is not because land is 'productive'[16] but because land comes to be owned by one set of units. Nor is it because land is 'scarce', for, whether land is scarce or not, those who own it will make a claim on the produce.

What the owners claim for the mere fact of ownership is in the nature of a transfer from those who work to those who do not work. But it is no longer a horizontal transfer as in the case of the rudimentary economy, but a vertical one, from below to above. This is one aspect of the 'belowness' and 'aboveness' that Hicks refers to as part of the features of traditional economies. But since he does not take serious note of the distinction between single unit and multi-unit economies, but classifies all pre-market economies as traditional, he is not able to appreciate some of these differences which, however, are very crucial ones. Multi-unit economies, therefore, come to have a vertical transfer, in addition to all the horizontal transfers that link the units, especially exchange. It is usually, though not necessarily, a transfer from those who have relatively less physical resources to those who have more and thus becomes part of the source of their enrichment.

There are, therefore, many forces working in the system that tend to bring about a polarisation between the Ha and Hb type of households, and an understanding of them is important to get to know the working and evolution of the composite economy. At the same time, one should not jump to the conclusion that a total polarisation of the economy into these two types is either natural or inevitable. For one thing, as noted already, the reverse processes can also be in operation: some Hb units may get reduced to Ha status, some Ha units can become Hb also. More importantly, some units are neither Ha nor Hb. They may retain most of the features of a rudimentary economy. Particularly, where needs are limited, it should be possible for households whose availability of physical resources are satisfactory in relation to their P/W ratio to be self-sufficient units, producing internally all their requirements. They may not have to borrow; they may not want to lend. They may neither lease in nor lease out. They may even decide not to enter into exchange, or may do it only very rarely. Since they have an agenda different from Ha and Hb households, we may designate them as Hc. Hc units, however, can get metamorphosed to Ha or Hb. The on-going processes may bring about any of these variety of transformation possibilities and there is not much more that we can say a priori about what is likely to be the case.

XVII

The economy has at least one more kind of units, the merchants. They certainly do not appear from thin air. Once money is introduced into the system, some of the surpluses that Hb households have, can get monetised paving the way for such units to transform themselves into merchants. In fact, for long, such units may remain mixed ones, retaining some features of *Hb* households and some features of merchant units. In any case, since the merchant units perform the new function of intermediation, we must recognise them as separate and distinct entities. We shall designate them as *M* units.

But the *M* units need not all be alike. Once trade begins to spread and opportunities become available to earn a living through the processes of buying and selling, they provide a new option for households with little or no physical resources to survive. Petty trades of all kinds, including most retail trade is of this nature. As traders, those engaged in such activities have to see that there is a positive difference between their selling price and their buying price, which is technically speaking a profit, but the quantum of money available to them is so small that what they make is barely sufficient for survival, leaving little or nothing for accumulation. Frequently, they have to combine trading with exercise of physical labour such as carrying goods from one place to another. Trade, therefore, offers to some the possibility to convert their labour power into goods that they require without the use of (much) physical resources. Such units may, therefore, be differentiated from those of merchant units per se. Since they will also be close to the survival level like the *Ha* units, we shall designate them as *Ma*, referring to the merchant units (proper) as *Mb* because of the resemblances they have to the *Hb* units. It may be noted too that these variety of units need not, and may not, remain pure types. *Ha* units may take on some *Ma* functions; combination of *Hb* and *Mb* functions is very likely, and so on.

Situations like this will give rise to one more kind of unit. Its nature, features and agenda are more difficult to describe. In the discussion on the rudimentary economy it was pointed out that an element of authority is a necessary component of that economy. Authority is partly related to the social system which is likely to be hierarchical. But usually it performs functions which may not be directly related to economic activity but makes heavy demands on resources and labour—defending the members and the territory against external aggression. One way or the other, therefore, the exercise of authority and those who exercise authority will come to have a bearing on the economy and will have to be recognised as a constituent of the economy. Since the economy is basically a group phenomenon, and since authority in some form is necessary to resolve the tensions between individual members of the group and the group as such, there is no reason why it should not be treated as part of the economy which can, and does, influence it in more ways than one.

The nature of authority, its functions in the economy and claims on it certainly change over time. In a rudimentary economy the focus of authority is very clear. But in a multi-unit economy where the units are substantially self-sufficient, authority may turn out to be much more diffused. However, unlike in the rudimentary economy where authority is internal, in a multi-unit economy authority may come to be seen as external to most units but, of course, internal to the system as a whole. Hence, some functions of authority become more pronounced in that context. That different contractual relationships emerge in such a system has been noted already. Even where these relationships are governed by custom and are, thus, institutionalised, wherever there are contracts, there is need for a third party to enforce them and interpret them. This is a role that authority performs. The authority, in this case, may reside in a military leader or a spiritual head, or even with a group of people. Second, wherever there is money, some authority is needed to back it. When a metal like gold is the basis of money, its purity has to be ensured by the image of the person who guarantees it. The guarantee is required more when paper money appears later. The acceptability of money, its basic characteristics, is a function of the power that guarantees it and the faith that those who deal with money have in the person or agency that exercises power. Authority may also be related to ownership and it is particularly relevant in the historical context of the kind of economy we have been dealing with where ownership means a variety of claims. It is not unusual for a monarch or a religious head to claim that all land and other resources available to the members of the economy belong ultimately to him. Whether put forward by a religious leader or a secular person, such claims are usually defended by invoking divine sanction.

These different functions of authority lead to those exercising it to make claims on what is produced in the economy making it necessary for a transfer from other units in the system. It is a further vertical transfer from below to above and is in the nature of a rent-cum-tax.[17] In a system of the kind we are dealing with, the distinction between these two elements can hardly be established. It is likely too that the transfer from below is not to a single, identifiable agent or agency above. The transfer is unlikely to happen voluntarily. Hence, whoever may be the ultimate authority, the collection (extortion may be a more appropriate expression) will have to be entrusted to several decentralised intermediaries. In fact, a welter of intermediary agents is the more likely outcome under such circumstances with all the arbitrariness and confusion that goes with it.

The person or persons exercising authority may wish to reach out to most other units in the system. However, a close tie-up between authority and the merchants, especially the *Mb* units, appears quite natural. The merchants need protection; they want contracts to be enforced; and for these services they are willing to pay. Authority, on the other hand, is eager, indeed desperate, to get collections. Thus a closer link between the two may emerge. What comes to be known, at a later stage, as the nation state is often the outcome of and growth from such alliances of conveniences (Dobb 1963: Ch. 3, Hill 1969).

Many other forms of tie-ups may also naturally arise. We have already seen tie-ups between *Ha* and *Hb* units. In such instances the links are likely to be bilateral, between one *Ha* unit and one *Hb* unit, or between one *Hb* unit and many *Ha* units, but with different specific terms and conditions with each one of them. Similarly, *Hb* units and *Mb* units may have their special linkages. Groups of *Hc* units may come to have their special dealings too. Hence, although the multi-unit composite economy may have exchange and markets, they will not result in the economy getting 'integrated' by them. There will be many kinds of markets; but no Market as such, which is something that analysts and theorists impose on the situation. The economy will not be integrated by any single principle, institution or agency. A plurality of heterogeneous units, a variety of links, different forms of tie-ups, criss-crossing transfers, vertical and horizontal—these are the features of a multi-unit composite economy.

That such was the real-life situation of most present-day national economies, of Europe and Asia in particular, can be seen from a study of the economic history of these regions. For countries like India it was not the experience of the remote past alone. The description given above would have been valid for many parts of rural India at least up to the time of independence: in some parts it bears a very close resemblance even today. If standard economic theory does not accommodate or even faintly reflect such real-life experiences, it is a verdict on that theory. What is significant is that the description of the multi-unit composite economy is useful for understanding a major problem of the present day world. A moment of reflection will show that it is a very apt representation of the emerging global economy. But here I anticipate what should come a little later.

XVIII

Expressions such as feudalism, capitalism and socialism are used both in popular and professional discourses on economic matters. Each one of them refers to economic systems or social formations in which economic systems are embedded. They are labels put on a variety of aspects—groups and their interactions—and are useful for quick identifications. But as labels they are external to what they refer to and give only the barest of indications about what is within. In sections XIII to XVII, I have attempted to provide an internal view of what is commonly referred to as feudalism as consisting of groups that are primarily concerned with the production of goods required for their own use and who interact with one another in that process through a variety of ways including exchange. It has at least two more kinds of groups, merchants who specialise in trade and those who exercise authority. The fact that economic arrangements of this kind are not merely things of the past but may be equally good descriptions of familiar contemporary situations shows how important it is not to go by labels alone.

I shall now move on to the economic order which bears the label of capitalism. The attempt, again, will be to enter into it to gain an internal view in terms of groups or units and their interactions. The treatment will be highly selective. In particular, I shall skip the discussion and controversy about the transition from feudalism to capitalism[18] and concentrate on my chosen theme of the differentiation that takes place as an economy evolves over time.

A units-and-links exposition of a capitalist economy is not unusual. In fact, there are two familiar versions of it. The first is the text book representation of the capitalist economy (of course, leaving out the adjective 'capitalist' in an attempt to emphasise the timelessness of the economy and to claim for the representation a 'universal' appearance) as consisting of households and firms. Households sell to the firms the factors of production which the firms convert into goods and sell them back to the households. This perennial flow back and forth is interpreted as exchange without or with the mediation of money, conveying the notion that exchange is exchange irrespective of the form it takes, once again implying a timeless universal activity. Since the activity is exchange, both parties are supposed to enter into it in their own interest and are shown to benefit from it. As for the two parties, households and firms, they are taken as 'given'. The givenness prevents the examination of some crucial questions. One is curious to know, for instance, why the households which possess the factors of production do not produce the goods they want but go through the rather devious route of selling their services to firms and getting back goods from them. One is also curious to know why the firms do what they do or why they exist at all. A possible answer is that what is being attempted is a simple representation of a real-life situation and that everyone knows that in real life households and firms do exist, though that is a rather naive justification. The fact of the matter is that the representation is not concerned with the units at all, but their links, exchange, to represent which the units have to be shown as engaging in buying and selling. As was noted in the previous chapter, the parties shown in the representation are not drawn from real life at all. Even at this elementary level, they are dummies brought in to perform some assigned tasks. Beneath all of this, there is also the attempt to establish (via appropriate assumptions and constructions) that the (capitalist) economy based on exchange and markets is one that is beneficial to both parties, then generalised to include all participants—thus to arrive at the principle of harmony, or the Principle of All-Round Advantage as Hicks has chosen to call it. It is not necessary to point out how simplistic the whole thing is but it is important to note that such is the basis of what claims to be the science of economics.

The second units-and-links version of the capitalist economy is that associated with Marx. Reflecting on the empirical phenomenon he observed in Great Britain, where capitalism was emerging, Marx divided its basic units into two sharply distinct groups—capitalists who owned all means of production on the one hand and workers who were deprived of everything other than their labour power on the other. For capitalism as a system of production to emerge and develop, argued Marx, two very different kinds of commodity possessors must come face to face and into contact: on the one hand, the owners of money, means of production, means of subsistence, who are eager to increase the sum of values they possess by buying other people's labour-power; on the other hand, free labourers, the sellers of their own labour-power. The polarisation that Marx indicates, it may be noted, is the logical culmination of the differentiation of households into *Hb* and *Ha* types. There has been a tendency to suggest that the kind of polarisation that Marx implies has not happened in capitalist economies and that, therefore, his analysis of capitalism is not empirically valid. It is not right to say that Marx's treatment of capitalism depends crucially on there being *only* the two opposing groups mentioned above. Marx was very much aware of the existence of other groups or classes and, in fact, was critical of Ricardo for overlooking this fact. Marx's characterisation of capitalism is meant to convey two basic aspects of capitalism: that capitalism is an economic order that can function only on the basis of wage-labour (unlike pre-capitalist systems where the bulk of those engaged in production were owner–producers); and second, that the distinction between the earnings of labour (wages) and the earnings for ownership (profits) is crucial for understanding the working of the capitalist economy. Unlike the textbook version featuring harmony as the underlying principle of the capitalist economy, Marx's version also underlines the innate element of conflict of interests in the capitalist system.

In spite of the differences in perceptions and implications, however, the two units-and-links versions of capitalism have one thing in common, viz., the complementarity of the two units. In the former version, firms cannot function without households and vice versa; in the latter, similarly, capitalists cannot function without workers, nor can workers function without capitalists. It is for this reason that the capitalist economy is frequently assumed to be an integrated system unlike its predecessors which were seen to be not adequately knit together. In the households-and-firms version of the capitalist economy, exchange is considered to be the integrating factor with its principle of All-round Advantage; in the capitalists-and-workers version, the system, though consisting of heterogeneous primary units, is claimed to be held together by the insatiable desire of the capitalists to accumulate surplus value.

In either case, the capitalist system would appear not to conform to our characterisation of the economy as a loosely knit entity consisting of units with different agenda interacting through a variety of links. The question to consider, therefore, is whether a representation of the capitalist economy compatible with this characterisation is possible without, of course, sacrificing what one knows to be the essential features of capitalism. I shall concentrate on this issue. Towards the end of section XVII, we had arrived at a multi-unit composite economy consisting of plurality of heterogeneous units, a variety of links, different forms of tie ups, criss-crossing transfers, vertical and horizontal. The units we have seen so far are Ha, Hb, Hc, Ma, Mb and that hitherto unnamed unit, 'authority'. Since this last has already been shown to emerge as the state, let us identify it as S. There is no reason why a capitalist economy in real life cannot have any, or all, of them. But a capitalist economy must have some more. Let us see why.

A broader interpretation of the household units is necessary to move forward. In the preceding section we were dealing with an essentially agrarian economy producing 'corn'. The rationale was that the basic substantive economic principle is survival of the members and that, therefore, production must initially be grains or 'corn'. But since the second substantive principle indicates the desire of members to rise above subsistence where that is possible, it is legitimate to accept that more corn and more than corn will be produced over time. The better endowed *Hb* units are the ones who are likely to move to these additional productive activities which is a reflection of the surplus they have and are able to command. On this basis we may think of the *Ha* units as those at the verge of subsistence and the *Hb* units as those with surplus. We have noted the nature of their interdependence. The intermediate category, *Hc* units, are primarily concerned about their internal matters, though they may come to have some horizontal transfers, including exchange, to further their interests. We shall refer to them as the self-reliant units.

XIX

Over time the *Hb* and *Mb* units will become preoccupied with the surplus they can come to have, the former through production and the latter through trade. As production increases and gets diversified, the two types of units will come closer because increases in production cannot be sustained for long without first selling what is produced; later it will become production for sale. Similarly, trade too cannot be sustained for long without links with production. If we look into the history of the emergence of capitalism, it can be seen that it is this need to link production and sales in the pursuit of surplus that marks its beginning and feeds its development (Dobb 1963: Ch 4). What kind of units will these producer–trader hybrids be? There need not be any ambiguity about their agenda; they are out to make profits or surplus. Indeed, this may become their single point agenda in which they display the genes of their *Mb* predecessors. The connection with the *Mb* units is closer still. Like them they play a role of intermediation; what they produce is not to satisfy their needs but to meet the needs of others.

Soon the new units will come to have a feature hitherto not widely prevalent, though not entirely unknown. Unlike households, tribes and so on which are groups based on the affinities of flesh and blood, these new capitalist units will be basically *contractual groups* of persons initially informally, and later formally, coming together for the sole purpose of making profits through explicitly formulated methods. Such contracting or incorporation is a new institutional arrangement which will become more formally established when another institutional arrangement, that of limited liability, supplements it. Hence, these units will come to be known as companies or corporations in common parlance. The term that economic theory uses for them is 'enterprises' or 'firms'. We shall identify them as the *F* units. In Max Weber's terminology, they are the economic organisations.

Let us look at the *F* units—these special units of the capitalist system—more closely. The first thing to note about them, though it is frequently not noticed at all, is that their emergence and existence presupposes authority, the state. As contractual units they have no possibility of formation or functioning apart from the authority that sanctions contracts and adjudicates between contesting parties if and when the need arises. All assertions (yes assertions, not arguments) that capitalism is a self-regulating system and functions best when the state withdraws completely are nonsensical. So crucial indeed is the dependence of a capitalist economy on the state that a writer bluntly but rightly says: 'Remove the regime of capital and the state would remain, although it might change dramatically; remove the state and the regime of capital would not last a day' (Heilbroner 1988: 105).

The second thing to note about the *F* units is that their *raison d' etre,* of making profits, in fact of *maximising* profits, depends on sustaining the mutual interaction between production and trade. This cumulative interaction accounts for the expansionary tendency of capitalism which reinforces the natural tendency of exchange, especially exchange mediated by money, to 'break through all local and personal bonds' and to 'develop a whole network of social relations entirely beyond the control of the actors'. Consequently, the introduction of capitalism usually results in a perceptible spurt in economic activity with the volume and variety of goods registering rapid increase. It also leads to constant and continuing changes in the processes of production through technological inventions and innovations. As output increases and incomes at different levels go up, there will also be organised attempts to persuade people to buy because the increase in production can be maintained only if there is a corresponding increase in buying also.

Third, therefore, the *F* units will tend to exert their influence on all other units in the system. Their impact on the *M* units, both *Mb* and *Ma*, is obvious. But will they also impact the *H* units? Yes, and in many ways. The underlying effort of the *F* units in this regard will be two-fold: to ensure that enough labour power is available to them from the *H* units and to convert *H* units from owner–producer status to worker–consumer status. The processes too will be two-fold. In the first instance the *F* units, acting primarily in their role as *Mb* units, will enter into deals with the household units to provide them the necessary inputs and to purchase their outputs. Under normal circumstances, the upper hand in both these transactions will be of the *F* units which, therefore, will be in a position to determine the terms of the transactions in their favour. They may strengthen it further by acting as money lenders to the household units in need of loans, especially consumption loans. The long-run effect of these transactions is likely to be for the *F* units to take over the means of production of the owner–producers and reduce them to the status of those who have nothing other than their labour power to sell. Marx described this process as primitive accumulation. The households that are likely to be affected are the *Ha* types and the ones in the *Hc* type close to the lower level. The *F* units using the advantage they are likely to have in production and the control they come to have over the markets, make direct inroads into the *Hc* units also by competing them out of production.

The approach of the *F* units to the *Hc* units at the higher level and the *Hb* units generally will be somewhat different. These, it will be recalled, are fairly well endowed in terms of physical resources. The effort, therefore, will be to induce them to part with their physical resources and to offer them attractive terms in respect of their labour power also. The effort will be facilitated by a further institutional arrangement that will emerge out of the separation of ownership and control whereby the households will still retain the ownership of resources, but leave it to the *F* units to manage them. In this process a new type of households will emerge which we shall designate as *Hd*, which own the means of production, but rent them out to the *F* units and lend them their services too in return for remuneration known, not as wages, but as salaries. The *Hd* households, referred to also as salaried households are, thus, the worker–consumers that the *F* units would like to see in the system. Superficially at least, they would appear to have much stake in the *F* units partly because they own them and partly because the *F* units manage their resources. These, then, are the undifferentiated households of the textbook version of the capitalist economy which, together with the *F* units (firms), become the complementing units in a harmoniously functioning system of circular flows. The *Hd* units may even appear to accept the agenda of the *F* units attempting to maximise the returns on their physical resources. To this extent the system may also appear to consist of homogeneous units, all claimed to be 'maximisers' with that kind of objective getting identified with economic rationality as well.

XX

The variety of processes described above may seem to be similar once the economy gets highly monetised and with new forms of markets also emerging. The growth in the monetisation of the economy is, of course, an aspect of the development of capitalism and its innate tendency to commoditise everything, including man and nature as Polanyi points out. Through monetised market transactions, goods and services of diverse kinds get reduced to homogeneous exchange values. Surplus too, which in an earlier period had to exist as distinct physical items, gets converted into 'liquid' form, or, at any rate, gets valued in money terms aggregated as capital. Along with this apparently homogenising, unifying process, social relations too tend to take new forms. As Marx points out, money begins to appear as objectified social relations making it possible for individuals to carry their social power (the power to purchase) as well as the bonds with society in their pockets. In earlier forms of economic organisations the individual related to others in specific forms—a specific form of labour and of product. This is changed when relations of exchange value become common, where individuals relate to others, not as their relation to one another but as their subordination to relations which subsist independently of them and which arise out of collisions between mutually indifferent individuals (Marx 1973: 157).

These changes, however, are largely illusory, but part of the brainwashing effort of those who have a vested interest in the accumulation of wealth and power in the abstract. A moment of reflection will show that capitalism does not iron out all qualitative distinctions between goods. In fact, its own logic rules out the possibility because only if goods are different, qualitatively and in terms of use values, will there be scope for choice and exchange. Indeed, a major thrust of the capitalist system is to project qualitative differences even where there is none or little: that is what product differentiation is all about, without which choice will get limited beyond a point, and the spread of exchange and markets will also get restricted. Similarly, though for accounting purposes capital may get homogenised through monetary valuation, in the actual process of production it is crucial to maintain the physical and qualitative distinction between different items of the capital stock. Capitalism, therefore, has a two-fold task: first, of generating and sustaining a variety of goods, and, second, of eliminating that variety for final reckoning by homogenising everything into exchange values of which money becomes the measure.

Capitalism does not succeed in destroying all group relationships either and in 'liberating' the individual.[19] Among the non-contractual groups that have existed in the past, at least, the family or the household continues well into the capitalist system. Theories relating to the capitalist economy have a vested interest in depicting the family as consumers who happen to come to have non-economic affinities. Some, like Becker, may even go to the extent of showing that the familial relationships including those of husband and wife, and parents and children, can be shown to be based on the logic of exchange and markets.[20] But the household is never a mere consuming unit. The household never loses its economic function of production if this term is interpreted to mean the interactions of labour with nature or physical resources to generate new use values. Within certain cultures the productive activities of households may be described and dismissed as 'household chores'. But a household is always a production unit, a consumption unit and a living unit combined into one (Sachs 1986: 1). In fact, only because individuals belong to such a group which takes care of their basic requirements and needs can they appear to be mere individuals in the market place.

Nor is this all. The firm too is a group or organisation with its own internal structure and hierarchies. Anybody who has experience in any firm knows this to be so. In recent years the transaction cost theorists have discovered it and are trying to convince their fellow neo-classical theorists that this is so.[21] Even theorists who normally adhere to a theory of individualist markets admit this fact when they examine the firm independently. Arrow, for instance, says 'A firm, especially a large corporation, provides another major area within which price relations are held in partial abeyance. The internal organization is again hierarchical and bureaucratic' (1974: 25). There is no doubt that a capitalist economy is more individualistic than those that preceded it. But the claim that all group considerations and arrangements disappear when capitalism gets established is a myth propagated partly by some economic theorists who have a vested interest in theories where the primary units are individuals, not groups. We go back to what we have demonstrated already: any real-life economy, including the capitalist economy, has to be basically a group phenomenon.

The growth of monetisation, especially the monetisation of the surplus, in a capitalist economy gives rise to a new set of intermediary units. With productive activity increasingly coming under firms, they become the locus where surplus is generated. But since households are the owners of productive forces, it is to them that the surplus accrues. However, they have no direct interest in using the surplus. Thus a distinction between those to whom surplus accrues and those who use surplus emerges, providing scope for intermediation. The units or agents who perform this intermediary role are banks, or the *B* units. In performing the intermediary role, banks establish a distinction between physical assets and *claims* on physical assets. The claims can be of different kinds and as they grow, they become easily marketable financial assets. In turn, further intermediation becomes possible and a host of financial intermediaries also emerges. Just as money initially performs the role of facilitating exchange, finance, initially, is a facilitator of production. And just as money comes to dominate exchange, finance will soon come to exercise dominion over production. When this happens, there will also be a tendency for the accent in the capitalist economy to shift from production to intermediation as the latter may appear to be a better option to make profits, especially quick profits. Proliferation of intermediation and the domination by intermediaries, therefore, are major features of the capitalist economy. Because intermediation has certain logic and dynamics of its own, a capitalist economy may give the appearance of being governed by its internal and, therefore, autonomous 'laws'; and so it is up to a point. But intermediation cannot function without explicit contractual commitments supervised and enforced by social agencies which, obviously, should not be governed by those laws. Hence, paradoxical though it may appear, the capitalist economy must be considered to be one of the most socially embedded and institutionalised economic orders. Strange indeed that economic theories of capitalism generally ignore this crucial aspect.

Markets and State

The main theme of this division is the nature of markets and the state in a capitalist economy. Section XXI points out that neo-classical theory terribly distorts the nature of markets in a capitalist economy. It is shown that under capitalism, markets are usually characterised by inequality in endowments and asymmetry of information, and section XXII shows that under such conditions there is no possibility of the capitalist system generating the kind of 'perfect competition' that neo-classical theory projects. It is also shown that the most important decision in a capitalist economy, the investment decision, cannot be based on market signals as the market does not provide signals about the future. Section XXIII deals with the crucial role of the State in capitalist economies so that it is misleading to argue that a capitalist economy is one that is regulated entirely by the forces of the market. Section XXIV looks at the variety of units under capitalism and the diverse kinds of interactions they enter into. It also refers to what may be described as 'non-economic' factors that have a bearing on capitalism and its transformation over time.

XXI

I shall now turn to an examination of the nature of markets under capitalism, specifically the claim that is made that the spread of markets that happens when capitalism grows will remove all the impediments on them that existed during the regime of pre-capitalist systems, and enable them to function almost as perfectly as some theories of markets, such as the general equilibrium theory of Walras, have demonstrated. It is on the basis of such claims that the capitalist economy gets identified with the market economy from which follows the argument that under capitalism, at least, 'leave it to the market' is the best policy option.

A critical account of the claims of the market at the logical level has been provided in the previous chapter. It was pointed out that the implications of a regime of markets have been derived from a carefully chosen set of 'givens'. Among them two basic ones were similarity of the initial endowments of the participants (the observation of Koopmans that the model 'would be best suited for describing a society of self-sufficient farmers who do a little trading on the side') and the symmetry of information. It must now be clear that these basic premises are not, and *cannot* be, applicable to a capitalist economy. A capitalist economy is not one where a little trading takes place on the side: it is one where practically everything—means of production and nature, labour power and the means of subsistence—is bought and sold. A capitalist economy is not, and cannot be, one of self-sufficient farmers who may trade the goods they produce but not their labour power. For, trading in labour power (forced by the whip of hunger or induced by the prospect of not having to face the risk of organising production) is the underlying condition of capitalism. If historical evidence can be relied upon, capitalism emerged and grew under conditions of enormous inequalities of endowments. Even if an initial equal distribution of endowments is postulated, the dynamics of capitalism based on the accumulation of surplus, the built-in tendency for the growing surplus to get concentrated under the control of a few and the changes in the technology of production resulting from it, will soon disturb the initial equality as Baran and Sweezy (1966) on the one hand and Galbraith (1967) on the other have demonstrated. Also, trading under capitalism is not directly between producers: it is mediated by merchants without whose involvement trade cannot proliferate the way it does.

These aspects have a bearing on the second basic 'given' of the market model: symmetry of information among the participants. We have already noted that once trade gets into the hands of merchants whose only interest in exchange is to make profits, it is unreasonable to maintain that information will be free and unbiased. It is certainly more reasonable to accept that traders will use information to their advantage. Logical theories of market elide this problem by concentrating on exchange that takes place without intermediation, but then this cannot be generalised. The inherent informational asymmetry when exchange as an activity becomes the profit-making activity of merchants gets further compounded under capitalism. To the extent that production under capitalism comes largely under firms, (that is, units specifically contracted for that purpose) the approach of sellers and buyers to exchange undergoes a change. Firms themselves are buyers in the sense that they have to buy their inputs from others and a lot of trade that takes place in a capitalist order is of that kind. But there are the final buyers, the households, who buy because they are prompted by the use value of the goods. The situation, therefore, is that the producers who become sellers want to sell goods on considerations of exchange value, while the final buyers wish to buy goods for their use value. This introduces an asymmetry in the exchange process itself with the sellers being in the

M–C–M′ form of exchange, but the buyers being in the *C–M–C* form. This asymmetry itself confers special bargaining power to the sellers who can use it to their advantage. As producers they are in a position to interpret to the buyers the use value of the goods they produce, and in most instances the buyers do not have the expertise to scrutinise the information that the sellers put out about the goods. Markets under capitalism, therefore, function under an inherent asymmetry of information.

The asymmetry may operate in the opposite direction also. When firms buy labour power, particularly on a contractual basis for a period of time like a month or a year, they are in no position to fully assess the quality of the commodity they buy or its performance potential over time. This problem, recognised in recent literature as the principal–agent problem, is also inherent to the market processes under capitalism as the sale and purchase of labour power is central to it.[22]

There is no reason to think that these instances of asymmetry of information will cancel each other out. On the contrary, they may reinforce asymmetry. In any case, it must now be clear that asymmetry of information will have to be accepted as the underlying condition of the exchange process in a capitalist economy and that, therefore, there is no legitimacy for the assumption made in theoretical writings of symmetry of information.

There is another aspect of markets under capitalism that is of considerable importance but which is generally ignored. Exchange, it has been noted already, is a transaction between two parties 'at the same level' insofar as both are owners. This formal similarity between parties holds when the seller has only his labour power to sell and the buyer is backed by substantial resource power. But apart from the asymmetry in bargaining power that this transaction implies, there is a further problem. In the capitalist order, a firm buys labour power not for resale but to put it to use for the generation of surplus value in production. The value added in production cannot be from the inert materials that are used along with labour in production such as raw materials, fuel, power, etc. It can come only from the human element in production, both physical and mental labour. It arises from the surplus that workers generate in all forms of economic organisations and forms the basis of the vertical transfer when it is appropriated from the workers on the basis of consideration of ownership.

In pre-capitalist orders this surplus is a good of some kind (corn) and is physically transferred from the actual worker below to the claimant owner above. Exchange as an activity is separated from that transaction. Under capitalism, where labour-power purchased and goods produced both become commodities, and where everything comes to be reckoned in terms of exchange value, surplus not only becomes surplus value but its appropriation becomes very much part of the combined production-exchange process through which the owners appropriate or realise the surplus value. Markets under capitalism, therefore, represent not only the horizontal transfer between parties at the same level, but also the (hidden) vertical transfer from worker to owner. The vertical transfer does not happen automatically. It is made possible by the institutional arrangement which sanctions and legitimises this mode of subtle surplus appropriation by those who claim ownership rights. Even granting that the means of production cooperating with labour power are owned by some person or agency other than the owners of labour power, there is nothing to say that the surplus should automatically accrue to the owners of the means of production. A different kind of institutional arrangement can make the owners of labour power the recipients of the surplus. It is, therefore, the institutional arrangement of capitalism that makes capitalist markets perform the vertical transfer also. To the extent that it happens, capitalist markets are not expressions of exchange pure and simple and they cannot possibly have all the characteristics that exchange, which is only horizontal transfer, is said to have.

XXII

A further question to be considered is the impact that competition will have on the nature of markets in a capitalist economy. One of the commonest assumptions is that it is the absence of competition that is responsible for markets remaining inadequately integrated in pre-capitalist and non-capitalist economies, and that with competition becoming a reality, there will be a tendency for markets and the economy as a whole to get unified through the regime of prices. There is no doubt that competition is an important factor in a capitalist economy, but the competition in a real-life capitalist economy is very different from what that term conveys in the theoretical discussions about markets.

Competition is real and can become intense in a capitalist economy because formally, at least, there is nothing to prevent anyone or any group that wishes to make profits, as merchant, as producer or as producer–merchant, from doing so. This freedom of entry is considered to be one of the essential features of capitalism in contrast with the variety of restrictions that prevailed in earlier economic systems. In the capitalist system, it is the competition by one's rivals, both actual and potential, that sets limits on the activities of the profit seekers. But for competition, a producer or merchant would be able to set himself up as a monopolist and make use of that position to exercise a large measure of control over the market including the setting of prices. Left to himself that is what each profit maker would want to do; but rivals, competitors, make it difficult. But no profit seeker would passively submit to the forces of competition that reduces his chances to exercise to some measure an element of monopoly power. If it is not possible to exercise it over the entire market, he would, through a variety of measures, non-price competition, product differentiation, etc., try to carve out for himself a segment of the market. In this effort advertising plays a major role. Product differentiation (real or imaginary) and advertising go hand in hand in the profit seeker's effort to retain control over a segment of the market. Hence, while there are some forces in the capitalist system that work to unify and integrate markets, there are others that result in segmenting and fragmenting markets. Getting a section of the buyers attached to oneself (by convincing them that what is being offered to them is better than what a rival can give, providing them credit and other facilities such as free delivery, etc.) and retaining them is something that every seller would aim at and succeed to some extent. That is what capitalist competition is all about.

Consequently, capitalist markets too have shown different forms of tie-ups at different stages of capitalist evolution. The putting out system was one of the commonest in the early stages—a merchant providing inputs to a manufacturer on the assurance that the output will be sold only to him. This transaction, therefore, ties up the labour of the manufacturer, credit, and the goods, usually on terms that the merchant decides. The truck system was another whereby workers employed by a producer were obliged to buy the goods they required from his retail shop. A careful examination of capitalist production and trade across the ages, and in different parts of the world, would show that the propensity to enter into 'deals' of this kind has been widespread. As we shall see later, it is a prominent aspect of the contemporary global capitalism. This is not surprising because capitalists always have to devise different ways of reaching out to labour power on the one hand, and capturing as much of the purchasing power of the public as possible on the other, because it is through these activities that they make profit and accumulate capital. These activities, in turn, shape the nature of the market.

Apart from these considerations from real-life situations, it is now being increasingly recognised from theoretical perspectives that instead of looking for the logic of the Market, it may be much more fruitful to search for the working of markets—market for primary goods, among them markets for quickly perishable goods ('fish') as distinct from storable ones ('corn'); market for manufactured goods; market for land; market for labour; market for money; market for credit; market for claims, and so on, where the operations are likely to be distinctly different (Hicks 1989).

But let us continue with capitalism and markets. One of the widely held myths about capitalism is that decisions made about economic activities are all in response to market signals. The fact, however, is that the most important decision, that relating to investment, is not, and cannot be, based on market signals. Investment decisions under capitalism are based principally on expectations about the future—a point that Keynes forcefully made against those who could not get out of the habit of thinking in terms of the timeless logic of the markets—and hence they cannot be guided by market signals, as the market has no way of signalling from the future to the present, though the decision makers no doubt make their own projections into the future. But such futuristic calculations are highly subjective. We are therefore led to the conclusion that the capitalist order with its accent on objective rationality depends heavily on subjective calculations. Nowhere is it seen as strikingly as in the transactions in claims which is emerging as one of the most important functions in the working of capitalism.

Two of the primary units in a capitalist economy—the households and the state—do not submit themselves fully to the logic or even the operation of markets even when they may participate in market activities. The internal structure of households is based on a work-sharing, goods-sharing, principle. In fact, the household in a capitalist economy must be thought of as a group of people held together precisely because they wish to be governed by non-market principles. Though they are economically active, their agenda is distinctly different from those of firms. Their economy consists of converting the resources they have, human and physical, into goods they need for use. It is in this sense that they are producing–consuming units. Their role in production comes to be underplayed and ignored only after 'work' gets defined, under the influence of the capitalist principle, as that which is done outside the household and for wages.[23] This is the reflection of certain institutional arrangements, although of late it has come to be projected as part of the innate logic of economics.

Households differ in their attitude towards markets and in their involvement with them. Once markets develop, the *Ha* units, particularly the extreme cases which have no non-human resources, have no choice except to be involved with markets. Since human resources alone are inadequate to be engaged in production, they have to sell their labour power for sheer survival. They are, as Bharadwaj points out (Raj et al. 1985: 335), compulsively engaged in market activities. Converting their labour power into money, they then convert the money into goods needed for survival. Even under such extreme cases they may be involved in some productive activity such as cooking, though many of them, especially in urban areas, may be buying the food they eat (Sachs 1986: 3).

The *Hb* households, those that have already been engaged in the purchase of labour power, would either tend to become fullfledged *F* units or get reduced to *Hc* units under capitalist influence.

The *Hc* units, peasants producing their own basic requirements being the typical case, will continue for a long time without much market involvement. There are two reasons for this. The first is the desire of some people to be their own masters, to be able to set their own pace and procedures of work, which does not disappear just because capitalism makes the institutional arrangement of working for wages widespread (Reddy 1984: 20–21 and 222–23). The second reason is the uncertainty of finding work for oneself and members of one's family even where labour power becomes a highly commoditised good. This is particularly true when one is conscious of the specific skills that constitute one's labour power. Under such conditions, however, the *Hc* units, though not involved in the market for labour and means of production, will have no choice except to be involved in the goods market for selling the goods they produce. Such is the case of the traditional artisans. Usually they enter into deals with some traders and may come very much under their control. They are likely to be the ones to be readily colonised by the commodity sector, as Sachs puts it, i.e., to be competed out by the *F* units which will produce cheaper substitutes for their wares. However, the fact remains that nowhere in the world has capitalism succeeded in weeding out the *Hc* units or producer households, not even in the most advanced of capitalist countries where they function actively as family business units (Braverman 1974).

It has been noted already that when capitalism grows, a new kind of households will emerge, the *Hd* units. They become the complements of the *F* units by preferring to rent out both their labour power and physical resources (monetised and converted into claims via the intermediation processes and institutions) to be managed by the *F* units. In fact, they also come under the capitalist ethos with their agenda becoming increasingly attuned to accumulation.

XXIII

That capitalism cannot function on its own without active support of the state has already been seen. Though we are primarily concerned with the market involvement of the state as a constituent unit of the economy, we may first deal with the broader involvement of the state in a capitalist economy. As already noted, the capitalist economy too is embedded in a larger social framework and it is the state that defines the legal premises within which the capitalist economy functions. Legal rights guaranteed by the state are the basic foundations of capitalism. Among them property rights are the most crucial. Adam Smith was very explicit about it.

It is only under the shelter of the civil magistrate that the owner of valuable property, which is acquired by the labour of many years, or perhaps of many successive generations, can sleep a single night in security. . . . The acquisition of valuable and extensive property, therefore, necessarily requires the establishment of civil government (Bk V, Ch I–II: 199).

The state also substantially influences the social relations of production particularly because of its power to determine conditions of labour, and in that sense directly intervenes in the accumulation process. Also, through its power to tax, the state enters into the realm of the utilisation of resources and through its spending patterns influences a variety of production patterns. And, of course, through the control it exercises on money and finance, it makes its presence felt on all economic transactions in a capitalist economy. The state, thus, is part of the very texture of a capitalist economy.

With such a unit present in the system, the markets can hardly be 'free'. Administration of money and finance, imposition of taxes, the nature of such taxes, the borrowing and lending patterns of the state—

all these have a direct bearing on the markets because they considerably influence the distribution of purchasing power in the system and also get reflected in the price structure. That apart, in most instances, the state becomes an active participant in the market through the variety of goods and services it buys and sells. In this regard too it has a unique position because of the right it has to confer purchasing power upon itself. It is, perhaps, not necessary to elaborate these aspects in view of the vast body of evidence that is available of the manner in which states in capitalist economies have been directly intervening in market processes in recent times.[24] This i one area where theory is hopelessly out of touch with the real-life situation.

In the light of the descriptions given above, we must conclude that in spite of the fact, and often because of it, that markets expand under capitalism, they continue to be as diverse, as fragmented and as capricious as under earlier economic orders reflecting the heterogeneity of the constituent units of the economy and their diverse agenda. Indeed, because of the inherent inequalities in resource endowments and the resulting differences in bargaining power, the equally inherent asymmetries of information, and the constant attempts by the major participants to segment markets in their effort to exercise control over them, markets under capitalism can never become perfect. Hence the claim that markets tend to become more perfect under capitalism, and that the capitalist economy gets integrated because of the perfect and unhindered working of the markets is a myth that some theoretical systems have invented and continue to perpetuate. Capitalism did not, and could not have ushered in a 'market economy' or 'market society' if these expressions are meant to convey situations where a perfectly functioning market system takes over the working of the economy. As a writer has commented about the capitalist order:

> Rather than speak of market society for the new social order that resulted, it would perhaps be better to speak of 'market culture'. The advantage of the word *culture* is that it at least raises the possibility of a disjuncture between perception and reality and forces us to interpret rather than blindly accept language used to describe or restructure social life. . . . Market culture . . . in the simplest terms, consisted of three elements: a set of (wrong) perceptions, a language through which these perceptions were formulated, expressed and debated, and a set of (misguided) practices partially but imperfectly

shaped in accord with these perceptions. Market society was a mirage (Reddy 1984: 1).

XXIV

Some aspects of the evolutionary process of capitalism arising from its accumulative thrust and the constant change in production technology that it necessitates have been widely recognised in the literature such as Schumpeter's treatment of 'the perennial gale of creative destruction'. But usually such changes are traced through the effect that they have on the organisation of production. Without going into the details of those changes, I have concentrated on the overall transformation that capitalism comes to have tracing it through the units-and-links schema. One of the inferences that can be made from the units-and-links analysis is that in real-life situation capitalism is likely to be a multifaceted as well as a multilayered entity. Capitalism manifests itself in the spheres of trade, production and finance, not necessarily in that order, and not certainly in isolation. More significant, perhaps, capitalism may function at different levels and through different strategies. At one level, it may just be an attempt to reach out to the isolated traditional producers in a locality and to wean them away from their customary social and local boundaries into a wider arena through the market process. At another level, the effort may be to bring together a large number of workers under one roof to subordinate them to the mechanical rhythm of mass production. At yet another level, the method may be to link up production units in different places, exercising the principle of centralised coordination of decentralised production. A large network of relationships may emerge among these different layers through a variety of deals and tie-ups. Such being the case, there is no reason to think that the lattice of a capitalist economy in terms of units-and-links is any different from that of pre-capitalist economies. This is why the transition from pre-capitalist to capitalist order is usually long drawn out and various forms may coexist for long also.[25]

There is one more aspect that remains to be examined for an adequate understanding of the capitalist economy and its contemporary transformation. The involvement of the state in the functioning of a capitalist economy is an expression directly of the unavoidable exercise of authority and indirectly of the impact of larger social considerations in its working. It is a further reminder that even a capitalist economy, often thought of as the most individualistic of economic systems is embedded in a communitarian set up. What is the community within which capitalism is embedded and functions? In a historical sense, the emergence of capitalism is accompanied by the breaking down of locationally limited communities such as a manor or a village, thereby providing individuals, the more enterprising among them in particular, an opportunity to liberate themselves from a number of constricting regulations and to move out to new opportunities. Undoubtedly, it was part of the propensity of exchange mediated by money to break through local and personal bonds, and hence merchants were among the first to go out of, or beyond, the old community arrangements. But not surprisingly, the collapse of the sense of community at the local level was accompanied by the search for a sense of belonging at a higher level. As parochial loyalties were getting eroded, individuals were in search of a larger community to identify themselves with. Such was the background to the emergence of the 'nation' as a larger community with a new ruling class, closely associated with merchants, to accept leadership and exercise authority in the new community (Dobb 1963: Ch. 3, Hill 1969). The nation and the nation-state were very closely associated with mercantile activity during the period that later came to be designated as the mercantilist era. The rationale of commercial activity (often accompanied by military activity) at this time was that through the acquisition of precious metals, the nation was getting enriched. From there it was easy for Adam Smith to take the next step to show that the wealth of a nation depended not on international trade, though trade was important, but internal production and increase in productivity. With that, the close link between capitalism and the nation was well established and it has continued to be so since then. It finds expression in the statement that a former President of one of America's biggest corporations made and that gained wide currency in that country that what is good for General Motors is good for America.

Whatever might have been the reasons for the links between capitalism and nationalism, it is a fact that the social and cultural aspects associated with nationalism have considerably influenced the evolution and features of capitalism in different parts of the world. No doubt capitalism has some universal features (but was this not true also of the pre-capitalist economic systems?) but invariably they have found expression through the specific social ethos of different nations. German and French capitalisms had features different from British capitalism. American, Japanese and Russian capitalisms too had their distinct identities. Nobody will deny that Indian, Mexican, Nigerian, Indonesian and Korean capitalisms today have their own specific features. This is partly because capitalism itself changes over time, but also because as a real-life economic order it is always located within the social and cultural specificities of its home. Over time, if the economic features of capitalism tend to influence other aspects of social life, they, in turn, influence capitalist development also.

There is no set pattern of these interactions either. Examining the history of the evolution of capitalism in Britain, Polanyi points out that while international trade may have had a kind of natural evolution from the early days, the development of internal trade owed much to state interventions; that land and labour had remained *extra commercium* for a long time; that when capitalists attempted to make them commodities there was a great deal of social resistance; that at one stage the state agreed with the capitalist argument that the threat of hunger was the only way to get poor people to work and abolished a variety of social arrangements which ensured that no member of society was subjected to the whip of hunger; and so on.[26] Later history showed that under the influence of society at large, British capitalism became something of welfare capitalism with legally binding minimum wages and a variety of protective measures for workers, employment guarantees and unemployment benefits and other humanistic measures. It is well known too that in more recent times there has been a retreat in Britain from many of the social security provisions. Other capitalist nations show their own distinctive track records of capitalist development which will make it clear that, for better or for worse, capitalist economies have never functioned apart from broader social influences.

The ideologues of capitalism, of course, try to establish that in capitalist societies there are two distinct *loci* of authority—the economy and the polity, resulting from the emergence of the former as an autonomous sphere with its own immutable (capitalist) principles and laws. Sometimes the distinction between the two spheres is traced to the differences in their basic premises: the polity has one person one vote as its basic principle; the basic principle of the economy is one dollar one vote. Such flippant arguments may come in handy for those who want to establish the independence of the economy as a prelude to asserting the independence of economics as a separate field of study. But they go contrary to all we know about the nature of social relationships and of power in society.

The historical experience has been that where capitalism has emerged and grown, it has been with the involvement of the polity represented by the state, always active and, in some instances, even aggressive. A common practice in the early days was protecting domestic capital against foreign capital through state action. Or it might have been to contain some social problems that the working of capitalism generates, instability and unemployment, for instance. In more recent times, political power and the instruments of administration have been used in many countries to promote economic growth, as has been witnessed in Japan, South Korea and other Asian countries.

The Emerging Global Economy

Up to now the analysis was confined to a single national economy concentrating on internal units and their interactions. But once a capitalist economy is taken up for examination, the analysis cannot be limited to a national economy because the innate expansionist tendency of capital does not respect national boundaries. Capitalism is intrinsically transnational as it demonstrated from its very early stage through the process of colonialism. This aspect of capitalism finds a new organisational manifestation via the multinational corporations (MNCs) which now play a major role in the emerging global economy which is conceptually different from the international economy that mainstream economics deals with. The units of the international economy are national economies. But in the emerging global economy, MNCs, which both in terms of their activities as well as ownership patterns, cut across national boundaries with agenda different from national economies must also be recognised as units. Hence the units-and-links approach is suited to deal with the newly emerging patterns of tie-up between them, the national economies and the units within national economies. That the MNCs are new players in the global economy with their own agenda is established in section XXV. The features of the global economy arising from this fact and the associated growth and global movements of finance capital are discussed in section XXVI. It is argued also that what are shown to be new features of the global economy can be seen to be a more adequate description of national economies as well than what mainstream economics is able to provide.

Section XXVII makes a brief attempt to locate the emergence of socialist economies in the evolutionary paradigm developed in the chapter.

XXV

From the early days nation states have lent their support to capitalist enterprises to reach out to other parts of the world. The global spread of capitalism, therefore, was as much the result of the political and military support as that of the inherent capitalist tendency to go beyond geographical and political boundaries. The early manifestation of this activity was colonialism and imperialism, the classic example, of course, being the British political and capitalistic domination over India. In the economic sphere the visible aspect of this arrangement was the presence in India of British capitalist corporations producing goods using Indian labour power and Indian physical resources. The goods could have been meant for British consumers or, as Britain had already emerged as the emporium of Europe, meant for consumers in some other country in Europe or in some other British colony. A new pattern of capitalist operation was emerging linking capital from one country, labour from another and buyers from a third. As against national capitalism, multinational capitalism was making its appearance. Practically all European countries, where capitalism first emerged, resorted to this procedure of locating their productive operations—plantations and oil and mineral extraction, primarily—in other parts of the world to take advantage of physical resources located there as well as of the cheaper labour power available in other countries and then to transport their produce to yet other locations. Arising from this arrangement were the multinational corporations, MNCs, a variant of the F units under capitalism.[27] The MNC operations received a high boost after the Second World War when, under the US military, political and economic leadership, there was an active promotion of American private investment in Europe and other parts of the world. In the 1960s and 1970s foreign direct investment by corporations from the USA, Britain, Germany and Japan increased very rapidly, and in the 1980s the MNCs became a high profile phenomenon in the global capitalist scene. By the early 1990s, some 35,000 MNCs with around 170,000 foreign affiliates that they controlled accounted for roughly 16 per cent of the world's productive assets. Not all of them were giant corporations, but the top ones among them have turnovers larger than the GDPs of· many member countries of the United Nations.

In many respects the emergence of these entities marks a new phase of capitalism. First and foremost, they are new players on the global scene active in many countries and thus exerting influence over many domestic economies. Some of them are transnational not only in the sense of having multinational activities, but also having multinational ownership, their shares being held by citizens of different nationalities. In what is increasingly described as the global economy, they, therefore, constitute a new type of units along with national economies and their constituent units. They have also made a big difference to the patterns of production and trade in the global economy. In terms of production they have led to two major changes. The first is a new international division of labour resulting from MNCs farming out the production of the goods that they manufacture to different parts of the world. The manufacture of automobiles which today involves the assembly of more than 4,000 components is a typical example. Ford Escort, which is assembled as a car in the UK and Germany, has its parts produced in 15 different countries; France, Canada, USA, Spain, Italy, Switzerland, Japan, Austria, Denmark, Norway, Belgium, the Netherlands and Sweden, in addition to the UK and Germany. Second, the organisation of production also undergoes a major change. Increasingly, sub-contracting and sub-subcontracting are becoming the nature of organising production which, therefore, brings a marked difference in the links between units. It also affects the payment arrangements at different levels, commissions and piece rates replacing wages as the standard mode of payment except perhaps at the lowest level where employment of labour on wage contracts is still practised. International trade and the pricing of goods moving across national boundaries also get affected. A good deal of movement from one country to another is now taking place *within* firms, more in the nature of interdepartmental movements. The firms concerned are, therefore, in a position to price them with considerable freedom in order to circumvent the tariff regulations of the countries involved. Such 'transfer prices', thus, are a new feature of international trade.

Through the variety of their international activities the MNCs come to have direct dealings with the currencies of many national economies. Through their buying and selling operations they are also in a position to influence the values of national currencies. The variation in the value of leading currencies provides an excellent opportunity for speculation and the MNCs take advantage of it. They are also in a position to influence the capital markets through their dealings in stocks and shares all over the world facilitated by the revolutionary changes in the communications technology. Another area where the

MNCs are active is in buying and selling enterprises as such in different parts of the world.

As a result of these activities of the MNCs during the past couple of decades, the international economy has become much more integrated than it ever has been through the operation of the market. So dominating has finance been in these transactions that the term 'market', especially in its global dimension, has come to mean the *capital* market, the transactions in securities and currencies which have come to greatly outstrip the transactions in goods and services. The *Trade and Development Report, 1990* of the United Nations Conference on Trade and Development (UNCTAD) pointed out that by the end of the 1980s the *daily* volume of foreign exchange trading in major currency markets almost reached the average *monthly* volume of world trade and that the annual increase in the size of international banking alone amounted to nine times the total foreign direct investment made across all borders.

Not surprisingly the new opportunities that global markets in finance have brought about have also led to the MNCs coming to concentrate their attention on finance itself. Not that they have given up the production of and trade in goods. But as Peter Drucker, the leading authority on corporate business has observed:

> Ninety per cent of the transnational economy's financial transactions do not serve what economists would consider an economic function. They serve purely financial functions. These money flows have their own rationale, of course. But they are in large part political rationalities, anticipation of government decisions as to central bank interest rates or foreign exchange rates, taxes, government deficits and government borrowing, or political risk assessment (Drucker 1990: 127)

XXVI

With all these changes rapidly taking place, the international economy, or the global economy as it is more appropriately being referred to of late, has been undergoing a major transformation. There is something of a crisis of perception associated with it. An *international* economy is viewed in terms of the relationships or transactions among the various participants consisting primarily of trade in goods and services and the movement of capital. But how is a *global* economy to be perceived?

The use of macro concepts usually applied at the level of national economies—aggregates of income, employment, investment, etc.—is a possibility, but not particularly enlightening as at the global level aggregation of these variables across the units that constitute it appears very artificial. This is mainly because the units within the global economy, the national economies, are known to be and recognised as separate and distinct entities with decision making powers of their own and because there is no corresponding decision making authority at the global level. In other words, the global economy cannot be represented solely in terms of some aggregate quantities, or merely in terms of the links between its constituent units. To understand the global economy, it is necessary to know something of the structure and agenda of its constituent units. An *internal* view of the units is called for, but standard economic theory has no procedure of doing so. International trade theory, for instance, takes the units, the national economies, as given and assumes also that they are similar except for differences in factor endowments. International trade theory is thus basically an extension of internal trade theory based on the assumption of utility maximising homogeneous participants.

But for two reasons such an approach is not satisfactory for dealing with the global economy now. The first is that some new units have emerged (MNCs) whose special feature is that they cut across the old units, the national economies. Standard international trade theories have no place for these new units. In fact, to locate them it is necessary to see the national economies in terms of their constituent units because the new units cut across national boundaries by establishing links with units *within* national economies thus making the boundaries of national economies rather blurred. Secondly, the old and the new units must be presumed to differ in their structure and agenda. The new units as modifications of F units in the capitalist economy are contractual bodies which can be disbanded if the need arises. A national economy does not have that facility. More important still, it is reasonable to assume that the new units have a single point agenda, of striving for the highest return on the capital at their command. The agenda of national economies hardly ever come up for discussion. In international trade theory, there is the silent assumption that as in any exchange relationship, the parties involved are 'maximisers', but theorists who take such a view will be hard put to say what it is that national economies are supposed to be maximising. Obviously, they cannot be considered to be maximising profits as firms are taken to do; they cannot be considered to be maximising utility as households are assumed to do. There is little choice except to accept that the agenda of national economies consist of a number of specific tasks: some targeted employment for their members; some degree of stability for the internal price level; some manageable level of payment to/from other national economies; some measure of protection for the environment, etc.

The palpable differences in the agenda also bring about changes in the manner in which the units relate themselves to one another. Again, in international trade theory, the interaction between the parties is confined to the exchange process, at the most to bargaining about quantities and prices in a bilateral situation which is assumed to be neutralised as the number of participants increases. The nature of interaction between the national economies and MNCs, both treated as constituents or sub-economies of the global economy, is of a very different kind. In the confrontation between them, both have internal strategies which the other can only partly know. Part of the internal strategy is to *anticipate* the counter moves of the opponents and on that basis to revise one's own internal strategy. The ability to do this depends very much on the internal structure of the parties concerned. (The national economies may have to go through several legislative procedures in revising their internal strategies while the MNCs may be in a position to attend to this task more quickly and with less exposure, for instance.)

Such game theoretic interactions are coming to be increasingly recognised in economic theory, but as long as economic theory is not in a position to accept the internal structure and the differences in agenda of the units in a system, and is not able to view the economy as an evolving entity, strategic interactions can only be treated as exceptions. This is the bind that economics is in today: the world around is changing rapidly, but economic theory approaches it with a model meant to emphasise eternal changelessness.[28]

It is, therefore, not surprising that the new features of the emerging global economy are being recognised by non-economists. John H. Holland of the Division of Computer Science and Engineering of the University of Michigan in a stimulating paper has given seven special features of the global economy (Holland 1988: 117–18) which I substantially reproduce.

Holland begins by pointing out that the global economy has features that, *in the aggregate,* make it a difficult subject for traditional mathematics, and then goes on to list the following:

(*a*) The overall direction of the economy is determined by the inter-action of many dispersed units acting in parallel. The action of any given unit depends upon the state and actions of a limited number of other units.

(*b*) There are rarely any global controls on interactions—controls are provided by mechanisms of competition and coordination be-tween units, mediated by assigned roles and shifting associations.

(*c*) The economy has many levels of organisation and interaction. Units at any given level typically serve as 'building blocks' for cons-tructing units at the next higher level. The overall organisation is more than hierarchical, with all sorts of tangling interactions across levels.

(*d*) The building blocks are recombined, and revised continually as the system accumulates experience—the system adapts.

(*e*) The arena in which the economy operates is typified by many niches that can be exploited by particular adaptations.

(*f*) Niches are continually created by new technologies and the very act of filling a niche provides new niches. Perpetual novelty results.

(*g*) Because the niches are various, and new niches are continually created, the economy operates far from an optimum. Improvements are always possible and, indeed, occur regularly.

Economists will have to admit that the non-economist's account given above provides a better understanding of the real-life global economy that they are becoming part of now, but which they fail to see because they are so completely blinded by the theories they hold dear to them. Holland also indicates why traditional economic theory cannot handle the features of the emerging global economy. According to him the global economy, like the central nervous system, ecologies, immune systems and the process of evolutionary genetics, is an example of *adaptive non-linear network* (ANN). ANNs are quite different from the manner in which traditional economic theory depicts the economy. The building-blocks or units of traditional economics are fixed rational agents that operate in a linear, static and predictable environment (the 'givens' of neo-classical theory). ANNs allow for intensive non-linear interactions among large numbers of changing agents. These interactions are characterised by limited rationality, adaptation and increasing returns. ANNs do not act in terms of stimulus and response, they *anticipate*. Participants in the system build up their own models of the system and use them to make predictions and determine their course of action. Their effort is not to be subject to the system, but to influence and alter the system to their advantage.

Holland does not provide any underlying reasons for the characterisation of the global economy. If one is willing to accept these features of a real-life functioning *global* economy, and reexamine one's basic notion of the economy itself, the chances are that they will be seen to be features of the real-life economy at practically *all* levels, global, national or local. For, these features are not related to the spread or geographical coverage of the economy, but on the manner in which its units, their environment and patterns of interaction are perceived. As I have been trying to bring out in this chapter, the economy at any level and at any time can be (*must* be) seen as a large number of heterogeneous units entering into a variety of patterns of interactions and undergoing change through such interactions—or an evolving complex entity. The change in perception is radical indeed making it possible to have a much better comprehension of real-life situations. This claim may become more meaningful if one were to start with the global economy free from conventional theoretical treatments and to work downwards and backwards into the national (capitalist) economy, and the local (feudal) economy.

XXVII

In the next chapter I shall spell out the major implications of the different perception of the economy that I have been attempting to convey. But in order to provide a more adequate understanding of the evolution of the economy over time one more task remains to be done. The expression 'evolution' may convey the impression of naturalness and inevitability. Given the three substantive essentials discussed in section III, particularly the second and third, the economy has an inbuilt tendency to keep moving forward and upward. To be more specific, the desire of human beings to improve their economic situation when conditions are favourable for it, and technological progress will provide the economy a measure of momentum for expansion. More goods will be produced; more variety of goods will become available; the patterns of production will change. But if the economy is not merely goods, or even human relationship to goods, but basically an aspect of human relationship to one another, there is no reason to expect that the changes that come about will be socially neutral. On the contrary, it is more reasonable to assume that some will be favourably and others will be adversely affected. If so, accompanying even what may appear to be upward movement or positive changes, such as a general increase in production, there will be social tensions, conflicts and opposition, and these too must be considered as part of the evolutionary process. Hence, the evolution of the economy cannot be thought of as a smooth, continuous process, although concentration of attention on the *logic* of change, without reference to *concrete historical social processes* may give that impression. In real life, change unavoidably has discontinuities and reversals. Even what may appear to be logically most compulsive, such as the growth of markets and the spread of capitalism does not happen without deliberate and organised human intervention on the one hand, and equally vehement protests on the other, as the studies of Karl Polanyi et al. (1957), E.P. Thompson (1980) and William Reddy (1984) have clearly shown and amply documented. These deliberate efforts on the part of organised groups to bring about or prevent changes must also be included in what is referred to as the evolution of the economy over time.

Of such efforts the most spectacular has been the Soviet Revolution of 1917 which, in social affairs, must be taken to be as significant as the first flight into space in the technological realm. It was an attempt of an organised group of people via the political processes (by a drastic realignment of power structure in society) to bring the economy directly under social control. The power structure was altered by taking away ownership rights from those who exercised it so far to their own advantage and legally vesting ownership with society a as whole to be used in the interest of *all* its members. It was an attempt to break down the exclusive use of resources by those who claimed ownership and to bring about an inclusive economy, in that respect similar to a tribal economy. Other consequential institutional changes followed. Exchange and markets which were closely linked up with ownership had to be drastically altered and substantially curbed. With that the role of money had to change too, all of which indicated how what are often considered to be well-established natural institutions can be changed by human volition. The organisation of production had to be changed too as production was no longer meant to satisfy the growing wants of the few, but to meet the basic needs of all as a matter of top priority. Norms of distribution also were radically altered.

These changes did happen. And an economic system fundamentally different from what existed before, in terms of units and links, did function. It was also emulated in other parts of the globe. And in an exceptionally short period of five to six decades, almost a third of humanity came under economic systems directly under social control. But then suddenly, within a period of three or four years in the late 1980s and early 1990s many of them collapsed also, including in the land of the birth of these systems. Those that remain are in a process of major readjustments.

It is not my intention here to take up a critical evaluation of the achievements and drawbacks of these attempts to bring about through conscious human effort economic systems different from what humanity had seen so far. We are too close to the events to be able to assess them adequately. However, a few facts may be recalled. While they existed, and where they still exist in some form or the other, they did succeed in their primary objective of making the economic order firmly and explicitly embedded in a larger social and political order and in making the economy largely inclusive. In the initial stages they also succeeded in getting the economy to perform adequately in terms of increased production and productivity. But as production expanded and the technical and social interrelationships in the economy become more complex, they failed to devise proper measures to provide incentives and to coordinate the diverse processes and interests. Beyond a point political commands were seen to be inadequate to stimulate and guide the economy. In other words, the institutional arrangements did not respond adequately to the requirements of a changing economy. The collapse of the systems too did not happen 'naturally'. Those who were not getting enough benefits from the system had to organise themselves against those who had come to have vested interests in keeping it going without necessary changes. Once again changes were brought about not through the internal momentum of the economy, but by mobilising larger social forces.

At the global level these transformations also must be considered as part of the evolutionary process of the economy. A major consequence of these changes has been that in the global economy today there are national economies whose internal structure and agenda are different from what was the case up to the late nineteenth century and consequently the links among them are also likely to show greater diversity.

If these are the realities what kind of economics will be required for the future? This is the question to be examined in the next chapter.

Notes

* For an explanation of the title see the appendix to this chapter.

1. See section III for an explanation of the term 'agenda'.

2. Marx (1973: 83) depicts groups as 'definite and limited human conglomerates'.

3. I am myself guilty of this error because I have described markets as being set in the context of two other institutions, households and the state See Kurien 1993a.

4. Quoted by Kisch (1989: 31).

5. Cf Myrdal (1953: Ch 6); Levine (1977: Ch 1)

6. See 'The emerging global economy' below.

7. For the significance of this approach for an understanding of the Indian Economy see Kurien (1992b: Chapters 7 to 9 in particular).

8. Since the unit has to be a group to emphasise *internal* interrelationships, the primary unit of analysis *cannot* be a Robinson Crusoe.

9. Chayanov (1966) makes the dependency ratio a major factor in the analysis of peasant households.

10. For a discussion of this aspect see Sahlins (1974) and studies referred to there.

11. The expression 'redistributory system', here, carries the same meaning as in Polanyi, 'The Economy as an Instituted Process' in Polanyi et al. (1957).

12. This is how Adam Smith saw 'savage nations' in the Introduction of *The Wealth of Nations*.

13. However, subsequently Hicks stated:

    Once upon a time I was giving a lecture, based upon my *Theory of Economic History*. When it was over, I was asked: are you a follower of Marx, or of Adam Smith? I am glad I replied, without hesitation: both! Certainly I have learned something from each of them (Hicks 1989: 1).

14. Exchange can be, and frequently is, converted into transactions involving 'deferred payments'. But when it happens, the activity ceases to be exchange per se, and becomes one of lending and borrowing with associated contractual obligations whether formal or informal. Exchange is best treated as a transaction between parties which does not have an intervening time period.

15. The shopkeeper ... makes market continuous in time by being ready to do business on any day, not just on market days. He may also do something to make it continuous in space, if he goes forth, or sends his agents to go forth to fetch from neighbouring centres things he can profitably sell in his own centres, and for which he can

offer in return things that are available in his own place. In this way trade can grow, it can grow gradually (Hicks 1969: 29).

16. If the term 'productive' only implies that labour alone cannot produce corn, it holds good even in a rudimentary economy where what is produced with the cooperation of land goes entirely to the workers who produce it. Also, rain, apart from land, is required to make labour productive, but no share of production is set apart for rain. But once water comes to be 'owned', a share of the produce is claimed by the owner.

17. Hicks (1969) refers to it as the 'revenue economy'.

18. The 'transition debate' originally between Paul Sweezy and Maurice Dobb is ably summarised and commented on by Hilton (1985).

19. Dumont (1977) takes the position that the emergence of economics as a separate field of study during the early days of capitalist development itself shifted the emphasis to the individual as against the primacy that pre-capitalist societies gave to society as a whole. See Kurien (1985) for a critical appraisal of Dumont's position.

20. The economist who has been consistently propagating this position is G.S. Becker. See Becker (1976).

21. Williamson (1975, 1985) argue the case for viewing firms as hierarchies. See also Simon (1991).

22. The pioneering work on the principal–agent problem is Ross (1973). See also Joseph Stiglitz's discussion of the problem and the reference to the literature in *The New Palgrave Dictionary of Economics*, Vol. III.

23. See section IX in Chapter 5 for a critical account of this concept of work.

24. World Bank (1993) has a detailed examination of the prominent part played by the state in the economic development of the East Asian countries which till recently were considered to be examples of the 'miracle of the market'.

25. However, it does not mean that there is no difference between economies of different periods. On the contrary, the unit-mix of the system changes and the nature of links among the units changes in the evolutionary process. The argument has been that an understanding of the interrelated changes is necessary to appreciate how economies evolve over time.

26. Polanyi (1944). passim.

27. *The Economist*, 27 March 1993, has a comprehensive survey of the MNCs. See also Grou (1985), Jenkins (1987), Gill and Law (1988).

28. See the discussion in the Appendix.

APPENDIX

'The Economy as an Evolving Complex System' is the title of an unusual kind of publication, not widely known to scholars in India (Anderson et al. 1988).

The publication consists of the proceedings of the Evolutionary paths of the Global Economy Workshop, held in September 1987 in Santa Fe, New Mexico, USA, under the auspices of the Santa Fe Institute which has, as one of its major objectives, the study of the science of complexity. The participants of the Workshop were economists, physicists, natural scientists, computer engineers, chaos theorists and medical scientists, mostly from the United States, but also from Europe and South America. The Foreword to the publication states the objective of the Workshop as follows: 'The purpose of the workshop was to explore the potential usefulness of a broadly trans-disciplinary research program on the dynamics of the global economic system, by bringing together a group of economists and a group of natural scientists who have developed techniques for studying non-linear dynamical systems and adaptive paths in evolutionary systems.' The publication indicates that recent developments in the global economy, especially in the realm of finance, posed new problems to economists who, because of the essentially static nature of their analytical system, were finding it difficult to comprehend the complexities of the emerging global economy dominated by finance. Scholars from other disciplines familiar with evolutionary processes, and computer scientists modelling evolving complex systems, were sharing their experience with the economists. In this process they had some comments to make and questions to raise about economics as a field of enquiry. This is what makes the publication unique.

The volume provides glimpses about the rethinking that is going on in some branches of science, biology, physics and physiology in particular. Scholars from these disciplines suggest that some of the recent developments in their fields could be profitably applied in economics. In the paper on 'Neural Nets for Economists', Eric B Baum (of the Jet Propulsion Laboratory, California Institute of Technology) suggests that the modeling of a 'complicated, poorly understood dynamical system', namely the human brain, may be useful for economists. Michele Boldrin (University of California, Los Angeles) makes out a strong case for the application of chaos theory in economics. David

Ruelle (of I.H.E.S., France) reviews the ideas of 'chaotic' dynamics and their possible applications to economics. Stuart A. Kauffman (School of Medicine, University of Pennsylvania) states: 'Like living systems bootstrapping their own evolution, an economic system bootstraps its own evolution' and suggests that the 'web' concept used in biology can be profitably applied to understand that process of evolution. Richard Palmer (Department of Physics, Duke University) shows how the development of *spin glass* theory has enabled the application of statistical mechanics to diverse complex systems and suggests that the extension of this theory may be used in economics, especially to deal with combinational optimisation problems.

The emphasis in some of these papers is clearly on techniques but, in the Report of the Final Plenary Session, there is a section on questions that natural scientists posed to economists, and their responses. One of the questions was: 'Why do economists downplay or ignore the role of psychological, sociological and political forces in economic systems?' It is reported that answers from the economists included: 'such forces really aren't important'; 'they are being studied in certain specific cases' etc. There is also the comment: 'None of these answers was entirely satisfying to the natural scientists, and their variability concerned some of us' (p. 258). In short, the natural scientists were looking for the substantive issues in economics while the economists weren't going much beyond formal statements. This issue became more focused in the second question. 'Rational Expectations (RE) theory with infinite foresight appears obviously wrong. Why is it so well accepted?' (p. 259). The summary of the discussion says:

Perhaps 'obviously wrong' is too strong, but most of the natural scientists were certainly disturbed by this theory. . . . There seems to be too much emphasis on determinism in RE theory especially since even deterministic dynamics does not necessarily allow long-term predictions because of the divergence of trajectories. Similarly, any requirement for a *unique* answer appears groundless in such cases. Multiple equilibrium are seen as natural (and perhaps even expected) by the natural scientists but not by the economists.

In other words, determinism, uniqueness, etc., which economists consider as the essential elements of 'scientific' analysis and for which they hold on to RE assumptions, appeared to the other scientists as anachronistic and, indeed, to go against scientific procedures as they understood them.

The economists tried to respond to the question in various ways, but apparently the differences in the basic understanding about 'science' continued. For, the report goes on to say:

'Several ways of improving the RE models were suggested. One was to add a modicum of irrationality. Although this makes some sense and has been tried, in practice it is not liked because of its ambiguity; there are too many different ways of being irrational, whereas rationality is presumed unique. This demonstrates again the desire for unique deterministic answers. In fact, many economists are hoping for a theory that is much *more* deterministic than RE (p.278).

In a summary of the Workshop, Kenneth Arrow admits that economics based on general competitive equilibrium (GCE) theory and linear stochastic systems cannot be claimed to be adequate to comprehend and explain a wide range of empirical problems.

The presence and persistence of cyclical fluctuations in the economy as a whole of irregular timing and amplitude are not consistent with a view that an economy tends to return to equilibrium state after any disturbance. The persistence of unemployment undermines the assumption that prices and wages work to reduce imbalances between supply and demand. Equilibrium theory would tend to suggest that as technology spreads throughout the world, per capita national incomes would tend to converge, but any such tendency is very weak indeed. Similarly, different ethnic and class groups and economic regions within a country show only fitful tendencies to converge balanced by the equal likelihood of divergence. Instead of stochastic steady states, we observe that stability tends to vary greatly over time. . . . The securities markets have always shown great volatility, while the international financial markets, on which currencies are exchanged, have shown virtual disorganisation since exchange rates were allowed to float, although most economists would have regarded free-exchange rate movements as an aid to stabilization (p. 278).

In the light of these blatant shortcomings Arrow expressed the hope that economics would learn and benefit from the experience of other disciplines.

The most promising piece in the volume from the point of view of any serious rethinking about the conceptualisation of and analytical procedure in economics is by John H. Holland, Division of Computer Science and Engineering of the University of Michigan, with the title, 'The Global Economy as an Adaptive Process', which is dealt with in the text of the Chapter in section XXVI.

In Chapter 5 I comment on what economists, especially neo-classical economists, consider to be the nature of science and the analytical procedures arising from it.

5

RETHINKING ECONOMICS

'Newtonianism' in Neo-classical Economics

I

What is the nature of the economy? Economics as a body of knowledge, is an attempt to answer that question, just as physics tries to explain the physical world. In both cases the underlying assumption is that the field of enquiry is some aspect of reality and that what the intellectual effort produces must illumine and explain that reality, but should not be allowed to become a substitute for it.[1]

If there is a reality referred to as 'the Indian economy', my involvement with it has shown that economic theories in general have not been particularly helpful in throwing light on the many complex aspects of that reality. In particular, neo-classical economics, in which I had my grounding and which claims to be universal, was found to be too limited to comprehend it and make sense of it. A selective survey of the evolution of economics as a field of study has shown a plurality of approaches to economic problems. Instead of trying to make a selection from among them I have tried, in Chapter 4, to lay bare the characteristics of real-life economies as they evolve over time. The understanding of real-life economies as evolving complex entities necessitates a rethinking of economics as a subject of study. I have neither the desire nor the competence to restructure economics, though I am convinced it is necessary. What I propose to do in this concluding chapter is to suggest, in rather general terms, how it may be done.

II

In Chapter 3 I have indicated that the pioneers of neo-classical economics were engaged in the task of taking over the various strands of economic analysis of the classical school, particularly of Adam Smith and David Ricardo, unifying them and providing them a rigorous scientific orientation. The model they had accepted was Newtonian physics and in view of the enormous prestige the discipline had at that time,[2] imitating it was thought to be a great achievement. In fact, a great deal of what may be described as the Newtonian approach had seeped into practically all branches of knowledge long before the pioneers of the neo-classical school appeared on the scene, for it was widely held that Newton had discovered the language that nature speaks and obeys. 'The term "Newtonian" was now applied to everything that dealt with a system of laws... even to all situations in which natural order on the one side and moral, social, and political order on the other could be expressed in terms of an all-embracing harmony' (Prigogine and Stengers 1984: 29). John Locke, thus, claimed to be a philosopher of 'natural law' and aimed to produce a comprehensive theory of society based on the properties of human nature; Helvetius later compared the role of the principle of self-interest in the social world to the role of the law of gravitation in the physical world; Bentham picked it up and produced a social total out of it, the greatest happiness of the greatest number; and in his *Theory of Moral Sentiments*, Adam Smith showed himself to be a philosopher in the natural law tradition and carried the same spirit into his *Wealth of Nations*.

As briefly indicated in Chapter 3, the founders of the neo-classical school made a conscious effort to fashion the science of economics according to the Newtonian principles. Among them five at least, had a special bearing on neo-classical economics. First, Newtonian science postulated a universe of order and precision with programmed internal laws of its own. To discover these immutable, universal laws of the universe was the role of science. Science, therefore, came to be identified with uniformity, universality, precision and predictability. These attributes of science, however, were achieved through the process of abstraction whereby the phenomenon studied was prepared and isolated, until it approximated some ideal situation that was possibly unattainable physically, but conformed to the conceptual schema adopted. It was within such a closed or 'canned' segment of reality, carved out through mental and experimental operations that regularities and uniformities were observed and on the basis of which predictions were made. The neo-classical propensity of making even far-fetched assumptions (e.g., constant returns to scale as a basic assumption in production) for 'convenience of analysis' can be traced back to this Newtonian approach.

Second, as Capra points out: 'The Newtonian model of matter was atomistic ... Newton assumed matter to be homogeneous. The basic building block of matter could be of different sizes, but consisted of the same stuff' (1983: 51). The system and its basic units were so closely connected in Newton's concept of the physical universe that it was immaterial whether one started from the system and worked down into its primary units or started from them and worked up to the system. The system, thus, is simply its units or parts put together. This is the basis of neo-classical economics taking homogeneous individuals (all self-interested despite other differences) as the basic units in the economic universe and treating the economy as the sum of its individuals. True, the individuals get partitioned into producers, consumers, etc., but that is only a matter of analytical procedure.

Third, the system is mechanical in structure, the 'great machine of the universe'. The reason is spelt out by Prigogine and Stengers. 'Why did the clock almost immediately become the very symbol of world order?' they ask, and go on to say: 'A watch is a contrivance governed by a rationality that lies outside itself, by a plan that is blindly executed by its inner workings. The clock world is a metaphor suggestive of God the Watchmaker, the rational master of a robotlike nature' (1984: 46). Neo-classical economics has taken over this view as well. The economy, left to itself, is a well-functioning machine, the rationality of whose component parts is to perform in such a way as to keep the machine in working condition. The rational behaviour that neo-classical theory attributes to the 'agents' in its economic system is not related to any independent objective that they may have, but what the analyst imposes on them to achieve *his* objective of showing that the system is in a state of equilibrium. The justification of this imposition also is Newtonian. If the universe is rational, so must its agents (or parts), for the universe is thought of as nothing other than its component parts. If the clock has a rationality, its spring must share the same rationality: indeed, the spring cannot have any rationality other than its role as a component of the clock. Neo-classical theory has this same attitude towards the agents of its system. All of them, including the much celebrated 'sovereign' consumers *must* play the role assigned to them (by those who have constructed the system); they are simply 'role-playing zombies', to borrow an expression from Law and Lodge (1984: 225). Designing the system in this manner has other implications too. Referring to scientists following Newton, Roger Hausheer has remarked that, 'they sought all-embracing schemes, universal unifying frameworks, within which everything that exists could be shown to be systematically—i.e., logically or causally—interconnected, vast structures in which there should be no gaps left open for spontaneous, unattended developments, where everything that occurs should be, at least in principle, wholly explicable in terms of immutable general laws'.[3] A great advantage, indeed, for those who want to make everything predictable, in principle, at least.

The fourth feature that neo-classical economics has taken over from Newtonian science can also be shown to be derived from the depiction of the system as a machine. A clock has motion, but no change. Taking the principle over to social systems (including the economy) the implication is that there is no temporal transformation. It is on this basis that neo-classical economics insists that the central problem of economics remains the same always, being that of scarcity. When the central problematic of the subject is defined in this manner, it has its consequences on the analytical system as a whole. The main agents have to be identified as consumers and producers insisting on a separation between the consumption and production decisions as a necessary and crucial aspect of the analysis, however ahistorical the procedure may be. That separation, in turn, becomes the basis for the laws of supply and demand which, then, have to be treated as universal. The accent on timelessness and universality that may appear to be the theoretical strength of neo-classical economics, however, becomes a major analytical limitation in that the theory does not, and cannot, provide any guidelines for the identification of specific economic problems, temporal and spatial in nature, that require to be examined and interpreted.

Finally, the mechanical analogue that neo-classical theory has taken over from Newtonian science also defines its procedure of enquiry. Since the system, its structure and its rationality can all be taken as given, the observer can view it from outside and can understand it by reasoning alone. On this aspect the Newtonian basis of neo-classical economics is reinforced by the Cartesian heritage. Descartes, it is well known, considered the world as characterised by order and rationality and claimed that the world could best be apprehended through an appeal to human reason alone. Neo-classical economics demonstrates this dependence on a priori reasoning. So strong is the emphasis on logic in neo-classical economics that two writers have expressed the view that 'in reality most standard economists were descendants not of Isaac Newton, but Rene Descartes' (Wilber and Harrison, in Marr and Raj 1982: 245)

III

Neo-classical theory's reliance on the postulational method which Koopmans refers to as 'the logical structure of our economic knowledge' (1957: 132) provides justification to this contention. Without going into the details of the method which I have dealt with elsewhere (Kurien 1970: Lecture 1) the privileged position it gives to logic and the manner in which it relates a priori logic to empirical facts may be briefly examined depending largely on Koopmans' exposition (1957, Essay 2).

Koopmans quite explicitly states that economics is an empirical science and that progress in economics comes about through continual interaction of observation and reasoning. However, he also says that it is impossible to say which comes first, observation or reasoning. His treatment of the postulational method leaves little doubt that procedurally at least, if not ontologically, reasoning is accorded priority.

The postulational method draws a sharp distinction between what Carnap designates 'syntactical' and 'semantical', or between reasoning and recognition of facts in theory formulation, for the better protection of both, according to Koopmans. At the syntactical level, theory is taken to be of the form 'If P then T', where P is the postulate and T theory, derived according to the rules of inference from the postulate, or a set of postulates. The postulates are analytic a priori propositions which are concerned with the meaning of words and their truth or falsity can be shown by pure reason, prior to observation. At the formal level, therefore, theory is a derivation from the set of postulates and is certain and universal in the sense that, given the postulates, the theory (or set of theories) must necessarily follow. Theories which are but formal statements assume substance when a transformation is made from the syntactical to the semantic level where they take the general form 'Since P, therefore T'. The transformation is achieved if there are objects in the world of experience which have the properties formu-

lated by the postulates. Where this condition is satisfied, the transformed semantic version comes to have the status of a scientific theory,
a statement about the empirical or real world. A scientific theory,
therefore, consists of two conceptually distinct aspects—a formal
frame which is logical in its structure and has no connection to reality,
and an empirical content directly related to the realities of the world of
experience that the science concerned deals with. As already noted, it is
this separation of the syntactical and the semantic that is distinctive
about the postulational method.

That separation poses an immediate problem of establishing the
nature of the relationship between the logical and the factual which is
widely discussed in the literature. Initially it was thought that facts
verify the logic. But soon it turned out that the same set of factual data
was compatible with different theories, sometimes even competing
theories or hypotheses derived on the basis of logical inferences.[4]
Hence it had to be admitted that while an empirical test may be used to
reject a theory, it could not form the basis for confirming or accepting
it. Granted that facts are finite, but a priori theoretical propositions
could, conceptually at any rate, be infinite, this was hardly surprising.
There was, therefore, a shift from verification to the Popperian concept
of falsification. According to this view, a test for a robust scientific
theory is whether it is empirically falsifiable. While conceptually falsification appears to be a more satisfactory alternative, it shares with
verification an underlying problem of the postulational method: the
assumption that 'facts' exist out there, somewhere, to be gathered and
processed without being influenced by (or contaminated by) theoretical
considerations. Such cannot be the case if 'facts' themselves are embedded in or derived from theoretical formulations.

In view of these difficulties of working out the links between logical theories and emporical facts, the tendency in economic analysis
has been either to indulge in various forms of 'data massaging' to get
them to conform to one's favourite theories or to get away completely
from the messy world of facts and to concentrate on the neat and
secure world of logic where the mind reigns supreme. It is the latter
that has brought to economics the prestige it has acquired in recent
decades for rigour and precision, but which has also tended to take it
away from real-life problems as I have indicated in Chapter 1.

There are more serious problems associated with the postulational
method which can be brought out with specific reference to Koopmans'

handling of it. When he is not directly dealing with the postulational method, Koopmans has a proper appreciation of the interaction of reasoning and observation in economics. He also recognises the extraordinarily difficult task of uncovering the foundations on which economic knowledge rests. 'How much of it is derived from observations, how much from reasoning? From what assertions does the reasoning start?' (1957: 131). These certainly are the foundational questions. Let us see how Koopmans deals with them.

On the question of the basic assertions from which reasoning starts, Koopmans uncritically accepts Samuelson's position, expressed in his *Foundations of Economic Analysis*, that a wide variety of problems arising in diverse parts of economic theory are manifestations of a single principle—maximisation under constraints. Koopmans says that he is not concerned with the realism of that statement, but that he accepts the fact 'that a large body of economic thought has taken off from such premises' (Koopmans 1957: 5). When he turns to postulational analysis later on, the statement about maximisation under constraints becomes one of the postulates defined as 'any premises used in any piece of economic analysis, which are not themselves conclusions from earlier parts of the reasoning in the same piece of analysis' (ibid: 132). Koopmans, therefore, tacitly admits that the basic premise of economics is the *logical* proposition about maximisation under constraints. However, he invokes Lionel Robbins' well-known statement that everyone knows the postulates of economics to be 'indisputable facts of experience relating to the way in which the scarcity of goods which is the subject-matter of our science actually shows itself in the world of reality' (ibid: 135). So, the postulates are not merely syntactical statements: they have already been transformed into semantical statements by interpretation. The interpretation is achieved (as Koopmans admits) by the use of 'certain key words, such as consumer, worker, entrepreneur, commodity' (ibid: 132–33).

Some comments are necessary on this issue. The moment economic theory takes on semantic interpretation, it comes to have reference to some specific form of economy at some particular period in time. Even in a postulational sense, the universality of economic theory is only 'hypothetico-deductive universality', confined strictly to the realm of logic, and not to the realm of the economy or economies. This is not indicative of the nature of theory. Rather, it is an affirmation of reality, that the nature of the economy (and consequently terms related to it) is geo-historically conditioned. That is what terms such as consumer, worker and community testify. Second, while in the realm of theory construction taken in the abstract, a separation between the syntactical and the semantical appears feasible and desirable, in the actual process of theory formulation in a particular field of enquiry such a separation is hardly practicable.

Koopmans realises this and admits: 'We have thus been led to the realization that neither are postulates of economic theory entirely self-evident, nor are the implications of various sets of postulates readily tested by observation' (Koopmans 1957: 142). So, the syntactic-semantic separation is not a distinction between reasoning and facts, as is normally assumed, but is related to the very process of reasoning suggesting that except perhaps in the realm of logic and mathematics there is no such thing as reasoning in the abstract. Reasoning in a particular field of enquiry can only be in terms of its own substantive aspects. On this Adam Smith was not wrong, after all!

Koopmans' treatment of the postulational nature of economic theory leads him to some tight corners when he enters the world of reality after the extensive tour of the realm of logic. Recognising indivisibility and the related increasing returns to scale as important features of real-life production processes, he is forced to admit that these aspects of reality are abstracted from the model of competitive economy whose logic he had expounded using the postulational method (1957: 148). Pursuing the theme further he concedes: 'We have not mentioned such obvious departures from perfect competition as product differentiation in order to emphasize that recognition of the 'physical' aspects of reality mentioned above already destroys the basis of the theory of competitive equilibrium' (ibid: 147). In other words, the theory of competitive equilibrium is based on such obvious 'facts' as that individuals can arrange their preferences in an order, and that there are more than one factor of production, but other obvious 'facts' like indivisibility and product differentiation destroy it! It is then clear that the theory of competitive equilibrium expounded with meticulous rigour is not intended to throw light on real-life problems, but simply to demonstrate the manner in which inferences can be logically drawn out, if the validity of the premises is not called into question. Nor can such theories be considered as first approximations to a complicated reality. One is entitled to know how the assumption of perfect divisibility is a first approximation to the problem of indivisibility or how the assumption of free and perfect information can be thought of as the first approximation to the problem of informational asymmetry. The fact is that theories like a smoothly functioning competitive economy, are not meant to be approximations to reality. Instead, they are meant to suggest what conditions are necessary if a complex rugged reality is to approximate the neatness and smoothness of a mentally constructed image. That is a very different task indeed, and a perverse one at that.

Features of a Complex Economy

IV

Whatever may be the merits of a theoretical system such as neo-classical economics, its limitations become strikingly evident when pitted against *any* real-life economy. In attempting to be a concept of the economy that transcends time and space, it has become far too empty to be meaningful; a mere caricature of reality, possibly a sophisticated one that demonstrates an exceptionally high level of architectural skills. Morishima puts it well when he says that General Equilibrium Theory presents 'an exaggerated and deformed view of economic society' (1991: 69). If real-life economies are rugged, uneven and multilayered, is it possible, or even proper, to represent them as flat, smooth, level grounds with straight lines and right angles? That is the question.

How, then, are real-life economies to be approached? What I have attempted in Chapter 4 is a procedure to do so, to move away from 'the logic of concepts to the logic of reality', to use an expression of Godelier's (1972: 131). That procedure involves three closely related aspects: recognising the economy as an organic totality of objects and relations or a 'system'; specifically tracing these objects and relations; and capturing their transformation over time. When they are taken together they depict an evolutionary complex system of the kind that has been narrated in Chapter 4. The three aspects mentioned are so intimately connected that to separate them is to do violence to the totality that they represent, and yet for expository reasons it has to be done. I shall, therefore, deal with them in the order given earlier, taking care to see that the discussion does not become too abstract.[5]

The term 'the Indian economy' conveys something of the sense of totality. However it captures that sense only partially, and somewhat misleadingly, if it only refers to the standard macro perspective. The macro perspective is an aggregation achieved by converting all objects that constitute the system (the variety of goods and services) into a uniform value category. For certain purposes this is a useful procedure although some questions will have to be raised about it later. But it gives the impression that the economy is simply a collection of goods and services. What happens to the agents in the system, the consumers, producers and others whose role is recognised as part of whatever is designated as the economy? Also, what about the lower-level totalities that these agents form part of—the consumers in their households, for instance, and the producers in their farms and factories? If, therefore, households and factories also form part of the Indian economy, it is a totality somewhat different from the sum of the goods and services. In fact, when households and factories are also recognised as part of the Indian economy, the possibility of aggregation (of the kind done in the case of goods and services) almost disappears and yet the notion of the totality has to be retained. It is, therefore, necessary to think of the totality or the 'whole' that is the Indian economy, not as a sum of its parts, but as a totality of partly autonomous and reciprocally interacting parts.

It follows too that the totality of the Indian economy has to be seen as having other totalities within it, or a collection of interacting totalities. These totalities within, or subtotalities, are related to the Indian economy in two ways: they are at different levels and they overlap in terms of their own parts. The totality that is the economy, therefore, is a multi-layered one with a distinct internal structure of its own, a dimension missed when a macro view is adopted which is just a view from outside, so to say. The perception of the economy as a totality with an internal structure is reinforced when the Indian economy, in turn, is seen as a subtotality within another totality, the global economy. Chapter 4 has referred to these subtotal parts as subeconomies.

The sense in which the expression 'total' (or 'whole') is used will become clearer when the second aspect, 'parts', is examined. It has been indicated that standard economic theory takes individuals as the basic element or part of the economy, although there is no attempt to aggregate the individuals to form the economy; when the aggregation is done it is only of goods and services. Chapter 4, on the other hand, has insisted on considering *groups* of individuals as the parts of the economy. This is not because individuals are unimportant in studying the economy, but because as a matter of fact, individuals do not exist and function as individuals, but only as members of some groups. Groups were seen to be different kinds of individuals in relation to one another. In a sense, groups are also totals with their own internal structures. Structured relationships of individuals within groups were identified as institutions and when such groups are taken as the unit of analysis, the units were shown to be in relation to one another within the economy, again through forms of institutions.

Capra uses the word 'holons' coined by Arthus Koestler to refer to these parts or subsystems which are both wholes and parts. According to him each holon has two opposite but complementary tendencies : 'an integrative tendency to function as part of the larger whole, and a self-assertive tendency to preserve its individual autonomy' (1983: 27). These two tendencies hold the system together, but also cause changes in it, as was shown in Chapter 4 while dealing with the relationship between individuals and groups.

The groups, parts or units within the system that is the economy must, therefore, be seen in terms of their own structure and character-istics on the one hand, and in relationship to one another and thus to the system as a whole on the other hand. In respect of their own characteristics the parts are likely to be diverse and heterogeneous and the patterns of relationships will display considerable variety. Hence, the economy must be treated as a totality of heterogeneous units and a variety of relationships. Because of this heterogeneity and variety, the units and the relationships must be specifically examined, each in terms of its own distinct features.

But more than an anatomical or morphological enquiry (of the units, in particular) is necessary. For, neither the units nor the rela-tionships remain invariant over time. The units have their internal dynamics that bring about change. Change comes from outside also because of the relationships that the units have with others. The inter-action of the internal and the external leads to the transformation of the units, to the metamorphosis of the relations and to changes in the composition of the units within their larger totality. It is a combina-tion of these that comes to be perceived as the evolution or transfor-mation of the system. The system, then, is always in a state of flux and change, in which there will be elements of both continuity and discontinuity.

Real-life economies, especially at the national level most common in the study of economics, can be seen to have all the three aspects indicated earlier: they are systems with subsystems within them; these subsystems are heterogeneous with a variety of relations among them; and they are constantly in the process of change—evolutionary com-plex systems, for short.[6] The complexity that this view of the economy communicates may appear to be difficult to handle at first, but the professional task of an economist is to make sense of that bewildering and complex entity just as a physician has the responsibility to enlighten those who approach him about the working of that equally complex system, the human body.

V

It would have occurred to the discerning reader that the treatment in section IV earlier is a systematised version of the detailed discussion of the economy taken up in Chapter IV. The order has been reversed: in Chapter 4 the emphasis was on the *evolution* of the economy as a complex system, whereas section IV begins with complexity and goes on to show that the evolutionary process is an intrinsic aspect of it. It is important to note also that the systematised version of section IV is built on the substantive themes dealt with in Chapter 4. A brief re-statement of those themes will be helpful to move on to a discussion, later in this section, of the implications of viewing the economy as an evolving complex system.

The economy, consisting of a set of social relationships related to the decisions and actions that human beings unavoidably get into as they strive to ensure subsistence and go beyond it, deals with the material and mental factors that make their attempt possible and successful. In studying the economy, the basic units have to be groups of individuals held together by structures and agenda for action. The evolution of the economy consists of the structuring and altering of the nexus of relations within groups and between groups and the resulting transformation of the groups themselves. At the lowest level, the internal structure, agenda and the pattern of inter-group relationships are related to the extent and manner of control that groups have over physical resources. Groups tend to get differentiated on that basis. At a slightly higher level, the relationships among groups come to be mediated which, in turn, gives rise to groups specialising in the mediatory role. The nature and functioning of a multi-unit economy undergo changes when intermediation comes to have a major role because apart from the basic asymmetry in terms of control over physical resources, it will also alter the inherent information asymmetry among the groups leading to greater differentiation among them. At this stage, conflict of interest between groups emerges as a major factor in their relationship.

At a still higher level, the pursuit of surplus becomes the objective of some groups in the system and a further asymmetry is introduced between those who are able and eager to pursue surplus in the abstract and those who are concerned with the diversity of goods. A further differentiation appears when claims to the surplus and transactions in such claims, as well as the intermediaries dealing with them, come to occupy prominent place in the system.

National economies are a confluence of such wide variety of participating groups, objectives, strategies and activities. National economies, such as India's are even more complex because they contain within them the many stages that other economies may have jettisoned in the process of evolution.

There can be no doubt that a complex totality of that kind can be penetrated only by entering into it through its constituent parts, the groups or 'organisations'. And yet this is one of the most neglected areas in standard economics though its significance is beginning to dawn on the profession. In a recent writing Stiglitz presents the issue thus:

> Most production in modern economies occurs within organizations, and this production is regulated only to a limited extent by prices. . . . Many of the organizations which play an important role in resource allocation, including governmental organizations, are not profit-maximizers. These observations make it clear that if economists wish to understand how resources in modern economies are allocated, we must understand what goes on inside organizations. Even if the Arrow–Debreu model accurately depicted how market economies behave—that is the relations between and among households and firms—it would provide insight into only a fraction of all economic activity. (1991b: 15).

But how are economic organisations to be studied? Herbert Simon whose contributions in this area have been widely recognised indicates a procedure in a recent paper, though the discussion is confined to organisations of production (1991).[7] Noting that motivations (the criterion that standard economic theory associates with organisations) are certainly important in understanding organisations, Simon points out that in a typical production organisation or firm where most members are employees, they cannot be expected to have the maximisation of profits by the firm as *their* motivation. From this perspective, it is necessary to examine the internal composition and heterogeneity of members and motivations within the firm. Associated with it are the elements of authority, hierarchy and coordination which must also be taken into account in analysing an organisation. Equally important is the sense of loyalty that must be considered along with the variety of reward structures. Simon acknowledges that while these aspects must first be seen as internal to the organisation, their effectiveness and relative significance are matters decided by society at large. Another point that Simon makes is that these issues in general are common to organisations in general, although their nuances may vary depending on whether the organisation is a profit-making, non-profit or governmental one.

The discussion on groups in sections III and IV of Chapter 4 has already touched upon many of these issues by insisting on the need to understand the internal structure of groups. But a checklist of items that go to make a group is not adequate to understand its internal structure. If the group is a structured totality (at its level), it is important to establish through specific empirical enquiries how the group has constituted that totality. This is particularly so because unlike production organisations which Simon deals with, the economy as envisaged in Chapter 4 consists of many more groups of diverse features and characteristics, households, intermediaries and the state. In fact, while it is useful to categorise groups in this manner, the argument has been that they get differentiated over time and that, therefore, without freezing the catego ries (for instance, into distinctly different ones as 'households' and 'firms' as neo-classical theory does) it is necessary to identify the groups temporally and spatially (i.e., contextually in the broad sense of the term) and to analyse them in terms of their specificities. It is an empirical task, not a mere logical exercise. But it is more than a fact-finding enquiry, particularly of a purely quantitative nature. What is called for is an approach informed by the 'logic of reality'.

Two major ingredients of that approach may be indicated. The first is a recognition, as Arrow has pointed out (cf. Chapter 4, section III), that to understand groups (or organisations) history is an important aspect. To become historical in this sense is to trace the lattice of links of the past and to comprehend their bearing on the internal structure of the group. Second, granted that the internal structure responds to links of the present also, the group can be understood only in terms of the variety of links or relationships that currently shape its agenda and activities. Thus, the group has to be situated within a diachronic and synchronic context.

When such an attempt is made, each group can be seen to be 'a specific structural complexity' (to borrow an expression from Charles

Bettleheim) with unique features of its own, like individual species in the biological sciences. But if the group is studied not as an end in itself, but as a part of a larger totality, a grouping of the groups will be permissible and possible because there will be other ones with similar characteristics, and in any case groups as analytical categories are constituted totalities.[8]

This implies that groups have to be probed inwards into their constituent units and outwards into larger groups of which they are the constituent units. It is such probing that enables one to capture the heterogeneity of the group on the one hand, and the many institutionalised patterns of coordination within groups and between groups on the other hand. Once it is recognised that the totality that one is concerned with consists of parts at different levels, it will be necessary to direct the enquiry at different levels as well. This aspect is accepted in economics as the macro and micro views of the economy. However, it is more in the nature of viewing a clock and its parts, both being taken as given. But if the economy is thought of as a complex system, its different layers are essentially a matter of perspectives. The procedure may be explained with reference to a simple illustration. A ball of thread will appear like a dot when viewed from a great distance, as a three-dimensional solid when viewed at a closer range and as a single dimensional long piece of thread rolled into a ball-like appearance when examined closer still.[9] Each one of these is a valid observation though none of them provides a 'full' or 'correct' description of the entity being observed. There is no way of combining the observations to get a 'comprehensive' view of the entity, and yet the three together provide a much better understanding through description of what is named a ball of thread. The same is true of visualising a statue of which one has been able to see only two-dimensional photographs taken from different angles. Here, again, the many photographs cannot be put together to produce a 'true' image of the statue, but the perceptions from the different angles lead to a better comprehension of the entity concerned. Similarly, producing different cross-sectional two-dimensional profiles is a standard procedure in trying to probe into a complex organ like the human heart.

A constantly changing economy is far more complex than a ball of thread, a statue or a human heart. There is no way of capturing it or depicting it fully and different procedures have to be used to comprehend its nature and working. The error lies in absolutising any one of these procedures or in insisting that in the final analysis every one of them can be reduced to some one pattern. Even the micro and macro approaches to the economy which show that inferences drawn from one need not be valid in the other warn against the common, but erroneous procedure of reductionism.

In *The Economy* (1992b) I had suggested that what is needed to envisage the economy as consisting of its variety of units and their diverse interactions is a 'micro-global' approach. But since then I have realised that such an approach, while it is better than other standard procedures, is still rather inadequate. Two reasons may be indicated. First, working on *Global Capitalism and the Indian Economy* (1994), I have come to have an appreciation of the vast difference between the perception of the economy and its operations in terms of *real* analysis and in terms of *financial* analysis. Economists on the whole are much more at home in the former and their perception of the economy, even of the inter-national economy, is essentially in terms of *real* variables. But those who perceive the same inter-national economy in terms of finance see it as an integrated global economy whose characteristics and working then appear to be very different from the way economists have traditionally thought of the inter-national economy. The second reason is a more familiar one in the context of studies on economic development. Even where there is no explicit units-and-links analysis, it is common practice now to treat the less developed (national) economies as consisting of two different segments or sectors usually referred to as the organised and unorganised sectors or the formal and informal sectors. If these two sectors are viewed in terms of the units-and-links approach, what is being conveyed is that the (national) economy consists of two different alignments, one of them consisting of modern production units catering to high income consumers and the other traditional production units servicing low income consumers. It is presumed that the links between the units is organised or formal in the former and unorganised or informal in the latter. In fact, such dualism is considered to be one of the distinguishing features of the less developed economies.[10] This dual economy conceptualisation is neither robust nor realistic. Anyone who is familiar with the ground realities of these economies will know that the stone wall or iron curtain that 'theory' sets up between the two sectors do not exist at all, and that there are many forms of close links between the two.[11] But there is an underlying principle in the dual economy conceptualisation—that the units within the system and their links establish different circuits which can be separated out in some instances, but are more often of a criss-crossing nature. This is not a peculiarity of the less developed economies either. Recent studies of real-life developed economies show that they too have different circuits within them and that they tend to overlap.[12] If further proof is required of the real-life counterparts of criss-crossing circuits, even a quick look at the global economy will bring out several of them. Criss-crossing circuits within real-life economies constitute one area where economic theories have completely distorted the perception.

If these real-life issues are to be taken seriously, one has to admit that there are no easy procedures and that there are vast areas of ignorance in the economists' perceptions of the working of the economy at different levels. But as a writer has remarked, ignorance is not just a blank space on a person's mental map; 'fashioning better maps of our ignorance is an important step towards knowledge'.[13]

VI

To gain further insights into the nature of an evolving complex economy, let us examine the relationship between the human beings and physical resources within the system reflecting on the treatment of the theme in Chapter 4. The first thing to be noted is that this relationship, so crucial in understanding a wide range of specific economic problems, especially the nature of production, is mediated through groups, underlining the social embeddedness of the economy. In the treatment of the rudimentary economy, the specific aspects of that relationship within which such a social context have been dealt with. Moving a step beyond, it can be seen that the relationship between human beings and physical resources is the first basis of the differentiation of the groups: the *Ha* households experience resource constraint while the *Hb* households are under labour constraint. In turn, this asymmetry greatly influences the relationship between the groups. The introduction of money brings in a new pattern of controls over resources and this new factor further influences the relationship between groups. It gives rise to a new process within the system, intermediation, and a to a new kind of group specialising on that process. From then on, there is a tendency for economic activities to become quickened and for both production and trade to expand mutually reinforcing one another up to a stage. The increased production results in the augmentation of surplus which becomes the basis of further differentiation, a new process of intermediation and new forms of controls over resources and over the labour power of human beings.

These are, in one sense, historical processes, and in another sense contemporary realities as the present is made up of the past and is its repository. Hence, at any given time the functioning of a (national) economy will be shaped by the social and institutional arrangements of the past that have a bearing on the distribution of resources among the groups that constitute it, and the generation of surplus within the system, its appropriation and patterns of utilisation. All these aspects, therefore, must also be specifically and empirically enquired into in trying to come to grips with the nature of the economy. This is particularly so because relationships within the system, the working of markets, the processes of lending and borrowing are all heavily dependent on such institutional parameters. The tendency to treat them as given and hence not subject to scrutiny and change is not valid, though very much a part of standard economic analysis.

These institutional parameters have a bearing on the long term stability of the groups and consequently of the system as a whole. The groups, it has been noted already, hold together two opposing tendencies, the attempt of its members to assert their individuality and independence on the one hand, and their readiness to submit to a collective on the other. These account for conflict and harmony in the group. Because of the heterogeneity of the members it is unlikely that they will view all situations and issues alike. This is specially true about their responses to signals from outside: some may see in them opportunities; others may think of them as threats. The internal structure of the group, especially how heterogeneous it is within, will, therefore, determine whether it will hold together or not when confronted with situations that they do not routinely deal with.

The attitude of the members towards physical resources is one of the main determinants of their heterogeneity and consequently of the stability of the group. The classic example is India's village economies before the colonial era and their disintegration as a consequence of the colonial impact. Using the stylised form of Chapter 4, a typical pre-colonial village economy could be presented as a composite system consisting of Ha, Hb and Hc households. The first two depended on land for their livelihood, while Hc consisted primarily of service households. Within the *Jajmani* system, there was a complementarity of functions of these members that held the group together in 'harmony' in spite of the many forms of injustice. But the colonial forces succeeded in weaning away some of the *Hc* households from the group by offering them better prospects outside. The internal integrity of the group was thus disrupted leading to their disintegration.[14] Such instances are not a thing of the past either. In the contemporary commercialisation of agriculture in villages the landed *Hb* households perceive new opportunities to improve their position while for the landless *Ha* households, it is, for a variety of reasons, a threat to their activities and existence.[15] It is, of course, not necessary that the *Ha* households are always the losers; the point is to note the differential perceptions of the members of a group about new situations, their differential impacts and, frequently, the attempt of the beneficiaries to project the changes as being advantageous to the group as a whole. At a different level the same phenomenon can be seen when a new situation presents opportunities of prospects to those whose main objective is to augment their surplus while those who strive for survival interpret it as a threat.[16] In fact, if one is searching for a single clue to the understanding of the working of national economies such as India's, it will be the differing perceptions of those whose primary interest is the augmentation of the surplus and of those whose main concern is survival.

A broader interpretation of these asymmetries of attitude towards resources and perceptions of opportunities is necessary. This can be illustrated with reference to two of the major types of groups or units in most modern economies, households (*H* units) and firms (*F* units). Households seldom consider human labour in the abstract. They think of their members as particular individuals with distinct physical features and mental faculties. A main item on the agenda of the households is to develop the physical and mental abilities of their members: material resources are a means to that end. In terms of the substantive essentials, it may be stated that survival and growth of their members is the primary objective and rising above that level is the secondary objective of households. The significance of households is that among all the units in the economy, the birth, growth and survival of human beings are their direct responsibility. At one stage in history, they are solely responsible for these vital tasks: at other times and under different arrangements, other units in the system may partially take over some of these tasks.

The *F* units, on the other hand, have a different orientation and agenda. Augmenting resources and exercising control over them is their primary task. They may come to have some interest in the well-being and personal growth of their members, but this can be only a secondary concern of theirs. An appreciation of these differences of the major units in the economy towards human beings and resources is important for an understanding of the working of the economy.

However, the significance of these differences can, and does, change over time. At a certain level of performance of the economy, and with necessary institutional arrangements, the F units can turn out to be specialised agencies to which the households delegate the function of augmenting resources because of the facilities that the F units as contractual entities come to have to raise productivity through specialisation in production, organisation of work and technological innovation. If and when this happens, the F units may be thought of as managers of the surplus resources of the H units carrying out certain objectives specifically assigned to them. This complementary relationship between the F units and the H units, of course, holds good only for a subset of the H units, designated in Chapter 4 as Hd. If this distinction is not taken note of, the complementary relationship between the F units and the H units will be an exaggeration or distortion.

These considerations suggest that the working of the economy at any given time can be grasped only by taking into account the asymmetries in the distribution of resources, the differentiation of the major units of the system that take place over time and the differences in interests and perceptions of the groups concerned. It may be worth examining how different theoretical systems have dealt with these issues. Classical theory recognised the resource asymmetries of the major participants of the economy and the differences in sectional interests related to it. But it assumed (with some evidence to support it) that capital accumulation and growth would benefit, in the long run at least, all classes in society. Marx, in *Capital*, by taking into account the F units and the Ha units featured the element of conflict in the system. Neo-classical theory by accepting the Hd units as the symbol of households concentrated on the complementarity of households and firms and thus presented a picture of harmony attributing it to Adam Smith's 'invisible hand'. Granted that in real-life economies both the elements of harmony and conflict are present, what is required is to explore how these different aspects of social relationships are mediated through the organisational and institutional structures of the economy and society.

Among the units of any national economy the state occupies a unique position. As already indicated, this is partly because, in most instances, the state is a major direct participant in the economy, but more so because of the manner in which its decisions and actions impact on all other units even when it does not attempt any direct coordinating role. The state determines a great deal of the agenda of the economy at the national level which the lower-level units have to take into account in shaping their agenda and activities.[17] The state also exerts influence on all inter-unit links, including the market, especially in situations where money and credit have significant roles in the system. But the state is not an 'unproblematic empirical given' (to use an expression of Bob Jessop) as is often taken to be. Its nature has to be theoretically examined and the structure of its relationships to the rest of the units in the system has to be empirically established.

VII

In concluding the treatment of the features of a complex economy,   a reference is necessary to the frequently considered question: 'What holds it together?' This search for the integrating principle is a hang-over from Newtonian science and is based on the assumption that unification and simplification are the essence of science. A theoretical system dealing with diverse elements may require an integrating principle for its completeness. But in real-life situations it is unlikely that there is a single unifying strand holding together a complex system. In fact the search for a unifying or integrating principle is more likely to be a conscious or unconscious attempt at reductionism which is neither necessary nor permissible under all circumstances. An integrable system has as its underlying principles the notions of homogeneity, harmony and a single-dimensional rationality. These are not compatible with a multiple, heterogeneous, temporal and complex entity such as a real-life economy. In the broadest sense the economy exists because society exists. More pertinently, the economy is always in the process of being constituted wherever human beings are trying to make a living and to rise above mere subsistence where it is possible to do so. Then, the real issue is to figure out how the economy with its rich and irreducible diversity and plurality is functioning and not to become excessively concerned about the integrating principle. Economists can afford to abandon the search in a dark room for a black cat that is not there anyway!

The operational part of the principle of integration is the aggrega-tion of the performance of the economy into a single number called

GNP. This is a facility that few other disciplines have in their own spheres and economists are naturally proud of their achievement. Taken as a mere approximation it may serve a useful purpose. But it is important to note that it is a crude approximation based on rather shaky premises. First, it is readily admitted that GNP does not take into account the total performance of the economy, but only those goods and services that get valued through exchange and the market processes. It can be seen that this view of what constitutes a good or service is closely linked to a concept of work which identifies it with work done for payment. This concept of work will be critically examined in the next section, but it is clear that it is derived from a certain institutional arrangement of what is considered to be economic activity. Hence, what is measured as aggregate income may capture only a part of what is actually generated. How far removed it can be from what is supposed to be measured can be seen from Sach's statements: 'Non-market economic activities are by no means restricted to tribal and primitive peasant economies, where they play a predominant role .... In industrialised countries about half of the total working time of society goes to daily *household* chores, not speaking of an embryonic "social sector" where people indulge in collective, voluntary production of services and goods' (Sachs 1986: 2). A fortiori what does not get captured by the market process and hence does not get reflected in GNP is much larger in economies like that of India.

The problem, however, is not confined to estimation, but goes straight and deep into the very notion of measurement underlying the GNP calculation. Lionel Robbins must have been one of the earliest to point this out, before (Keynesian) national income measurements became common. Robbins touched upon two related problems. 'Valuations which the price system expresses are not quantities at all. They are arrangements in a certain order.... Value is a relation, not a measure' (1935: 56). Hence the procedure of quantifying the value of goods and services is not valid at all, for it is an attempt to quantify an *order*. Second, the ordering itself depends crucially on the initial distribution of spending power. If that distribution changes, valuation will change too. 'By the very fact of distribution, relative valuations would necessarily alter. The whole "set" of the productive machine would be different. The streams of goods and services would have a different composition' (ibid: 58). Robbins illustrates the problem by pointing out that lawyers, doctors, the proprietors of rare sites, etc., enjoy high incomes because there are people with high incomes who value their services highly, but that if the initial spending power is redistributed, their services will come to be valued very differently, even if the technical efficiency of their services may remain unaffected.

Hence, while figures like GNP may be used for limited purposes and with great caution, to arrive at a more meaningful idea of the performance of the economy, the scanning of the economy from different angles and at different levels will be necessary depending upon the purpose for which it is done. Such a procedure is not likely to be unit neutral either. To judge performance, for instance, it will be necessary to know not merely how much has been produced in the aggregate, but also the kind of goods produced.

The aggregation and measurement of the performance of the economy, then, is largely a matter of some conventions and too much of significance cannot be attached to figures thus derived. In the case of an economy of multilayered structures and heterogeneous units it is even questionable whether there can be a single criterion for the evaluation of the performance of the economy. In a situation of resource and information asymmetries and differences in agenda, the performance of the economy is likely to be viewed differently by different participants or group of participants and hence is unlikely to be unit neutral. Where the system performs on the basis of resource power, for instance, it will be under the domination of those who wield that power and its performance will be directed to their advantage. What they consider 'goods' may be 'bads' from the perspective of other constituents of the system. Hence, just as the performance of the economy has to be scanned from different angles and at different levels, the audit of that performance has to take into account the differences in perspectives. It may be noted that criteria such as Pareto optimality which claim to have some socially neutral technical norms for the evaluation of the performance of the economy are based on assumptions that in the first place remove all social asymmetries and generate a robot-like 'economic man' who submits to what theorists want him to do. In games of that kind any result that one wants to can be generated and for over a century that has been the preoccupation of the 'science of economics'. Recognition of this fact is the initial step towards a meaningful understanding of real-life economies.

Substantive Issues

VIII

If it is recognised that the attempt to devise a predictable model based on artificially contrived assumptions (on the mistaken notion that science implies the search for regularities, prediction and measurement) has been the main reason for economics getting distanced from real-life economic situations, the way to move forward is to emphasise, as the classical economists did, the substantive aspects and relationships. But economists have a habit of thinking that the substantive issues relating to the economy are all known and remain invariant and hence the professional responsibility is to go on perfecting new tools to deal with old problems as Koopmans stated when he reviewed the state of economics in the middle of the century. That view is widely held even now.

There are, of course, substantive essentials common to all economies as have been identified in Chapter 4. But because the economy is an evolving process, the manifestation and implications of the substantive themes have to be contextually explicated. The significance of this procedure to understand real-life economic problems will be examined here with reference to four key concepts, needs, wealth, work and rewards. A moment of reflection will show that these are basic to the economy and to economics. There is another observation that can be made about them which, perhaps, is less obvious. They are all related to human interactions and are, therefore, institutionally derived and defined. It is because these basics are institutionally embedded that economics, the systematic exposition and explanation of the economy, cannot but be situated in an institutional milieu.

The recognition of needs, or what are frequently referred to as 'basic needs', is now quite common in development economics, that is, policy related economics, as has been demonstrated by the prominence it occupies in the Declaration of the World Summit for Social Development of the United Nations.[18] But needs have almost completely disappeared from theoretical discussions. One author goes to the extent of saying: 'When they have in mind a professional commitment to orthodox, non-Marxist theory, economists react to attempts to use the concept in their presence with the same sort of instantaneous conditioned reflex that champions of sanitation manifest, swatters in hand, when swarms of houseflies invade their kitchens' (Braybrooke 1987: 11). It was one of the achievements of neo-classical economics to jettison 'needs' from theoretical discussion, substituting for it wants or preferences. But classical writers had a different perception of needs. The centrality of human needs in the writings of Marx and Engels has already been noted. The opening sentence of the *Wealth of Nations* recognises the provisioning of 'the necessaries and conveniences of life' as the basis of the study of political economy.

The early writers were clear about another aspect too: needs certainly have a physiological or physical dimension, but they are primarily a matter of *social* norms. Adam Smith was quite explicit about it. 'By necessaries I understand not only commodities which are indispensably necessary for the support of life' [he wrote] 'but whatever the custom of the country renders it indecent for creditable people, even of the lowest order, to be without. . . .' After illustrating it with reference to linen shirts as being a necessity even for the lowest order in his days, he continued: 'Under necessaries, therefore, I comprehend not only those things which nature, but those things which the established rules of decency have rendered necessary to the lowest rank of people' (Bk V, Ch II–II: 351–52). It is not easy to specify what 'the rules of decency renders necessary' and in that sense there is an element of vagueness in Smith's notion of necessaries, but he is quite clear that needs are socially embedded. Levine is right when he says: 'Economics becomes a science only when the renewal of the species becomes a social act so that the species is itself constituted as a social reality, therefore, when the original object of economic activity becomes a social object' (Levine 1977: 6).

The social nature of needs is powerfully, though rather perversely, brought out by the manner in which commercial advertisements determine what one needs, notwithstanding the assertions of neo-classical theory that it is personal preference, uninfluenced by anything else in the system, that forms the basis of economic analysis. But in Chapters 2 and 3 I have shown that on the rare occasions when that theory searches for its social foundations, it is led to admit that a group of human beings who somehow provision their basic needs is the underlying assumption of theoretical analysis.[19] While theory can simply *assume* that such conditions exist, for the vast majority of human beings conditions for survival and for tolerable living in society are far from assured. This has been so in the past; and is so now and is likely to continue to be so in the future. Hence a major task of economic analysis is to examine why conditions assumed by theory do not hold good in reality. This is happening to some extent, and what Braybrooke aptly describes as 'course-of-life needs' occupy a more prominent place in economic studies today than was the case even a quarter of a century ago. One has only to refer to the manner in which poverty and hunger have entered as themes of economic enquiries to realise that such is the case.

If one takes a broader view, it is not only issues relating to basic needs alone that social realities are forcing economists to take up. At the other end, what was once considered the mundane world of finance, and hence relegated to Departments of Commerce and Management, has begun to engage the attention of economic theorists. Hence from the lower and upper ends, course-of-life needs are re-entering, and quite forcefully, into the world of professional economics. It is the result of the growing awareness of the ordinary people about their rights (that is, their claims on society) and may, therefore, be thought of as part of an on-going political and democratic process which only goes to show (as has been argued in Chapter 4) that the economy is open to other forces not only at its outer boundary, but also 'within' it. Economics as a discipline may from time to time escape into the orderliness and security that closed systems provide, but these can only be either conscious retreats into abstraction to gain mental clarity or aberrations not so recognised. The pressures of life will always be at work to bring it back to real-life situations.

There are reasons to think that such pressures will continue and intensify. Because, as people become conscious of their needs and rights, they are also becoming aware of the fact that only through organised social action can they be realised. Economic changes of the past have contributed to that awareness. A farm household that produces the bulk of its requirements may think that its own efforts and the blessings of the nature are responsible for its well-being. But a farm household that produces for the market realises how dependent it is on the rest of society for the success of its enterprise, even for its daily food. A salaried household becomes even more conscious of its utter dependence on a host of others for all its requirements. The fact that one's resource power and the use of money may succeed in hiding this sense of dependence is another matter. The central substantive theme of the economy as an evolving complex entity is the growing interdependence, the growing social intercourse, of human beings—through the direct exchange of goods they produce, through exchange mediated by money, through the direct use of surplus, through the intermediation of that surplus—the emergence of a multi-unit, composite, complex, economy, in short. This is essentially a social process. The growing awareness that one needs others for one's survival and development is one aspect of it. There is another aspect which is a little more technical and may not readily enter into the thinking of untrained minds: that the more that an individual enters into interaction with others, and the more intermediation that such interactions come to have, the less control that he or she as an individual will have over them. They become distinctly *social*, of and by individuals and groups of individuals, to be sure, but beyond their immediate control. The economy, in the future, will be more and more of such relationships.

The social orientation of needs and the method of meeting needs reflecting this fact will be further reinforced by the collective action that is increasingly becoming necessary for the satisfaction of needs. Fresh air is a need that every individual has for healthy living and was once assumed to be freely available. But today in most urban areas only carefully planned collective action will ensure that the air that one breathes is tolerably unpolluted. It is being recognised too that droughts and floods are not natural calamities, as they were once considered to be, but very much the consequence of human actions and can be checked and avoided by collective effort at different levels. There are also signals that indicate that the very survival of the human race on planet earth is at stake and collective actions at the global level are required to prevent calamities. Few of these are matters that can be handled through personal preferences and the operations of markets. And yet they will feature prominently as economic problems for city and national governments and for bodies at the supranational levels.

A further issue arises from them. As the emergence of economics as a separate field of study was closely associated with the growth of the capitalist economic order, limitless growth had become the unexamined commitment of the discipline and contribution to growth had come to be the validating principle of economic policies. There can be no doubt that if population is increasing and if living conditions are to be improved the production of goods and services, or wealth, according to classical terminology, must continue to increase. But then such increases must be specific goods in relation to specific needs, both individual and collective. However, this is not what economics means by growth. Growth in economics is the increment to the exchange value of goods and services produced on the basis of the manner in which resource power happens to be distributed in the system. There is nothing to guarantee that a growth of that kind ensures the production of goods and services required, though it may correspond to the desires of those who are in a position to bid for the goods and services they desire. In any case, there is nothing to validate the position that the economic objective must be to see that such growth should be as high as possible.

Here, again, pressures from real-life situations will force economics to reconsider whether limitless growth is desirable or even possible. Already in countries where growth in the abstract was almost a matter of worship, it is coming to be noticed that much of it turns out to be 'jobless growth' making it impossible for most people to become its beneficiaries. Equally growing is the concern that the pursuit of growth today may be at the cost of growth tomorrow because of the depletion of natural resources and the destruction of the environment. It is also being realised that all over the world, a substantial share of 'growth' is in the form of weapons of destruction which serve no purpose except to make some people rich and powerful while exposing the vast majority to conflicts, insecurity and death. As these issues that still remain the concern of specialists seep into the consciousness of people at large, there will be demands that economics must abandon its false pretense of neutrality and suggest specifically the goods and services whose production must increase indicating the rate at which they should increase. Such decisions can be done only on the basis of what is desirable and not on what is desired. In this sense there can be no doubt that economics of the future will be a study of need-based economies.

IX

What has been stated shows the close connection between needs and wealth. The two are complementary. The purpose of wealth is to meet needs. This link between needs and wealth is seen from the fact that when need was thought of as the physical requirement for survival, food, (corn) represented the specific good to meet that need and land which yielded that good was the symbol of wealth. The link between the two is significant from another point as well. As Levine has indicated, it is the link between needs and wealth that gives needs a social character and makes needs self-limiting. By contrast, 'when being wealth becomes an end in itself, independent of any structure of need, the finiteness of need breaks down. If the idea of acquiring wealth in order to be as wealthy as possible becomes an element of my personality structure, then my need for wealth can never be satisfied since it does not fix upon a discrete group of useful objects' (Levine 1988: 58). It may be recalled that it was when capitalism shifted the accent on production from a search for useful objects to a quest for wealth in the abstract that neo-classical theory replaced the concept of needs with a social and self-limiting connotation by the concept of wants claimed to be unlimited and individualistic.

Economics of the future, by restoring the primacy of social needs will have to work out the appropriate link between needs and wealth. But this will not be easy because the capitalist system which led to an increase in the variety and diversity of goods also led to a homogenisation of wealth as the exchange value of goods, thus removing the association between specific objects and wealth, and giving wealth the notion of resource power or economic power in the abstract. Further, the intermediation in the sphere of surplus and wealth has introduced much fluidity in the patterns of ownership of wealth. Up to a point this fluidity was (and is) advantageous to production as it allowed a separation of ownership and use of wealth facilitating concentration of attention on the technical aspects of production. The phenomenal increase in production under capitalism was to a large extent the result of this institutional arrangement for the separation of the actual use of wealth from its ownership. But beyond a stage, individuals and groups, though not society as a whole, will be able to use claims on wealth as a means to increase wealth through transactions of the claims themselves, just as merchants have the possibility of enriching themselves through the buying and selling of goods. Once this happens a disjunction can be caused between production and the acquisition of wealth, the latter becoming a specialised activity in itself with many consequences on the rest of the economy. The marketing of claims is not subject to the restraints that production and the costs of production exert on the marketing of goods and hence easily comes under the influence of speculation introducing extreme volatility in the volume of transactions and in prices. As prices on claims are usually considered to be indicative of the health of the economy, such fluctuations have their bearing on the rest of the economy as well. Further, the more abstract wealth becomes with the associated elusive notions of ownership and control, newer forms of conflict may be expected between the ownership of that abstract wealth on the one hand and the ownership of the diverse, heterogeneous and personal labour power on the other. It is legitimate to expect that the manifestation of such conflicts will transcend the boundaries of national economies and also the domain of economics as a discipline.

The discussion in Chapter 4 has suggested that preoccupation with claims on wealth and transactions in them across national boundaries have become distinct features of global capitalism in recent years and that these activities have their impact on most national economies and their constituent unit.[20] In the coming years the variety of institutional changes they imply and their differential impact on different sections of society will become matters of public concern and economics will be under pressure to re-examine concepts of wealth, ownership and control. This will be particularly so in countries such as India where phases of capitalism from the earliest to the latest coexist and interact.

Creation of wealth for the satisfaction of specific needs and increasingly for further creation of wealth will, in turn, necessitate reconsideration of the concept of work. In the evolution of economic thought work has been one of the haziest concepts, but standard economic theory has succeeded in giving it a precision and measurability.[21] This notion of work was spelt out by Hicks more than half a century ago and continues to be reaffirmed or implicitly assumed since then: 'People earn their living in all sorts of different ways—by manual work, by brain work, in factories, in offices, and on farms, in dull ways, in interesting ways—but the thing which is common to all ways of earning one's living is the doing of work for which one is paid, doing work and being paid for doing it. . . .' Hicks went on to say: 'It appears that the whole of economic activity of humanity (that vast complex of activities which we call the Economic System) consists of nothing else but an immense cooperation of workers or producers to make things or do things which consumers want. . . .' (Hicks 1942: 11 and 14). The identification of work with what is done for payment or wages that these passages represent has many analytical advantages. Apart from giving the concept of work precision and measurability, it also makes the supply of labour, the primary input in production, a function of price, thus making production a market related activity and providing a rationale for a market oriented economic system. By a subtle reference to humanity as a whole, such a system is made universal and with the equally subtle reference to cooperation it is conveyed that the system is one of harmony. Hicks, probably was not deliberately distorting these aspects. He was simply relying on professional terminology to achieve a worthwhile professional objective of showing how what different people do in different ways to make a living can all be added up and summed up as income, (or as wealth using the old terminology). Since it is typical of standard economic theory's procedure of claiming universality and scientific precision, a look at how these are arrived at will be worthwhile.

Let us concede that making a living by working for payment is. common enough these days, and was so even half a century ago when Hicks wrote these words. But it is an *institutional* arrangement to make a living, a fairly recent one in the long history of humanity; even now it is not the *only* arrangement by which people make a living.[22] In fact, taking humanity as a whole, for the vast majority involved in making a living, it is *not* the commonest arrangement as can be seen from the experience of peasant households who make a living without working for others and women all over the world engaged in household activities directly related to living, but are not paid for putting in the effort! That economic theory can blatantly overlook these facts which go contrary to its 'universal laws' and can rest them on convenient but unexamined institutional premises while pretending to be institutionally neutral, are typical of its procedures of theorising and the effort to appear to be scientific! And we are dealing with a concept that is central to understanding economic activity and should be considered the cornerstone of economic theory. Hence, if the concept of work becomes questionable, the edifice of economic theory will become very shaky indeed.

Yet, as in the case of needs and wealth, issues emerging from real-life force a reconsideration of the notion of work. First, even where people are working for others, payment is not always on the basis of 'work put in' (hours or days) but for 'work done'. That is, payment is both on time rate and on piece rate with a pronounced shift into the latter reversing the opposite trend of an earlier period. Clearly, it is a reflection of the changing institutional arrangement of work. Unlike in time rate arrangement, where the quantum of work can be measured (though not its intensity or quality), in the piece rate system there is no easy way of quantifying work performed. Second, for a variety of reasons many people now prefer to work on their own, marketing the outcome of their work, either in the form of direct services, or in the form of goods, instead of selling their labour-power as such. This may be because it gives them greater freedom and flexibility in the allocation of their time. It may be because they realise that their skills are too specific to be marketed directly. It may be because the nature of technology and the organisation of production generally make it possible and worthwhile to do so. Whatever the reasons, there is a great resurgence of a wide variety of self-employed occupations through which one can make a living and much more, without working for others and being paid for by them.

The third reason, and the one with far-reaching implications, for the concept of work coming in for critical scrutiny is related to all the activities done in the household, most directly and intimately associated with ensuring livelihood, and in which for long centuries women have had the major part. Economic theory, of course, does not consider these activities as 'productive' activities or 'economic' activities simply because they are not paid for and because they are not income generating. Economic theory's inability or unwillingness to recognise as work such activities—preparing the daily meals, washing, cleaning, and above all, bringing up and training the future productive workforce—which, in terms of real-life processes are the most crucial ones, reflects only the poverty of that theory and its alienation from life. There is now a burgeoning literature on this subject, most of them exposing the unreasonableness and injustice of the situation, many of them trying to make monetary estimates of the contribution of women attending to 'household chores'.[23] All these are necessary to make people, especially the males among them, conscious of the nature of the problem. But theory is largely immune to criticism that it is insensitive to issues of fairness and justice. The real challenge in this case is that it forces a review of one of economic theory's foundational concepts. There can be no doubt that theory will not be able to run away from this issue which is related to the life experience of half of humanity. In the decades ahead re-examining the concept of work will be one of the unavoidable tasks of economic theory.

X

The manner in which work is conceptualised is closely related to the problem of rewards, the settlement of claims on wealth. From this angle, it is easy to see why economic theory as it exists is comfortable with the notion of work as activity that is paid for. It is the view of those who pay, who think of the produce essentially as theirs, but recognise that a share of it has to be passed on to those who have 'worked' for it. Hence payment (and work as the justification for it) is not what links 'producers' and 'consumers' (as Hicks was at pains to establish), but defines the relationship between 'owners' and 'workers' in a set-up where ownership has been (through institutional arrangements) taken away from those responsible for activity. Payment for work done, or work as activity necessitating payments, therefore, is an indication of the separation between the two components of the labour process that underlies all economic activity, the distinctively human element, both physical and mental, on the one hand, and the physical and material on the other (tools, implements, machines, etc.). This separation is characteristic of capitalism and its organisational and institutional manifestations. The experience of humanity shows that such was not the case always. However, that separation has the advantage both in practice and in theory that work gets unambiguously defined and payment clearly determinate. It is certainly not general or universal as shown by patterns of the organisation of production prior to the emergence of capitalism and by many experiments undertaken by post-capitalist economic systems.

The question of rewards—in the broad sense as claims on the produce—is linked to yet another and deeper issue. What is the basis of the claim on the produce? Is it a quid pro quo for work as narrowly defined, or even for economic activity defined in the broadest possible terms? Or is it a right? If the latter, is it only the right of the owner (as recognised in different forms of economic system)? Or is it a fundamental right of any human being at least within the group that he or she belongs to, without any quid pro quo and without any other qualifications attached to that claim? If it is to be as unconditional and universal as implied by the last question, how is it to be made operational? In the discussion on the rudimentary economy in Chapter 4, this issue had already emerged, and it was seen there that a possible operational principle which recognises unconditionally everybody's claims on the produce is: 'To each according to needs; from each according to ability'.

Two observations may be based on this principle. The first is to note the close link between rights and needs. It is the recognition of needs that leads to rights. It is because the human being needs goods and services (produce) to be human that he/she comes to have rights over goods and services. It is the individual human being who has needs and rights; but the recognition of needs as well as of rights is social. Hence, as Marx cogently argued, the individual and the social are not antithetical: 'the individual is the social being' (Marx 1959: 98). The second observation is a further manifestation of this intimate individual–social link which may, however, appear to be a perverse one. If there is a close connection between rewards and need at one level, at another level rewards may decide whether the individual will perform according to his/her ability or not—the whole question of incentives in relation to rewards. A lesson that can be learned from the socialist experiences of the past is that while at rather low levels the meeting of needs may be considered as adequate reward, at higher levels rewards may decide how much effort will be forthcoming. A group that wishes to rise above the requirements of subsistence, therefore, must work out a structure of rewards that is satisfactory both to meet everybody's necessaries *and* to ensure that increase in production is *not* neglected for want of incentives. The classical solution to this ticklish problem was to proceed on the assumption that the convenience available to a few initially will become available to all in the long run. But subsequent experiences have shown that this 'trickle down' assumption may not work, or may not be acceptable in an age which is not willing to concede privileged position to any section of society. There need be no doubt that in the decades ahead finding a socially satisfactory reward structure that defines and settles the claims of individual members on the social product while at the same time sustaining a desirable rate of increase in production will be an important problem in all real-life economies, closely related to the re-examination of the nature of 'work' and of 'needs'.

That formulation also brings out the interconnectedness of the four substantive issues dealt with—needs, wealth, work and rewards—and the manner in which the individual and the social are intertwined through all of them. I have been arguing that the economy is one of the major expressions of the individual-in-society problematic. What has been attempted here is to spell out how that problematic is to be viewed concretely via the changing substantive ingredients of the economy. In Chapter 4 it was suggested that institutions are the links between the individual and the group or society. Hence the solutions to the set of problems dealt with are to be found by evolving appropriate institutions.

That is more easily said than done. The possibilities and difficulties of the task can be seen from the socialist experiences of this century. A very legitimate way of viewing these experiments is to think of them as the search for institutional arrangements—in the spheres of ownership and management of resources, the organisation of work and production, the definition and settlement of needs and rights—to deal satisfactorily with the eternal individual-in-society problematic. We may take China as an example. In the early years after the new regime was established in 1949, there was little dispute that the need of the vast majority of the people of the country was food and that the need could be met by channelling human effort on land. Institutional arrangements to ensure that land was put to use for the production of foodgrains and that human labour was directed to that task were, therefore, the first item on the social agenda. This was achieved by changing the pattern of ownership of land so as to conform to the social objective of ensuring the livelihood of all members. Private familial ownership of land which was the traditional pattern in the country was changed to bring land under collective use where men and women organised as teams would attend to all the farming operations. Meeting the basic need for food was the reward for the effort put in and a procedure of sharing the produce was worked out. Effort was directed partly to meet the infrastructural requirements necessary to increase production in the future. It would appear that while these arrangements were adequate to satisfy the main objective of a fair distribution of the produce among the members, it was not satisfactory from the point of view of increasing production.

To meet this problem, further institutional changes were brought about starting in the late 1970s. First, within the large collectives, the organisation of work, particularly the management of labour was delegated to smaller groups. Later the 'responsibility system' was introduced whereby land was contracted out to individual households which had to hand over a fixed quantity of output to the collective, but could dispose of any surplus as they deemed fit. The incentive to improve the position of one's family that this new institutional arrangement provided led to a substantial increase in the total produce in the early 1980s. The increased production also led to another major institutional change, the emergence and recognition of rural markets where the households could exchange their surplus with other farming households or with the producers of non-farm articles. The linking up of agricultural and non-agricultural production in this manner led to further increases in production, to greater diversification of economic activities and newer forms of links among production units.

The process of intermediation soon set in resulting particularly in the emergence of a 'capital market' for the transfer of agrarian surplus into large-scale industrial activities in the urban areas. The opening up of what was initially a closed economy followed, leading to greater interaction with the rest of the world including the entry of foreign capital into the country. The story is not over, and the institutional adjustments of an evolving economic order are going on.

The descriptive account of what happened in the Chinese economy over the past half a century is not meant to suggest that the changes came about naturally or were brought about without opposition and conflicts. It is also not meant to suggest that the sequencing of institutional changes that took place was the 'correct' line for China, or for any other country. A record of the past is recalled only to show the role of institutional changes in dealing with the needs-wealth-work-reward problem. The socialist experiments of the twentieth century deserve attention because they offer concrete instances of deliberate institutional adjustments in economic processes, some of which have been successful while others have failed. There is much to be learnt both from the successes and the failures.

The Economy and Economics

XI

Starting from a view of the economy as an experiential reality in Chapter 1, we have, through a process of analytical description, arrived at a different perception of the economy. What has to be examined now is the relationship between that perception of the economy and economics as a field of study, taking into account the substantive issues indicated in this volume. The analytical descriptions of Chapter 4 and the present chapter so far have already outlined the nature of the economics that is needed to illumine the economy that has been depicted. The close relationship between the two, the economy and economics, that has emerged is no accident. It is the essence of science understood in its broadest sense as a systematic enquiry about some aspect of reality, physical or social. Science, in that sense, has two basic features: it is a language; it has a subject. The relationship between the two is bound to be intimate. Once the nature of science as a discourse about an aspect of reality is recognised, it is no longer necessary to enter into the discussion as to whether economics is a science or not. That discussion is misdirected and is, not surprisingly, rather sterile. It is misdirected because it presumes that there is a body of knowledge, or at least a procedure of enquiry (identified usually as *the* scientific method) whose validity and sanctity have already been objectively established and in terms of which particular fields of study can be evaluated. This was the predominant view about science for a long time, when science tended to be identified with Newtonian physics, but it is no longer accepted by the community of scholars, including scholars in physics.[24] Most scholars are now inclined to think of science essentially as a language of communication that a group of specialists set up in their attempt to understand and explain some aspects of a vastly complex reality.[25] If so, there is no method apart from the subject matter.

This position has far-reaching consequences on the way one thinks about economics as a field of study and the way one goes about studying it. It calls for abandoning the postulational method with its emphasis on a priori reasoning as the basis of economic knowledge. Instead, familiarity with the actual working of the economy at the empirical level and an appreciation—even an intuitive appreciation—of the network of social relations that constitute the economy must be accepted as the introductory procedure in moving to the level of abstraction that the systematic study of the economy calls for. Granted that these relations change over time, the nature of abstraction itself becomes a matter of conscious decision. Abstraction required to understand an economy where most participants directly produce the goods necessary for survival will be different from what is required where the participants live by buying and selling. When the thrust of the economy shifts from survival to accumulation, again, the kind of abstraction required will be different. When trade in claims becomes more pronounced than trade in goods, a different procedure of abstraction will become necessary. When these variety of activities interact in any (national) economy, the kind of abstraction needed will be of yet another type.

The same principle will apply with appropriate modification when units of different kinds and at different levels are dealt with. The abstraction and analysis needed to comprehend the problems of a household economy and of a firm cannot be the same. Understanding the working of a national economy and of the global economy will also call for different procedures.

Sensitivity to these differences and a grasp of their rationale are the crucial preconditions for any attempt to reformulate economics as a field of study. Unfortunately, they are precisely the requirements negated by neo-classical theory's universalising a priori logic. It is the fear of losing the rigour of that logic that prevents many people from searching for alternate conceptualisations of the economy and alternate procedures of enquiry even when the major flaws of neo-classical economics are recognised.[26]

One of the requirements of the principle of contextual abstraction indicated above (as against the a priori abstraction of standard economic theory) is that economic knowledge must be built up through the constant interaction between the theoretical formulations that are in vogue and concrete instances that they are said to be applicable to. Standard theory has some form of interaction with concrete instances: they are the ones that are supposed to test the validity of the theory, or at least its range of applications. As Kuhn has argued, much of 'normal science' is of that kind and economics is no exception to it.[27] But what is suggested here is a different procedure. If it is recognised that the subject matter one deals with is always in a process of change, there never is a complete corpus of theory to fall back on which can illumine all aspects of even the selected areas of reality.[28] Concrete instances can be helpful to indicate refinements needed in theory to ensure its robustness. But the concrete must also be approached as a potential source of new knowledge that can help to modify, or reformulate the corpus of theory one already has. The real issue is to insist that economics is primarily an observational discipline, and only secondarily one of logical derivations.

For this purpose the concrete must be studied as thoroughly as possible with the accent on descriptive richness. Descriptive studies are at a low premium in economics, considered to be the professional occupation of 'institutionalists', not of theorists.[29] The mistaken notion of the nature of institutions and of theory that forms the basis of this view has been dealt with, and it is not necessary to repeat it. The social embeddedness of the economy makes it constantly open to influences from 'outside' at different levels thus frequently changing the very texture of the economy; only meticulous descriptive studies can capture these changes. Descriptive accounts are also necessary to ensure that abstraction which is unavoidable for systematising knowledge does not lead to an emptying of critical content.[30] Where, for instance, the heterogeneity of units is the essence of the problem, an abstracted homogeneity can be of no help in understanding it. Instead, a descriptive account that captures the differentiation and variety of units may reveal new forms of inter-relationships facilitating deeper understanding.

It is also important to consider what the purpose of a systematised body of knowledge is in relation to the segment of reality that is being studied. The common presumption is that the purpose of science is to be able to predict. While this may be a valid position to take in respect of sciences like astronomy or even physics to some extent, it is certainly not valid in the case of biology. Which goes to show that, again, the nature and purpose of a branch of science must be established in relation to its subject matter.

Prediction is a form of explanation, and often not a satisfactory one. When clouds appear, it is easy to predict that there will be rain, but that prediction provides no explanation about the phenomenon called rain. Similarly, on the basis of changes in prices, predictions can be made about demand, but that does not lead to an understanding of the problems of pricing or of purchasing. Further, most predictions, especially in matters relating social phenomena, rely heavily on ceteris paribus condition and their practical significance is, therefore, limited.

Prediction, as causal explanation, points out Mahajan, demonstrates 'why necessarily something happened'. According to him the narrative, on the other hand, explains how a particular event 'could possibly have occurred'. He goes on to say: 'Instead of considering a particular event as an instance of a general law that manifests an invariable and necessary relation between the antecedent condition and consequent event, it acknowledges that similar antecedent conditions do not always lead to or result in the occurrence of the same event' (Mahajan 1992: 83).[31] In trying to understand social phenomena, it is necessary to search for similarities which help in formulating general principles and for differences which are expressions of particularities. Concrete descriptive accounts offer the possibility of discovering the similarities and differences of instances both of which are germane to systematising knowledge. 'Things are similar: this makes science possible. Things are different: this makes science necessary' (Levins and Lewontin 1985: 141).

XII

Another issue frequently debated within the profession is whether economics is a positive science committed only to prediction or it is (or ought to be) a normative science equally concerned with prescription. There are those who tenaciously hold to the former position while others tend to agree with Pigou: 'If it were not for the hope that a scientific study of men's social action may lead not necessarily directly, immediately, but at some time and in some way, to practical results of social improvement, not a few students of these actions would regard the time devoted to their study as misspent' and that this is 'true of all social sciences, but specially true of economics' (1983: 4).

These divergent views will continue. They are, however, not related to the nature of economics as such, but on the nature of economics as a science, and are, thus, related to one's perception of science. A view of science that sees its role as the search for the pre-existing structure of a machine is likely to attach importance to prediction and those pursuing such a science may feel that objectivity demands that there should be no attempt to change the working of the machine in the attempt to grasp it. But what if economics is more like the science of medicine, 'an agglomeration of overlapping field of research' as Schumpeter thought it was? (1954: 10) Whatever may be the nature of medicine as a science, can its practitioners pretend to be interested only in prediction and refuse to make prescriptions?

In this connection, a critical review is necessary of what is usually referred to as the 'neutrality' of science. Neo-classical economics, because of its claim to be scientific, is said to be neutral between social classes. However, it does not take much effort to see that neutrality is achieved by first accepting a notion of society that is devoid of social classes and by working with a view of society as consisting of homogeneous individuals who are all aiming to achieve the same thing. A great deal about the nature of society is already built into what neo-classical economics considers to be scientific theory, and hence the claim to neutrality cannot go unchallenged. Or, consider the manner in which neo-classical theory establishes that individuals when they try to maximise their own utilities bring about social efficiency, and that, therefore, that concept of efficiency is neutral. That claim rests at least on private ownership of resources as a form of social organisation and markets as the institutional arrangements to facilitate production being based on the principle of division of labour. It also requires that the distribution of resources is such that no one can dominate the market to one's own advantage, that economies of scale in production are absent and that there is symmetry of information. Above all, it is based on a definition of efficiency linking it directly to individual preferences.

With so much achieved by way of construction, where is the scope for a meaningful discussion of neutrality? It may be noted too that neo-classical economists who swear by the principle of neutrality are not neutral between efficiency and inefficiency and view the science of economics as a means of ensuring efficiency. The socially neutral science must, therefore, be thought of as at least a goal-oriented one. Neo-classical economics, it may be recalled, does not claim to be an attempt to provide a neutral description of the working of the economy (any economy) but is a prescription for optimisation which is declared to be the universal economic problem.

Some of these paradoxes, apparent or real, can be resolved if it is accepted that science is not a discoverable entity with a predetermined package of procedures of its own, but is an exercise in building up a language and associated procedures to deal with some aspect of reality. The emphasis must, therefore, be on the production of science, (on the construction of science if that expression is more in tune with the status usually assigned to science) and not its practice alone. For, the production of science is not a matter of immaculate conception, but is very much a social activity in which the producers participate with their passions and prejudices. To those who put science on a higher plane than other human activities and think of scientists as those who are dedicated to the rational pursuit of truth and nothing but the truth, it may be disconcerting to know that the great Isaac Newton was a rather mean person who used his position as president of the Royal Society to protect his personal interest against professional rivals, and in that effort resorted to some devious methods.[33] It is well known that this was not an old and isolated instance either, and that similar happenings are quite common even today among distinguished scientists, including economists.

But the issue is not merely about the personal dispositions of the members of the scientific communities. More important is the bearing of the social ethos on the construction of scientific knowledge. The history of the development of economics bears testimony to it. It is hardly necessary to point out that the classical writers on the subject were immersed in the social and economic problems of their societies and their times. The same was true of Keynes. The early neo-classical theorists may appear to have been an exception, but if they were not directly concerned with the economic issues of their day, they were influenced by a major social theme of the nineteenth century, to shape all knowledge, including knowledge about human motivations and actions, according to the method of science which they uncritically accepted as *the* scientific method.

In view of this dialectical relationship between science and society, with scientific knowledge and methods influencing society in different ways and social factors entering into scientific procedures, perhaps in less visible ways, any claims to the social neutrality of science, any science, can only be considered as a manifestation of ignorance of those who should know better. It is not surprising that science as a human activity is socially embedded. The science of economics dealing directly with human enterprise will be more pronouncedly related to social processes and social institutions. To deny it would be not an expression of ignorance, but an act of deception.

An implication of the social embeddedness of the economy and of economics is that economic knowledge arises from practical knowledge and must remain closely related to it. In other words, practical knowledge is both the beginning and end of economic knowledge—its two terminals, so to say, with economic theory being the connecting link between the two. This metaphor needs some clarifications. That economic knowledge begins with practical knowledge may be readily conceded. But then what is the role of theory, of abstraction, logical inferences, and systematisation? My understanding is that the role of theory is not to produce a mirror-like reproduction of the reality that practical knowledge refers to, but to go beneath it, to explore the hidden interconnections, and thus to provide some coherence to the fragments that are the usual manifestations of practical knowledge.[34] It is this activity that I have referred to as 'editing' in Chapter 1. But what is this edited version supposed to do? Is it to be simply filed as a refined version of the original stuff? Filing has to be part of the process because it is not a once-for-all activity. And, as the files grow, some review of the files will become necessary, and also some reclassifications, some further editing.

That, indeed, is the task of the professional community in the field of economics. In that process the edited and the re-edited versions of practical knowledge will come to have a language of their own. It is the next stage that is crucial. What is to be done with the new language? As the professional discourse grows, it will have a tendency to become more and more refined and to become completely distanced from where it started. My complaint has been that economics as a discipline shows signs of falling into that trap of becoming addicted to its own language. When that happens, what may appear as the progress of the science is more likely to be a distancing of it from the real world. There may also be the feeling that greater refinement and rigour may lead to deeper insights.

Insight into what, is the question. As Einstein has remarked, 'Pure logical thinking can give us no knowledge whatsoever about the world of experience: all knowledge of reality begins with experience and terminates in it.[35] That is why the second terminal is important. Refined economic knowledge will become sterile unless it is again linked to practical knowledge. If the two are linked, the scientific knowledge of economics has the means of constantly renewing itself. It also has the possibility of lifting practical knowledge to a higher level so that the understanding of all members of society about economic realities can become clearer and more authentic. The professional economist, then, has a twofold responsibility to contribute to the refinement and renewal of the language of the profession, and to harness the knowledge and insights of economic science to enrich the general awareness of the complexities of the real-life economy. That is what his 'dual citizenship' involves.

Notes

1. This view presupposes that there is a reality apart from the perceptions of it, a theme that forms a major issue of debate in contemporary philosophy. I do not propose to enter into that debate. My position simply is that there are economic activities that human beings undertake, whether or not there are professionals called economists to observe them, interpret them and to produce theories based on them. It is in this sense that I have described the economy in Chapter 1 as an experiential reality.

    Readings particularly useful in this area have been Rorty (1980 and 1991) and Bhaskar (1989). I have found the latter specially helpful to clarify some crucial aspects relating to social theory. I agree with Bhaskar's observation that 'things in general exist and act independently of their descriptions,. . . [but] we can only know them under particular descriptions' (p. 152). That is one reason why 'particular descriptions' about nature, society, economy, etc., must be frequently kept under review.

2. Alexander Pope had proposed the following epitaph for Isaac Newton who died in 1727.

    > Nature and Nature's laws lay hid at night:
    > God said, let Newton be! and all was light

    Quoted by Prigogine and Stengers (1984: 27).

3. Quoted by Prigogine and Stengers (1984: 2).

4. In economics, one of the best examples of this possibility has been in the empirical verification of the consumption function where the same set of data was found compatible with Friedman's permanent income hypothesis and Duesenberry's relative income hypothesis. See Friedman 1957.

5. The writing of this section is based largely on my personal reflections over the years on the nature of the economy. But readings on dialectics which Engels described as 'the science of interconnections' and the works on what has come to be referred to as 'modern science' have been helpful in formulating the ideas. Of special help have been the following: Engels (1976), Godelier (1972), Kosik (1976), Althusser and Balibar (1979), Illyenkov (1982), Capra (1983), Prigogine and Stengers (1984), Levins and Lewontin (1985), and Bhaskar (1989).

6. The essence of complexity is seen differently by different writers. In Prigogine and Stengers (1984) it is the irreversibility of motion associated with thermodynamics that figures prominently in the notion of complexity.

7. However, Simon recognises that in many parts of Africa and the more rural portions of China and India, families and villages also will have to be treated similar to firms in which people work. His contention is that organisations in which people work are more important in understanding economies than markets where they exchange goods. He, therefore, suggests that even for modern economies the expression 'organisational economy' is more appropriate than 'market economy'.

8. Levins and Lewontin observe: 'At various times in the history of science important advances have been made either by abstracting away from differences to reveal similarity or by emphasising the richness of variation within a seeming uniformity. But, either choice by itself is ultimately misleading' (1985 : 141).

9. Gleick uses this example, originally suggested by the mathematician Benoit Mandelbrot, in a discussion of perceptions and measurements (1987 : 97).

10. Starting with Arthur Lewis' celebrated dual economy model of underdeveloped economies (Lewis 1954), it has been very common to think of them as consisting of two clearly separated sectors.

11. Many empirical studies have established the close connection between large-scale industries of the organised sector and small-scale industries of the unorganised sector. For instance, see Goyal et al. (1980), Banerjee (1988).

12. Reich (1991) shows how the United States of America may be thought of as having several economies within it.

13. Thomas Pynchon quoted in Winston and Teichgraeber (1988 : 84)

14. There are graphic descriptions of these processes in Dutt (1960) and Gadgil (1971).

15. In Chapter 1 of Kurien (1992a), I have dealt with a typical case of this kind.
16. See Kurien (1994).
17. In Chapter 9 of Kurien (1992a), I have examined at greater length the role of the state in modern economies.
18. The U.N. Social Summit was held in Copenhagen in March 1995.
19. Cf. Chapter 2, section III and Chapter 3, section XI. '
20. For a more detailed treatment see Kurien (1994).
21. There is an excellent account of the evolution of the concept of work in Gorz (1989).
22. Even in the Indian adaptation of Hicks' *Social Framework* authored by him and two Indian scholars more recently, the same concept of work is relied on. See Hicks et al. (1984). It shows how uncritically economists use their basic concepts once these become part of their vocabulary.
23. The literature is ably reviewed in Shanmugasundaram (1993). UNDP's *Human Development Report 1995* has women's work and gender inequality as the theme. According to the Report, in developed industrial countries roughly one-third of men's total work time and two-thirds of women's total work time is spent on unpaid activities. In the less developed economies with predominance of the rural sector a still higher share of women's total work time is in unpaid activities which, therefore, tend to go unrecognised as well. The Report has a select bibliography relating to women and work.
24. As works that deal with the changing perception of science the following may be mentioned: Capra (1983), Progogine and Stengers (1984), Law and Lodge (1984), Gleick (1987), Woolgar (1988), Bhaskar (1989), Stehr (1992), Silverman (1993).
25. 'Science is best treated, not as a discoverable entity, but as a discursive resource' (Woolgar 1988 : 45).
26. Other sciences, particularly biology, have developed rigorous procedures to deal with evolutionary processes in their realms. See Levins and Lewontin (1985), Anderson et al. (1988).
27. Kuhn says: 'Normal science means research firmly based upon one or more past scientific achievements, achievements that some particular community acknowledges for a time as supplying the foundation for its further practice' (1962: 10).
28. Bhaskar points out : 'Because of the historical (transformational) character of social systems, qualitatively new developments in society will be occurring which social scientific theory cannot be expected to anticipate. Hence for ontological, as distinct from purely epistemological, reasons, social scientific, unlike natural scientific, theory is *necessarily* incomplete' (1989: 84–85).
29. On the significance of description and its role in understanding social phenomena, see Amartya Sen, 'Description as Choice' in Sen (1983).

30. 'Abstraction becomes destructive when the abstract is reified and when the historical process of abstraction is forgotten, so that the abstract descriptions are taken for descriptions of the actual objects. The level of abstraction appropriate in a given science at a given time is a historical issue' (Levins and Lewontin 1985 : 149–50).

31. Mahajan adds: 'The narrative is essentially a signifier of a new type of politics and protest against the dominant rationality of the Enlightenment. In place of a single pattern of individual, social and historical development, it stresses difference: indeed, it celebrates difference. And it is this celebration that finds an expression in its emphasis on the study of history and its conception of historical events as unique particulars' (1992 : 101).

32. The comparison of economics to medicine has received renewed emphasis of late. In a recent presentation Arnold C. Harberger said : 'The analogy I like best is with medicine. Law and accounting do not fit because they are not inferential; in that sense they have no scientific component. Physics, chemistry and biology are all the opposite extreme: much more science than prescription. None of these fits as nicely with economics as medicine—a profession with one foot planted in medical science, the other in what we know as the practice of medicine' (Harberger 1993 : 1).

33. Stephen Hawking, presently holding Newton's chair as Lucasian Professor of Mathematics at Cambridge University says that his illustrious predecessor clashed with John Flamsteed who had earlier provided him with much needed data for *Principia*. After some court proceedings Newton was incensed and sought his revenge by systematically deleting all references to Flamsteed in later editions of *Principia*. Hawking also refers to Newton's dispute with the German philosopher Gottfried Leibniz as to who among them was the originator of that branch of mathematics now known as calculus. Newton had discovered it prior to Leibniz, but published his work much later. There were scientists supporting both sides. But most of the articles appearing in defense of Newton were originally written by Newton, though published in the name of his friends. Hawking goes on to say: 'When the row grew, Leibniz made the mistake of appealing to the Royal Society to resolve the dispute. Newton, as president, appointed an 'impartial' committee to investigate, coincidentally consisting entirely of Newton's friends. But that was not all : Newton then wrote the committee's report himself and had the Royal Society publish it, officially accusing Leibniz of plagiarism'. (Hawking 1988: 182).

34. Bhaskar points out that science is the move from manifest phenomena to the structures that generate them (1989: 69).

35. In his essay 'Method of Science' in Maddan (1960).

BIBLIOGRAPHY

Abramovitz, Moses et. al., 1959. *The Allocation of Resources* (Stanford, Stanford University Press).

Althusser, Louis and Etienne Balibar, 1974. *Reading Capital (London, Verso).*

Anderson, Philip W., Kenneth J. Arrow, and David Pines, eds, 1988. *The Economy as an Evolving Complex System* (Redwood City, Addison-Wesley Publishing Company).

Anikin, A., 1975. *A Science in its Youth* (Moscow, Progress Publishers).

Arrow, Kenneth J., 1959. 'Towards a Theory of Price Adjustments', in Moses Abramovitz, et al. 1959.

_____ , 1974. *The Limits of Organizations* (New York, W.W.Norton and Co.)

_____ , 1981. *Real and Nominal Magnitudes in Economics,* in Daniel Bell and Irving Kristol, eds, 1981.

Arrow, Kenneth J., and G. Debreu, 1954. 'Existence of an Equilibrium for a Competitive Economy', *Econometrica, July.*

Arrow, Kenneth J. and F.H. Hahn, 1971. *General Competitive Analysis* (Amsterdam, North-Holland Publishing Company).

Azariadis, C and Joseph E. Stiglitz, 1983. 'Implicit Contracts and Fixed Price Equilibria', *Quarterly Journal of Economics*, November (Supplement).

Bagchi, A.K., 1982. *Political Economy of Underdevelopment* (Cambridge, Cambridge University Press).

Banerjee, Nirmala, 1988. Small and Large Scale Units: Symbiosis or Matsyaanyaya?, in K.B. Suri, ed., *Small Scale Enterprises in Industrial Development* (New Delhi, Sage Publications).

Baran, Paul A., and Paul M. Sweezy, 1966. *Monopoly Capital* (New York, Modern Reader paperbacks).

Bardhan, Pranab, ed., 1989. *The Economic Theory of Agrarian Institutions* (Oxford, Clarendon Press).

Becker, G.S., 1976. *The Economic Approach to Human Behavior* (Chicago, University of Chicago Press).

Bell, Daniel and Irving Kristol, eds, 1981. *The Crisis in Economic Theory* (New York, Basic Books).

Bhaduri, Amit, 1983. *The Economic Structure of Backward Agriculture* (Delhi, Macmillan India).

_____ , 1984. *Unconventional Economic Essays* (Delhi, Oxford University Press).

Bharadwaj, Krishna, 1974. *Production Conditions in Indian Agriculture* (Cambridge, Cambridge University Press).

Bharadwaj, Krishna, 1978. *Classical Political Economy and¹ Rise to Dominance of Supply and Demand Theories* (Calcutta, Orient Longman).
_____ , 1985. 'A Note on Commercialization in Agriculture', in K.N. Raj, et al., eds, 1985.
Bhaskar, Roy, 1989. *Reclaiming Reality* (London, Verso).
Blaug, Mark, 1962. *Economic Theory in Retrospect* (London, Heinemann).
_____ , 1980. *The Methodology of Economics* (Cambridge, Cambridge University Press).
Bloch, Marc, 1965, *Feudal Society* (London, Routledge and Kegan Paul, Vol: I and II).
Boland, Lawrence, A., 1982. *The Foundations of Economic Method* (London, George Allen and Unwin).
Brahmananda, P.R., 1974. *Explorations in the New Classical Theory of Political Economy* (Bombay, Allied Publishers).
Braverman, Harry, 1974. *Labour and Monopoly Capital* (New York, Monthly Review Press).
Braverman, A. and Joseph E. Stiglitz, 1982. 'Sharecropping and Interlinking of Agrarian Markets', *American Economic Review,* September.
Braybrooke, David, 1987. *Meeting Needs* (Princeton, Princeton University Press).
Capra, Fritjof, 1983. *The Turning Point: Science, Society and Rising Culture* (London, Fontana Paperbacks).
Chakravarty, Sukhamoy, 1979. 'Keynes, Classics and the Developing Economies', in C.H. Hanumantha Rao and P.C. Joshi, eds., 1979.
Chayanov, A.V., 1966 (1925). *The Theory of the Peasant Economy,* Edited by Daniel Thorner et al. (Homewood, Richard D. Irwin).
Coats, A.W., 1962. 'Adam Smith: The Modern Reappraisal', in *Renaissance and Modern Studies,* (Vol. VI, p.38, Quoted by Deane 1978: 5).
Dandekar, V.M. and N.Rath, 1971. 'Poverty in India', *Economic and Political Weekly,* January 2 and 9.
Das Gupta, Ajit K., 1974. *Economic Theory and the Developing Countries* (London, Macmillan).
Dasgupta, A.K., 1983. *Phases of Capitalism and Economic Theory* (Delhi, Oxford, University Press).
Datta, Bhabatosh, 1978. *Indian Economic Thought: Twentieth Century Perspectives 1910–1950* (New Delhi, McGraw Hill).
Deane, Phyllis, 1978. *The Evolution of Economic Ideas* (Cambridge, Cambridge University Press).
Dobb, Maurice, 1963. *Studies in the Development of Capitalism* (London, Routledge and Kegan Paul, Revised Edition).
_____ , 1973. *Theories of Value and Distribution since Adam Smith* (Cambridge, Cambridge University Press).
Drucker, Peter, F., 1990. *The New Realities* (Delhi, Asian Books).
Dumont, Louis, 1977. *From Mandeville to Marx: The Genesis and Triumph of Economic Ideology* (Chicago, The University of Chicago Press).
Dutt, Romesh, 1960. *The Economic History of India, Vol. I, Under Early British Rule, 1757–1837* (Government of India, Publications Division).
Engels, Frederick, 1976. *Dialectics of Nature* (Moscow, Progress publishers).
Friedman, Milton, 1957. *A Theory of the Consumption Function* (Princeton, Princeton University Press).

Friend, Irvin and **Irwin V. Kravis,** 1957. 'Entrepreneurial Income, Saving and Investment', *The American Economic Review,* June.

Gadgil, D.R., 1971. *The Industrial Evolution of India in Recent Times, 1860–1939* (Delhi, Oxford University Press, Fifth Edition).

Galbraith, John Kenneth, 1967. *The New Industrial State* (New York, Signet Books).

—————— , 1973. *Economics and the Public Purpose* (Harmondsworth, Penguin Books).

Ganguli, B.N., 1977. *Indian Economic Thought: Nineteenth Century Perspectives* (New Delhi, Tata McGraw-Hill).

Gill, Stephen and **David Law,** 1988. *The Global Political Economy* (Baltimore, The Johns Hopkins University Press).

Gleick, James, 1987. *Chaos: Making a New Science* (New York, Penguin Books).

Godelier, Maurice, 1972. *Rationality and Irrationality in Economics* (New York, Monthly Review Press).

—————— , 1986. *The Mental and the Material: Thought Economy and Society* (Norfolk, Verso.)

Gorz, André, 1989. *Critique of Economic Reason* (London, Verso).

Goyal, S.K. et al, 1984. *Small-Scale Sector and Big Business* (New Delhi, Indian Institute of Public Administration).

Grou, Pierre, 1985. *The Financial Structure of Multinational Capitalism* (Warwickshire, Berg Publishers).

Guha, Ashok, 1981. *An Evolutionary View of Economic Growth* (Oxford, Clarendon Press).

Gurley, John G. and **E.S. Shaw,** 1967. 'Financial Structure and Economic Development', *Economic Development and Cultural Change,* April.

Hahn, Frank, 1981 'General Equilibrium Theory' in Daniel Bell, and Irving Kristol, eds., 1981.

Harberger, Arnold C., 1993. 'The Search for Relevance in Economics', American Economic Association, *Papers and Proceedings,* May.

Hawking, Stephen, W., 1988. *A Brief History of Time* (Toronto, Bantam Books).

Heilbroner, Robert L., 1988. *Behind the Veil of Economics* (New York, W.W. Norton and Co.)

Hicks, J.R.,1942. *Social Framework: An Introduction to Economics* (Oxford, Clarendon Press).

—————— , 1946. *Value and Capital* (Oxford, Clarendon Press, Second Edition).

—————— , 1965. *Capital and Growth* (Oxford, Clarendon Press).

Hicks John, 1969. *A Theory of Economic History* (Oxford, Oxford University Press).

—————— , 1989. *A Market Theory of Money* (Oxford, Clarendon Press).

Hicks, J.R., M Mukherjee and **Syamal K. Ghosh,** 1984. *The Framework of the Indian Economy* (Delhi, Oxford University Press).

Hill, Christopher, 1969. *Economic History of Britain: Reformation to Industrial Revolution* (Harmondsworth, Penguin Books).

Hilton, R.J., 1985. *The Transition from Feudalism to Capitalism* (London, Macmillan).

Hodgson, Geoffrey M., 1988. *Economics and Institutions* (Cambridge, Polity Press).

Holland, John H., 1988. 'The Global Economy as an Adaptive Process', in Philip W. Anderson, Kenneth J. Arrow and David Pines, eds, 1988.

Illyenkov, E.V., 1982. *The Dialectics of the Abstract and the Concrete in Marx's Capital* (Moscow, Progress Publishers).

International Labour Organisation, 1977. *Poverty and Landlessness in Rural Asia* (Geneva, International Labour Office).

Jenkins, Rhys, 1987. *Transnational Corporations and Uneven Development* (London, Methuen).

Jevons, William Stanley, 1970 (1871). *The Theory of Political Economy,* Edited with an Introduction by R.D. Collison Black (London, Penguin Books).

_____ , 1977. *Lectures on Political Economy* (London, Macmillan).

Kalecki, M., 1963. 'An Outline of Financial Policy for the Third Five Year Plan', in *Economic Strategy and the Third Plan,* Indian Statistical Institute, (Bombay, Asia Publishing House).

Keynes, J.M., 1936. *The General Theory of Employment, Interest and Money* (New York, Harcourt, Brace and Co).

Khatkhate, D.R. and D.L. Deshpande, 1965. 'Estimates of Savings and Investment, Indian Economy: 1950–51 to 1962–65', *The RBI Bulletin,* March.

Kisch, Herbert,1989. *From Domestic Manufacture to Industrial Revolution* (New York, Oxford University Press).

Koopmans, Tjalling C., 1957. *Three Essays on the State of Economic Science* (New York, McGraw-Hill).

Kosik, Karel; 1976. *Dialectics of the Concrete* (Boston, Reidal Publishing Company).

Kuhn, Thomas S., 1962. *The Structure of Scientific Revolutions* (Chicago, University of Chicago Press).

Kurien, C.T.,1967. 'Some Problems of Factor Allocations in an Underdeveloped Economy', in K.S. Sonachalam, ed., *The Theory of Economic Development* (Annamalainagar, Annamalai University).

_____ , 1969. *Indian Economic Crisis: A Diagnostic Study* (Bombay, Asia Publishing House).

_____ , 1970. *A Theoretical Approach to the Indian Economy* (Bombay, Asia Publishing House).

_____ , 1972a. 'What is Growth?: Some Thoughts on the Economics of *Garibi Hatao', Economic and Political Weekly,* December 23.

_____ , 1972b. 'Framework of a Plan to Eradicate Poverty in Tamil Nadu', in Malcolm S. Adiseshiah, ed., *Techniques of Perspective Planning* (Madras, Tamil Nadu State Planning Commission).

_____ , 1974. *Poverty and Development* (Madras, Christian Literature Society).

_____ , 1977. 'Rural Poverty in Tamil Nadu', in *Poverty and Landlessness in Rural Asia,* International Labour Organisation, 1977.

_____ , 1978. *Poverty, Planning and Social Transformation* (New Delhi, Allied Publishers).

_____ , 1981. *Dynamics of Rural Transformations: A Study of Tamil Nadu 1950–1975.* (Madras, Orient Longman).

_____ , 1982. 'Social Problems and Social Sciences', in *Relevance in Social Science Research,* Institute of Economic Growth (Delhi, Vikas Publishing House).

_____ , 1983. 'Indian Society in the late 1980s', *Mainstream,* May 14 and 21.

_____ , 1985. 'Social Factors in Economic Development: Some Methodological Issues', *South Asian Social Scientist,* July–December.

Kurien, C.T.,1987. 'The 1987–88 Budget and the New Fiscal Strategy', *Economic and Political Weekly*, April 11.

—————— , 1992a. *Growth and Justice: Aspects of India's Development Experience* (Madras, Oxford University Press).

—————— , 1992b. *The Economy: An Interpretative Introduction* (New Delhi, Sage Publications).

—————— , 1993a. *Markets in Economic Theory and Policy* (Calcutta, Orient Longman).

—————— , 1993b 'Indian Economic Reforms and the Emerging Global Economy', *Economic and Political Weekly*, April 10.

—————— , 1994. *Global Capitalism and the Indian Economy* (New Delhi, Orient Longman).

Kurien, C.T. and Joseph James, 1979. *Economic Change in Tamil Nadu* (Delhi, Allied Publishers).

Law, John and Peter Lodge, 1984. *Science for Social Scientists* (London, Macmillan).

Leontief, Wassily, 1971. 'Theoretical Assumptions and Non-observed Facts', *American Economic Review*, March.

Levine, David P., 1977. *Economic Studies: Contribution to Critique of Economic Theory* (London, Routledge and Kegan Paul).

—————— , 1988. *Needs, Rights and the Market* (Boulder, Lynne Reinner Publishers).

Levins, Richard and Richard Lewontin, 1985. *The Dialectical Biologist* (Cambridge, Harvard University Press).

Lowe, Adolf, 1965. *On Economic Knowledge* (New York, Harper and Row).

Lewis, Arthur W., 1954. 'Economic Development with Unlimited Supplies of Labour', *The Manchester School of Economic and Social Studies*, May.

Maddan, Edward H., ed., 1960. *The Structure of Scientific Thought* (New York, Houghton Miffin).

Mahajan, Gunpreet, 1992. *Explanation and Understanding in the Human Sciences.* Delhi, Oxford University Press).

Mahalanobis, P.C., 1955. 'The Approach of Operations Research to Planning in India', *Sankhya*, December.

Maki, Uskali, Bo Gustafsson and Christian Krudsen, eds, 1993. *Rationality, Institutions and Economic Methodology* (London, Routledge).

Malenbaum, Wilfred, 1962. *Prospects for Indian Development* (London, Allen & Unwin).

Malinvaud, E. 1991. 'The Next Fifty Years', *The Economic Journal*, January.

Marr, William M. and Baldev Raj, eds, 1982. *How Economists Explain: A Reader in Methodology* (Lanham, University Press of America).

Marshall, Alfred, 1961 (1890). *Principles of Economics* (London, Macmillan, Eighth Edition).

Marx, Karl, 1955. *The Poverty of Philosophy* (Moscow, Progress Publishers).

—————— , 1959. *Economic and Philosophical Manuscripts of 1844* (Moscow, Progress Publishers).

—————— , 1964. *Pre-capitalist Economic Formations* (Edited with an Introduction by E.J. Hobsbawm, New York, International Publishers).

Marx, Karl, 1971. *Capital,* Vols I, II and III (Moscow, Progress Publishers).

_____ , 1973. *Grundrisse* (Harmondsworth, Penguin Books).

Marx, Karl and **Friedrich Engels,** 1976. *The German Ideology* (Moscow, Progress Publishers).

Masani, Minoo R. 1949. *Our India* (Calcutta, Oxford University Press).

Morishima, Michio, 1991. 'General Equilibrium Theory in the Twenty First Century', *Economic Journal,* January.

Myrdal, Gunnar, 1944. *An American Dilemma* (New York, Harper and Row).

_____ , 1953. *Political Element in the Development of Economic Theory* (London, Routledge and Kegan Paul).

_____ , 1968. *Asian Drama* (London, Penguin Books).

North, Douglass C., 1978. 'Structure and Performance: The Task of Economic History', *Journal of Economic Literature,* September.

_____ , 1990. *Institutions, Institutional Change and Economic Performance* (New York, Cambridge University Press).

Parfit, Derek, 1984. *Reasons and Persons,* (Oxford, Clarendon Press).

Patnaik, Utsa, ed., 1998. *Agrarian Relations and Accumulation* (Bombay, Oxford University Press).

Phillips, Kevin, 1990. *Politics of Rich and Poor* (New York, Random House).

Pigou, Arthur C., 1938. *The Economics of Welfare* (London, Macmillan, Fourth Edition).

Polanyi, Karl, 1944. *The Great Transformation* (New York, Rinehart and Co).

_____ , et al., eds, 1957. *Trade and Markets in Early Empires* (New York, The Free Press).

Prigogine, Ilya and **Isabelle Stengers,** 1984: *Order out of Chaos* (New York, Bantam Books).

Raj K.N., 1979. 'Keynesian Economics and Agrarian Economies' in C.H. Hanumantha Rao, and P.C. Joshi, eds, 1979.

Raj, K.N. et al., eds, 1985. *Essays on Commercialization of Indian Agriculture* (Delhi, Oxford, University Press).

Rakshit, Mihir, 1982. *The Labour Surplus Economy: A Neo Keynesian Approach* (Delhi, Macmillan India).

Rao, Hanumantha C.H. and **P.C. Joshi,** eds, 1979. *Reflections on Economic Development and Social Change* (New Delhi, Allied Publishers).

Rao, V.K.R.V., 1952. 'Investment, Income and the Multiplier in an Underdeveloped Economy, *Indian Economic Review,* February.

_____ , 1953. 'Deficit Financing, Capital Formation and Price Behaviour in an Underdeveloped Economy', *Indian Economic Review,* February.

Raphael, D.D. and **A.L. Macfie,** eds, 1976. *Adam Smith: The Theory of Moral Sentiments* (Oxford, Clarendon Press).

Rawls, John, 1972. *A Theory of Justice* (Oxford, Oxford University Press).

Reddy, William M., 1984. *The Rise of Market Culture* (Cambridge, Cambridge University Press).

Reich, Robert B, 1991. *The Work of Nations* (New York, Alfred A.Knopf).

Reserve Bank of India, 1985. Report of the Committee to Review the Working of Monetary System (Bombay, The Chakravarty Committee Report,).

Ricardo, David, 1911. *The Principles of Political Economy and Taxation* (London, Everyman's Library).

Robbins, Lionel, 1935. *An Essay on the Nature and Significance of Economic Science* (London, Macmillan, Second revised edition).

Robinson, Joan, 1971. *Economic Heresies* (London, Macmillan).

_____ , 1972. 'The Second Crisis of Economic Theory', American Economic Association: *Papers and Proceedings,* May.

Rorty, Richard, 1980. *Philosophy and the Mirror of Nature* (Oxford, Basil Blackwell).

_____ , 1991. *Objectivity, Relativism and Truth* (Cambridge, Cambridge University Press).

Ross, S., 1973. 'The Economic Theory of Agency: The Principal's Problem, *American Economic Review,* May.

Sachs, Ignacy, 1986. 'Market, Non-market, Quasi-market and the "Real" Economy', Paper prepared for the 8th International Economic Association's World Congress, Delhi (mimeo).

Sahlins, Marshall, 1974. *Stone Age Economics* (London, Tovistock Publications).

Samuelson, Paul A., 1976. *Economics* (Tokyo, McGraw-Hill, Kogakasha, International Edition).

Say, J.B., 1841. *A Treatise on Political Economy* (Translated by C.R. Prinsep, Philadelphia, Grigg and Elliot).

Schotter, Andrew, 1981. *The Economic Theory of Social Institutions* (Cambridge, Cambridge University Press).

Schumpeter, Joseph A., 1954. *History of Economic Analysis* (New York, Oxford University Press).

Sen, Amartya, ed., 1970. *Growth Economics* (Harmondsworth, Penguin Books).

_____ , 1983. 'Description as Choice', in *Choice, Welfare, and Measurement* (Delhi, Oxford, University Press).

_____ , 1987. *Commodities and Capabilities* (Delhi, Oxford University Press).

Sen, Amartya, and **Barnard Williams,** eds, 1982. *Utilitarianism and Beyond* (Cambridge, Cambridge University Press).

Shackle, G.L.S., 1972. *Epistemics and Economics* (Cambridge, Cambridge University Press).

Shanmugasundaram, Yashodha, 1993. *Women Employment in India* (Madras, Allied Publishers).

Simon, Herbert A., 1991. 'Organization and Markets', *Journal of Economic Perspectives,* Spring.

Silverman, Hugh J., ed., 1993. *Questioning Foundations* (New York, Routledge).

Smith, Adam, 1964 (1776). *An Inquiry into the Nature and Causes of the Wealth of Nations,* with an Introduction by Edwin R.A. Seligman, (London Everyman's Library Edition).

_____ , 1976. *The Theory of Moral Sentiments,* Edited by D.D. Raphael and A.L. Macfie (Oxford, Clarendon Press).

Spiegel, Henry William, ed., 1952. *The Development of Economic Thought* (New York, John Wiley and Sons).

Stehr, Nico, 1992. *Practical knowledge: Applying the Social Sciences* (London, Sage).

Stiglitz, Joseph E., 1989. 'Rational Peasants, Efficient Institutions and a Theory of Rural Organization: Methodological Remarks for Developmental Economics' in Pranab Bardhan, ed., 1989.

_____ , 1991a. 'Another Century of Economic Science', *The Economic Journal,* January.

Stiglitz, Joseph E., 1991b. 'Symposium on Organization and Economics', *Journal of Economic Perspective*, Spring.

Thompson, E.P., 1980. *The Making of the English Working Class* (England, Penguin Books).

UNCTAD, 1990. *Trade and Development Report* (New York, United Nations).

UNDP, 1995. *Human Development Report 1995.* (New Delhi, Oxford University Press).

Walras, Leon, 1954. *Elements of Pure Economics,* translated by William Jaffe´ (Homewood, Richard D. Irwin.)

Weber, Max, 1978. *Economy and Society,* edited by Roth Gunther and Wittich Claus (Berkeley, University of California Press).

Williamson, O.E., 1975. *Markets of Heirarchies* (New York, Free Press).

_____ , 1985. *The Economic Institutions of Capitalism* (New York, Free Press).

Wintson, Gorden C and **Richard F. Teichgraeber,** eds, 1988. *The Boundaries of Economics* (Cambridge, Cambridge University Press).

Wilber, C.K. and **R.S. Harrison,** 1982. 'The Methodological Basis of Institutional Economics: Pattern Model, Storytelling and Holism, in William R. Marr and Baldev Raj, eds, 1982.

Woolgar, Steve, 1988. *Science: The Very Idea* (Chichester, Ellis Horwood).

World Bank, 1991. *World Development Report* (Washington, D.C. and Delhi, Oxford University Press).

_____ , 1993. *East Asian Miracle : Economic Growth and Public Policy* (New York, Oxford University Press for World Bank).

INDEX